AF207941

Wirtschaftssoziologie und Politische Ökonomie
Economic Sociology and Political Economy

herausgegeben von / edited by
Prof. Dr. Alexander Ebner,
    Goethe-Universität Frankfurt am Main

Band 1 / Volume 1

Stefan Stuth

Closing in on Closure

Occupational Closure and Temporary Employment in Germany

The Deutsche Nationalbibliothek lists this publication in the
Deutsche Nationalbibliografie; detailed bibliographic data
are available on the Internet at http://dnb.d-nb.de

a.t.: Berlin, HU Kultur-, Sozial- und Bildungswissenschaftliche Fakultät, Diss., 2015

ISBN   978-3-8487-3722-2 (Print)
          978-3-8452-8017-2 (ePDF)

British Library Cataloguing-in-Publication Data
A catalogue record for this book is available from the British Library.

ISBN   978-3-8487-3722-2 (Print)
          978-3-8452-8017-2 (ePDF)

Library of Congress Cataloging-in-Publication Data
Stuth, Stefan
Closing in on Closure
Occupational Closure and Temporary Employment in Germany
Stefan Stuth
193 p.
Includes bibliographic references and index.

ISBN   978-3-8487-3722-2 (Print)
          978-3-8452-8017-2 (ePDF)

1. Edition 2017
© Nomos Verlagsgesellschaft / edition sigma, Baden-Baden, Germany 2017. Printed
and bound in Germany.

For Christian, Lena, Janine and Ana
who helped me to keep on going

Acknowledgements

Writing and finishing a dissertation is a long process in which a lot of individuals contribute to the work in some way or other. Because I worked on my dissertation primarily in my leisure time, but also because I became a father during the process, it took me nearly five years to finish it. I thus had plenty of time to meet helpful people. In this section I'd like to acknowledge their contributions.

Most importantly, I'd like to thank my supervisors Jutta Allmendinger and Kim Weeden. Without their continuous support and sophisticated feedback I wouldn't have been able to finish my dissertation. Their advice and incisive critique helped me to broaden my perspective for the problems at hand. It laid the very foundations for a sharpened line of argument, theoretically and methodologically. I thank the WZB Berlin Social Science Center, which provided an excellent work environment that allowed me to engage in fruitful discussions with excellent researchers. I thank my colleagues Christian Brzinsky-Fay, Lena Hipp, Janine Bernhardt, and Ellen von den Driesch who commented on my drafts and with whom I engaged in constructive discussions about my work. The superior research infrastructure at the WZB allowed me to partake in an English writing clinic where researchers receive practical guidance regarding good and correct English writing. I am especially grateful that Roisin Cronin, who held these weekly individual writing sessions, was not only patient in telling me not to make the same mistakes over and over again, but also very successful in teaching me how to write well. Being part of the WZB also gave me the unparalleled opportunity to successfully apply for a six-month WZB grant that allowed me to finish my dissertation. Furthermore I am also much obliged to the Hans Böckler Foundation. Their funding of the project "The Institutional Determinants of Atypical Employment and Social Inequality in Europe" gave me access to the excellent research infrastructure of the WZB Berlin Social Science Center[1]. I would also like to thank Rose Batt, who gave me the opportunity to be a visiting fellow at the ILR School at Cornell University where I was able to discuss my dissertation in two workshops. At Cornell I had the necessary quiet time to start the long and slow process of rewriting my German dissertation sections in English and to get my theory straight.

Special thanks go to Jürgen Hoffmeyer-Zlotnik, who convinced me in a very early stage of my dissertation to analyze detailed 4-digit occupations instead of occupational groupings, as well as to Samuel Greef and Wolfgang

---

1   Grant # S-2010-342-4

Schroeder, who allowed me to use parts of their exceptional survey data on occupational associations and occupation-specific trade unions. I am very grateful to the team at the research data center of the Federal Statistical Office and the statistical offices of the *Länder*. They were helpful, friendly, and were almost always able to speed up processes so that I got my results in time and was able to meet my deadlines[2]. I would also like to thank Christian Ebner, Basha Vicari, Dörthe Gatermann, Steffen Kohl, Andreas Haupt, Martin Ehlert, Johannes Giesecke, Agniezka Althaber, Lena Ulbricht, Kyle Albert, Isabel Hageman, Clara Behrend, Lena Reichgard, Laura Jung and Daniel Staemmler who gave me advice, critical feedback or technical support.

Last but not least I would like to thank my parents and my wife for their support. Ana, thank you for your constant backing but also your impatience with me to finish my seemingly never-ending story. I would also like to thank my friends Steffen, Dennis, Marko, Mike, Dirk, Norman, Robert, and Christiane for their patience.

---

2 All results have to be checked first whether they meet the German data security and privacy laws or not, before the researcher gets his results handed out.

Table of Contents

List of Figures   **13**

List of Tables   **15**

List of Equations   **17**

List of Abbreviations   **19**

1   Introduction   **21**

2   Beyond the Norm—Temporary Employment Contracts and Occupations   **27**

2.1   Theories on the Determinants of Temporary Employment   28

2.2   The (Neglected) Occupational Perspective on the Labor Market   31

2.3   Occupations—An Elusive Concept   34

2.4   No Trespassing—The Mechanisms and Sources of Occupational Closure   37

       2.4.1   Credentialism   40

       2.4.2   Licensing   43

       2.4.3   Occupational Specificity   44

       2.4.4   Occupational Associations   46

       2.4.5   Unionization   49

       2.4.6   Human Capital, Internal Labor Markets, and Occupational Closure   49

2.5   Summary on Occupational Closure and Temporary Employment   52

3   Case Selection   **55**

3.1   Germany as a Textbook Example of an Occupational Labor Market   55

3.2   The Norm of Standard Work Arrangements and the Deregulation of Employment Protection Legislation in Germany   57

4 The Theoretical and Methodological Challenges of Operationalizing Closure Measures for Germany ... **61**

4.1 Credentialism—An Unbalanced Concept ... 61

4.2 Licensing—Two Definitions, Two Worlds of Licensed Occupations ... 64

4.3 Specificity—An Underexplored Niche ... 65

4.4 Associations—Two Different Measurement Strategies ... 67

4.5 Unionization—Industry-Level versus Occupational-Level Unions ... 68

4.6 Additional Distinctive Features of the German Labor Market ... 68

5 Data, Methods, Sample Selection, and Variables ... **71**

5.1 Methods ... 72

5.2 Sample selection ... 76

5.3 Variables ... 79

5.3.1 The Credential Inflation Index—A New Approach to Capture the Supply of Occupation-Specific Credentials ... 79
5.3.2 The Standardization Index ... 85
5.3.3 The Licensure of Tasks and Titles ... 87
5.3.4 The Specificity of Occupational Tasks ... 88
5.3.5 Occupational Associations and Occupation-Specific Trade Unions ... 90
5.3.6 Control Variables ... 91

6 Descriptive Statistics ... **95**

6.1 The Trends in Temporary Employment in Germany ... 95

6.2 Closure Sources and Their Bivariate Association with Temporary Employment ... 100
6.2.1 The Credential Inflation Index ... 100
6.2.2 The Standardization of Occupational Credentials ... 103
6.2.3 Occupational Specificity ... 105
6.2.4 The Licensing of Occupations ... 108
6.2.5 Occupational Associations ... 111
6.2.6 Occupation-Specific Trade Unions ... 112

6.3   Summary of the Descriptive Statistics   113

**7   Closing in on Closure—The Association between
          Occupational Closure and Temporary Employment   119**

7.1   Occupational Closure and Temporary Employment—Results   121

7.2   Occupational Closure, Human Capital, and Internal Labor
        Markets   128

7.3   Occupational Closure and Monitoring Costs   138

7.4   Occupational Closure and Additional Distinctive Features of the
        German Labor Market—Region and Gender Composition   144

7.5   Occupational Closure and High-Risk Populations   151

7.6   Solving the (Academic) Credentialism Conundrum   155

7.7   Sensitivity Checks   157

8   Summary   159

9   Conclusions   169

References   171

Index   191

List of Figures

Figure 1:   Temporary employment in Germany, 1993 to 2008   57

Figure 2:   The designer/graphic designer occupation as an example of the
operationalization of the credential inflation index, in the year 2004   85

Figure 3:   Temporary employment in the old and new German Länder, 1993-2008   96

Figure 4:   Temporary employment differentiated by age, 1993-2008   97

Figure 5:   Temporary employment differentiated by qualification, 1993-2008   98

Figure 6:   Temporary employment differentiated by public and private sector,
1993-2008   99

Figure 7:   Temporary employment differentiated by sex, 1993-2008   99

Figure 8:   The distribution of the mean credential inflation index values over the
deciles of the occupations for the years 2000, 2004, and 2007   101

Figure 9:   The mean rate of temporary employment differentiated by the deciles of
CIX for the years 2000, 2004, and 2007   102

Figure 10:   The mean rate of occupational incumbents with tertiary degrees
differentiated by the deciles of CIX for the years 2000, 2004, and 2007   102

Figure 11:   The distribution of the mean standardization index values over the deciles of
the occupations for the years 2000, 2004, and 2007   103

Figure 12:   The mean rate of temporary employment differentiated by the
standardization of vocational credentials in the years 2000, 2004, and 2007   104

Figure 13:   The distribution of unique and common sets of tasks over the deciles of the
occupations for the years 2000, 2004, and 2007   105

Figure 14:   The mean rate of temporary employment differentiated by the deciles of
occupational specificity (unique or common sets of tasks) for the years 2000,
2004, and 2007   106

Figure 15:   The distribution of narrow and wide sets of tasks over the deciles of the
occupations for the years 2000, 2004, and 2007   107

Figure 16:   The mean rate of temporary employment differentiated by the deciles of
occupational specificity (narrow or wide range of tasks) for years 2000,
2004, and, 2007   108

Figure 17:   The mean rate of temporary employment differentiated by licensed and
nonlicensed occupations in the years 2000, 2004, and 2007   109

Figure 18:   The distribution of the mean licensure (titles) over the deciles of the
occupations for the years 2000, 2004, and 2007   110

Figure 19:   The mean rate of temporary employment differentiated by the deciles of title
             licensure for years 2000, 2004, and, 2007   111

Figure 20:   Occupational incumbents' mean rate of temporary employment
             differentiated by their representation by occupational associations in the
             years 2000, 2004, and 2007   112

Figure 21:   Occupational incumbents' mean rate of temporary employment
             differentiated by their representation by trade unions in the years 2000,
             2004, and 2007   113

Figure 22:   The interaction between further education and standardization with regard to
             the probability of temporary employment   130

Figure 23:   The interaction between further education and the width of tasks with regard
             to the probability of temporary employment   132

Figure 24:   The interaction between further education and the commonness of tasks with
             regard to the probability of temporary employment   133

Figure 25:   The interaction between further education and the specific associations with
             regard to the probability of temporary employment   134

Figure 26:   The interaction between large companies and the credential inflation index
             with regard to the probability of temporary employment   138

Figure 27:   The interaction between the four levels of task complexity and title licensure
             with regard to the probability of temporary employment   141

Figure 28:   The interaction between two levels of task complexity and title licensure
             with regard to the probability of temporary employment   143

Figure 29:   The interaction between two levels of task complexity and the representation
             by specific associations with regard to the probability of temporary
             employment   144

Figure 30:   The interaction between the proportion of incumbents employed in the new
             Länder and title licensure with regard to the probability of temporary
             employment   146

Figure 31:   The interaction between the gender composition of occupations and the
             credential inflation index with regard to the probability of temporary
             employment   149

Figure 32:   The interaction between the gender composition of occupations and the
             degree of standardization with regard to the probability of temporary
             employment   150

Figure 33:   The interaction between the gender composition of occupations and the
             representation by trade unions with regard to the probability of temporary
             employment   151

List of Tables

Table 1: Description of individual-level and occupational-level sample sizes of the full sample and the final sample (pooled for the years 2000, 2004, and 2007) ... 78

Table 2: Descriptive statistics of occupational-level measures ... 114

Table 3: Bivariate correlations of the occupational-level closure variables ... 116

Table 4: Mean of the various closure sources by major occupation group ... 117

Table 5: A description of the estimated logit coefficients of the 1,118 separate stage-one regression analyses ... 120

Table 6: Pooled linear regression of temporary employment on the different sources of occupational closure, 2000, 2004, and 2007 ... 123

Table 7: Pooled linear regression of temporary employment on the different sources of occupational closure—full model with standardized coefficients, 2000, 2004, and 2007 ... 126

Table 8: Pooled linear regression of temporary employment on the different sources of occupational closure—with interactions between further education and the closure sources, 2000, 2004, and 2007 ... 128

Table 9: Pooled linear regression of temporary employment on the different sources of occupational closure—with interactions between firm-internal labor markets (large organizations) and the closure sources, 2000, 2004, and 2007 ... 136

Table 10: Pooled linear regression of temporary employment on the different sources of occupational closure—with interactions between managerial tasks (model 9), managerial/skilled tasks (model 10), skilled tasks (model 11), and routine/labor tasks (model 12) with the closure sources, 2000, 2004, and 2007 ... 139

Table 11: Pooled linear regression of temporary employment on the different sources of occupational closure—with interactions between the new Länder and the closure sources, 2000, 2004, and 2007 ... 145

Table 12: Pooled linear regression of temporary employment on the different sources of occupational closure—with interactions between gender, type of occupations, and the closure sources, 2000, 2004, and 2007 ... 147

Table 13: Explaining differences in the probability of temporary employment between young and middle-aged occupational incumbents within occupations using the different sources of occupational closure—a pooled linear regression with the individual-level stage-one logit coefficients of young occupational incumbents as dependent variable ... 153

Table 14: Explaining differences in the probability of temporary employment between occupational incumbents with low- and medium-level qualifications within occupations, using the different sources of occupational closure—a pooled linear regression with the individual-level stage-one logit coefficients of occupational incumbents with low-level qualifications as the dependent variable — 154

Table 15: Explaining differences in the probability of temporary employment between highly and moderately qualified occupational incumbents within occupations, using the different sources of occupational closure—a pooled linear regression with the individual-level stage-one logit coefficients of highly qualified occupational incumbents as the dependent variable — 156

List of Equations

Equation 1: The general form of the first step of the two-step multilevel model   74

Equation 2: The general form of the second step of the two-step multilevel model   75

Equation 3: The credential inflation index   82

Equation 4: The computation of the number of occupation-specific credentials that are awarded by the tertiary education track   83

Equation 5: The standardization index   87

Equation 6: The relative uniqueness of tasks and skills in occupations using the index of qualitative variation   89

Equation 7: The relative variety of tasks and skills within occupations using the index of qualitative variation   90

List of Abbreviations

BbiG	Vocational Training Act (*Berufsbildungsgesetz*)
BIBB/BAuA	Employment survey conducted by the Federal Institute for Vocational Education and Training (*Bundesinstitut für Berufsbildung* (BIBB)) and the Federal Institute for Occupational Safety and Health (*Bundesanstalt für Arbeitschutz und Arbeitsmedizin* (BAuA))
CIX	Credential Inflation Index
ISCED	International Standard Classification of Education
Gsoep	German socio economic panel
HwO	Crafts Code (*Handwerksordnung*)
IQV	Index of Qualitative Variation
KldB	German Dictionary of Occupational Titles (*Klassifikation der Berufe*)
MSE	Mean Squared Error
p10	The 10 percent percentile
p25	The 25 percent percentile
p50	The 50 percent percentile (median)
p75	The 75 percent percentile
p90	The 90 percent percentile
R	Correlation coefficient
RDC	Research data centers of the Federal Statistical Office of Germany and the statistical offices of the German *Länder*
SD	Standard deviation
Vif	Variance inflation factor

1   Introduction

Temporary employment contracts have increased in political and economic relevance in the last few decades. Policy makers have lessened the restrictions on the use of temporary employment contracts to allow employers to be more flexible when faced with external market shocks and to integrate more people into the labor market (Barbieri 2009; Hipp et al. 2015). The price of temporary employment is, however, low wages[3], poor working conditions[4], high labor turnover[5], and limited career chances[6] for the individuals who are actually temporarily employed (e.g., Kalleberg 2000, 2009, 2011; Standing 2011; Hipp et al. 2015).

---

3 Contrary to the theory of compensating wage differentials, research shows a negative association between temporary employment and wages. The theory of compensating wage differentials suggests that higher wages compensate employees for negative job characteristics like high levels of job insecurity (Rosen 1986). However, most authors argue and demonstrate that the relationship between job security and income is inverted because permanent employees have better bargaining positions than temporary employees (Pfeffer and Baron 1988, pp. 294-295; Bentolila and Dolado 1994; Groß 1999; Booth et al. 2002; Hagen 2002; Giesecke and Groß 2003; Polavieja 2003; Giesecke and Groß 2004; Groß and Wegener 2004, pp. 192-197; Mertens and McGinnity 2004; Giesecke 2006, pp. 259-299; Oberst et al. 2007; Campbell et al. 2007; Gash and McGinnity 2007; Brehmer and Seifert 2008; Gebel 2009, 2010; Elia 2010; Schäfer 2010).

4 Temporary employment contracts are also used to maintain a constant and high level of labor intensity by promising permanent contracts in exchange for constantly high levels of productivity (Loh 1994; Wang and Weiss 1998; Polavieja 2003, 2005). These arguments are in line with the efficiency wage model, which assumes that work motivation and productivity increase the more insecure the jobs are. The persistent fear of layoffs motivates otherwise work-shy employees and creates a constant pressure to work hard.

5 Individuals have better chances of getting employment but at the same time face higher risks of being laid off (Bentolila and Saint-Paul 1992; Bentolila and Dolado 1994; Cabrales and Hopenhayn 1997; Boeri 1999; Goux and Maurin 2000; Korpi and Levin 2001; Güell 2000a,b; Alda 2002; Blanchard and Landier 2002; Cahuc and Postel-Vinay 2002; Giesecke and Groß 2002; Giesecke and Groß 2003; Polavieja 2003; Boockmann and Hagen 2005a,b; Kurz et al. 2005; Giesecke 2006; Boockmann and Hagen 2006; Brehmer and Seifert 2008; Giesecke 2009; Gebel and Giesecke 2011).

6 Temporarily employed workers have fewer opportunities for skills and career development (e.g., Booth et al. 2002; Boockmann and Hagen 2006, pp. 125-127; Gebel 2010). However, the evidence is mixed. Some studies fail to show that present temporary employment contracts negatively affect later processes of occupational attainment or skills development (for career development see: Scherer 2005; for skills development see: Brehmer and Seifert 2008).

To understand who gets a "bad" temporary job and who gets a "good" permanent job, the majority of research focuses on individual-level or organizational-level explanations. These explanations stress the importance of firm-specific training, firm-internal labor markets, and the complexity of work tasks. High amounts of firm-specific human capital and complex work tasks increase employees' chances of becoming part of firm-internal labor markets that grant permanent employment contracts. Temporary employment is therefore often interpreted as a function of the firm-specific human capital that employees have acquired and the complexity of their work tasks (monitoring costs) (e.g., Uzzi and Barsness 1998; Goldthorpe 2000; Sørensen 2000; Masters and Miles 2002; Kalleberg et al. 2003; Polavieja 2003; McGinnity et al. 2005; Giesecke and Schindler 2008). However, general human capital, namely occupation-specific skills, is conspicuously absent from the discussion of the determinants of temporary employment. Accordingly, empirical data on temporary employment on the occupational level are rare. However, Stuth et al. (2009, p. 24) found that, for female employees, temporary employment varied strongly on an aggregated occupational level. For example, among all railway signalers (rails) and architectural draftsmen, there were no temporary employees, whereas up to 15 percent of medical doctors and gardeners were temporarily employed.

The exclusion of occupations results in two major shortcomings. First: It may lead researchers to overlook the role played by occupations in the fragmentation of the labor market. Labor demand and labor supply are coordinated by occupations, which fosters the occupation-specific fragmentation of the labor market (e.g., Kerr 1954, pp. 92-96; Stolzenberg 1975, pp. 648-649; Bielby and Kalleberg 1981; Grusky and Sørensen 1998, pp. 1210-1212; Grusky and Weeden 2001; Mouw and Kalleberg 2010, p. 402). To illustrate my argument: When seeking to hire a new human resources manager, an employer might not so much be interested in whether the candidate has, for example, a tertiary-level degree or high levels of cognitive skills. The prospective employer may instead be interested in the employee's training, education, or experience as a human resources manager. These qualifications and skills are related to occupation-specific task fields, and thus, a candidate cannot be reassigned from one occupational task field to another without the loss of productivity from an organizational-level perspective or without the loss of earnings from an individual-level perspective. Hence, the pool of possible candidates is restricted to those who have acquired the necessary occupational qualifications and skills. Second: Overlooking occupations may lead us to ignore important processes of occupational closure. In situations where the supply of employees with certain occupation-specific skills is scarce, or the demand exceeds the supply, processes of occupational closure may additionally alter the equilibrium between supply and demand to improve the position of the occupations' incumbents (e.g., Weeden 2002). Hence, an employer's decision whether to use permanent or temporary employment contracts is not merely based on the amount of specific human capital individuals possess and the difficulty of monitoring employees' productivity; the decision may also be based on the availability of the required occupation-specific skills (Masters and Miles 2002), whereas this availability may in turn be a result of processes of occupational closure.

To address the occupation-specific fragmentation of the labor market, as well as closure processes and their possible impact on the employers' human resource strategies, researchers must refocus from individual-level or organizational-level outcomes to occupational-level outcomes. While research on occupational-level outcomes is steadily growing with regard to earning inequalities, no such research exists with regard to temporary employment. To address these shortcomings, I develop and evaluate an occupational-level approach to temporary employment and will focus on the question: Why is temporary employment more common in some occupations than in others?

This occupational-level approach is derived from the literature on occupational closure and earning inequalities. Research in this relatively young tradition emphasizes that occupational fragmentation processes are artificially reinforced by the occupations themselves and thus significantly affect the hierarchy of occupational rewards (e.g., Weeden 2002; Groß 2009, 2012; Giesecke and Verwiebe 2009; Haupt 2012, 2014; Bol and Weeden 2014; Bol 2014). This reinforcement is based on closure mechanisms, which alter the equilibrium of occupation-specific labor supply and occupation-specific labor demand. These closure mechanisms are triggered by closure sources: the institutionalized practices of occupations through which occupational closure is established and maintained (Weeden 2002)[7].

In adapting this approach to analyze the determinants of temporary employment, I address conventional closure sources like licensure, occupational associations, and unionization and develop a new credentialism measure that allows me to assess the hypothetical link between the availability of occupation-specific credentials and temporary employment. I also introduce a new closure source, occupational specificity, which allows me to capture the exclusivity of occupational task niches and occupational task specialization. Task specialization is a feature that is often hotly debated with regard to its effect on employees' employment security (e.g., Emmenegger 2009; Streeck 2011). Based on these closure measures, I am able to address both shortcomings of

---

7 To account for the fact that occupational closure may exist without occupations actively pursuing closure strategies, Kim Weeden suggested using the term closure source instead of the term closure strategies.

conventional analyses of the determinants of temporary employment: the occupational fragmentation of the labor market and closure processes that may modify the occupational fragmentation of the labor market. Whereas the main thrust of this book is to establish the relevance of closure theory, I am also interested in expanding the conventional, organizational-level explanations (specific human capital, firm-internal labor markets, and the complexity of work tasks) by analyzing their interrelation with occupational closure. An empirical relationship seems inevitable because both theories focus on credentials and skills but from different angles (e.g., Weeden 2002; Werfhorst 2011).

The empirical analyses will focus on Germany as an ideal-typical case for studying the interrelationship between occupations, occupational closure, and temporary employment. Germany has an occupational labor market and is renowned for its strong link between the education and training system and the labor market (e.g., the apprenticeship training system), which reinforces the segmentation of the occupational labor market. Another reason is that employees' attitudes toward temporary employment are strongly based on the normative framework of standard work arrangements: Almost no employees want to have temporary employment contracts. This is an important precondition for the analyses, which are based on the assumption that employees will always choose permanent employment contracts over temporary employment contracts. Another reason is that the institutional setting in Germany is characterized by relatively strict employment protection legislation, which incentivizes employers to use temporary employment contracts to increase their external, numerical flexibility.

I use a two-step multilevel approach and base the analyses on a special version of the German Microcensus that allows for the analysis of detailed occupations. Although other scholars have used the German Microcensus to examine closure and earnings (Bol and Weeden 2014; Bol 2014) or to examine closure and the duration of employment breaks for family reasons (Stuth and Hennig 2014), no one has used it to study the impact of closure on temporary employment and no one has examined occupational closure at the level of detailed occupations.

The results provide evidence of great variation in temporary employment across the occupations, with a minimum of zero percent temporary employment up to a maximum of 64 percent temporary employment. The analyses confirm the argument that occupational closure influences employees' risk of temporary employment. Thus, occupations can shelter their incumbents from temporary employment contracts. Specifically, the occupational specificity closure source and the modified credentialism closure source have substantive and statistically significant effects on temporary employment. For example, the findings support the argument that an inflationary supply of occupation-specific credentials results in an increased risk of temporary employment.

In the next chapter, I will give a short introduction to the conventional theoretical arguments about the determinants of temporary employment and their shortcomings with regard to the relevance of the occupational level for the determinants of temporary employment. I will also introduce the occupational-level closure theory and the closure sources that I will use to establish the empirical link between occupational closure and temporary employment. In chapter 3, I establish Germany as an ideal-typical case for researching occupational closure and temporary employment. Chapter 4 critically discusses the conventional measures used for the various closure sources and introduces new measures and concepts. Chapter 5 describes my statistical method, a two-step multilevel model, and the sample selection at the individual level and the occupational level. It also describes the operationalization of the closure sources and the occupational-level and individual-level control variables. Chapter 6 contains the descriptive statistics, and chapter 7 delivers the results of the analyses. Chapter 8 presents the summary and chapter 9 the conclusions.

2 Beyond the Norm—Temporary Employment Contracts and Occupations

Modern Western industrial nations base their employment relations on the normative framework of standard work arrangements (Mückenberger 1985; Kalleberg 2000). The term "standard work arrangements" refers to full-time work that is performed on an indefinite basis at the employer's place of business under the employer's direction (Kallerberg 2000, p. 341). The social security systems of many industrial nations are based on the norm of "standard" employment. However, this norm is declining and temporary employment is in the ascent (e.g., Beck 1999; Kalleberg 2000; Heinz 2003, pp. 185-201; Gallagher and Sverke 2005; Blossfeld et al. 2006; Kalleberg 2011; Allmendinger et al. 2013). Temporary employment contracts are defined as contracts that have a fixed termination date or a fixed reason for termination. These contracts dissolve automatically if the specified date is reached or a contractually defined reason ceases to exist (e.g., when an absent employee returns from sick leave). Temporary employment contracts provide organizations with the flexibility to cope with fluctuations in the demand for goods or services[8], help them to keep costs low, and to gain advantages in (global) economic competition (Abraham 1988; Bollinger et al. 1991, pp. 187-188; Davis-Blake and Uzzi 1993, p. 193; Matusik and Hill 1998, pp. 681-682; Kaiser and Pfeiffer 2001; Hagen and Boockmann 2002; Boockmann and Hagen 2003; Hagen 2003; Pfeifer 2005, 2006; Struck 2006; Sesselmeier 2007; Hohendanner and Gerner 2010)[9]. Temporary employment contracts also provide

---

8 The literature on nonstandard employment differentiates between four basic organizational strategies for adapting to volatilities in the product market and economic cycles (e.g., Atkinson 1984; OECD 1986; Dragendorf et al. 1988, p. 113; Rubery and Grimshaw 2003; Keller and Seifert 2007; Bukodi et al. 2008, pp. 5-6): Numeric external strategies allow organizations to adapt to changes by recruiting new employees from external sources if needed and just for the time needed (e.g., temporary employment contracts). Numeric internal strategies do not depend on external resources, but use and reorganize the internal resources the organizations already have (e.g., part-time work, overtime). An adaptation to economic cycles that follows the external-functional pathway outsources internal processes (contract work). An internal functional path adjusts the qualification of the employees (increasing productivity and fields of assignment) or stimulates internal mobility processes (see Giesecke 2006, pp. 46-47).

9 Temporary employment contracts fulfill a buffer function that allows organizations to reconcile the available (future) manpower with the (future) product demand (Engels et al. 1986; OECD 1986, 1994; Pfeffer and Baron 1988; Abraham 1988; Bentolila and Bertola 1990; Bollinger et al. 1991; Davis-Blake and Uzzi 1993; Bentolila and Saint-Paul 1994; Booth 1997; Siebert 1997;

employers with an important instrument for human resources management (Bollinger et al. 1991, pp. 186-188). They are used to discourage undesired collective action that would lead employers to refuse to renew their employees' contracts (e.g., Mückenberger 1989, Davis-Blake and Uzzi 1993; Uzzi and Barsness 1998; Nienhüser 2007). Used as a screening instrument, temporary employment contracts serve as prolonged probationary periods that help employers predict the long-term productivity of future employees (Doeringer and Piore 1971; Abraham 1988; Korpi and Levin 2001; Boockmann and Hagen 2008). Temporary employment contracts that perform a screening function are thus often considered to serve as a bridge into permanent employment because they give potential employees the opportunity to demonstrate their skills and motivation (Abraham 1988; OECD 1998; Wang and Weiss 1998; Houseman 2001; Booth et al. 2002; Gangl et al. 2003; Zijl et al. 2004; McGinnity et al. 2005; DiPrete 2005; DiPrete et al. 2006; Gash and McGinnity 2007; Gash 2008; Gebel 2013). Additionally, temporary employment contracts are a necessary measure for employers who need to cope with internal personnel fluctuations due to, for example, sick leave (e.g., Seifert and Pawlowsky 1998; Houseman 2001).

The various approaches that explain the use of temporary employment contracts focus strongly on organizations. Therefore, it comes as no surprise that the determinants of temporary employment are primarily derived from theories that focus on organizations: firm-specific human capital, firm-internal labor markets, and transaction costs. In the next section I will introduce these theories and will critically review their assumptions. I will point out that the theoretical focus on organizations is not sufficient to explain the variation in employees' holding temporary employment contracts. Employees may benefit from various sources of occupational closure; these closure sources change the equilibrium between occupation-specific labor supply and occupation-specific labor demand, which might change the organization's management of occupational incumbents and thereby change their risk of temporary employment.

2.1 Theories on the Determinants of Temporary Employment

Who gets a temporary employment contract? There are three major theoretical approaches that explain when individuals are more likely to hold temporary

---

Bender et al. 2000; Houseman 2001; Kaiser and Pfeiffer 2001; Hagen and Boockmann 2002; Hagen 2003; Meyer and Pfeifer 2005; Pfeifer 2005, 2006; for a labor shortage perspective see: Barry and Crant 1994; Uzzi and Barsness 1998; Kalleberg et al. 2003).

employment contracts: human capital theory, internal labor market theory[10], and the transaction costs approach. All three theories concur that individuals are less likely to hold temporary employment contracts if they have a high amount of firm-specific human capital and if their productivity is difficult to monitor or to evaluate (e.g., Davis-Blake and Uzzi 1993; Barry and Crant 1994; Uzzi and Barsness 1998; Masters and Miles 2002; Giesecke and Groß 2003; Kalleberg et al. 2003; Polavieja 2003; McGinnity et al. 2005; Giesecke 2006; Giesecke and Schindler 2008). In these cases, both the employees and employers have an interest in long-term employment relationships. Employees seek stability whereas the employers want to exclude outside competition. To keep employees' productivity high in the absence of competition, governance structures like career ladders with highly stratified and distinctive job titles are introduced, which results in the emergence of internal labor markets (e.g., Edwards 1979, p. 21; Pfeffer and Cohen 1984, pp. 554-555; Goldthorpe 2000; Sørensen 2000; Polavieja 2003, p. 504).

The most important theory used by researchers interested in the determinants of temporary employment is human capital theory, which stresses the fact that employees differ in their productivity due to training and education (Becker 1962, 1964, Mincer 1974). Becker differentiates between specific human capital that is acquired on the job and general human capital that is acquired through schooling (for example: education, training, and higher education). General human capital increases the productivity of employees in a broad variety of organizations. Since investments in general human capital would be lost if employees moved from one company to another, employers would only provide general human capital if they didn't have to pay the costs (Becker 1964, p. 21). Specific human capital also increases the productivity of employees, but from the perspective of the employer, ideally only within their own organization. If employees with specific human capital switch employers, this would result in a loss, not only for their employer, but also for the employees themselves, since their gains in productivity (and therefore earnings) through specific human capital are not transferable to other organizations (Becker 1964, p. 27). Becker argues that employers try to secure their investments in specific human capital and posits that wage premiums are the best

---

10 The internal labor market theory is just one of many theories that are usually subsumed under the label of "segmented labor market theories". However, the majority of these segmentation theories (e.g., dual labor markets or open and closed positions) explain the characteristics of different labor market segments with the presence or absence of internal labor markets (Kalleberg and Sørensen 1979, p. 359; Pfeffer and Cohen 1984, p. 551). By addressing internal labor market theory, I will focus on the common base on which all the segmented labor market theories rest.

means to doing so. However, many researchers have applied his arguments to the use of permanent and temporary employment contracts, which employers might also use to secure investments in firm-specific human capital (e.g., Giesecke and Groß 2003, 168; Giesecke and Groß 2004; Mertens and McGinnity 2004; Kurz et al. 2005, pp. 64-65; McGinnity et al. 2005; Giesecke 2006, pp. 210-213; Gundert 2007).

The internal labor market theory builds on Becker's analysis but explicitly focuses on employers who use long-term employment contracts to secure specific human capital within firms (Pfeffer and Cohen 1984, p. 552)[11]. The long-term employment contracts are part of a governance structure that is specific to internal labor markets (Doeringer and Piore 1971; Braverman 1974; Marglin 1974; Edwards 1979; Gordon et al. 1982). Internal labor markets have a complex set of rules that determine the movements of employees between different jobs within their administrative units (Dunlop 1966, p. 32). Jobs are arranged in an orderly fashion, starting with port-of-entry jobs. These lines of progression constantly provide employees with the specific human capital that is necessary to move up the job ladder (Althauser and Kalleberg 1981, p. 130). They are combined with seniority entitlements. Both of these elements—the job ladder and seniority entitlements—bind the employees to the employers and the employers to the employees (Kalleberg and Sørensen 1979, pp. 359-360). The governance structures of internal labor markets protect their employees from the competition related to the external market (Thurow 1975; Sørensen 1983). Employees in internal labor markets thus face a low risk of temporary employment, whereas employees in external labor markets face a high risk of temporary employment.

The transaction cost approach combines the asset specificity of human capital theory with the governance structures of internal labor market theory. Starting with Williamson (1981, 1985), theorists have differentiated human capital by the degree of specificity and additionally by how separable or inseparable work relations are. The work tasks performed by various individuals may be inseparable in the sense that individuals' productivity cannot be assessed directly by measuring their output (e.g., teamwork) (Williamson 1985, p. 244). If employees have a high amount of firm-specific human capital that is combined with work tasks that are difficult to measure or monitor, organizations have to use additional governance measures to ensure that employees remain loyal to the firm. This is achieved through social conditioning and the

---

11 There is also the notion of occupational internal labor markets (e.g., Kerr 1954; Kalleberg and Sørensen 1979, p. 359). However, research on firm-internal labor markets dominates, while the notion of occupational internal labor markets is the least developed and explored concept of all internal labor market conceptions (Althauser 1989, pp. 148, 156).

provision of considerable job security (Williamson 1985, p. 247). According to the transaction cost approach, the interplay between employees' (absent) firm-specific human capital and employers' difficulty in evaluating their productivity determines the individuals' risk of temporary employment.

2.2 The (Neglected) Occupational Perspective on the Labor Market

While the previously mentioned theories frequently address specific human capital and transaction costs, general human capital is rarely considered by research on temporary employment[12]. The exclusion of occupations as a manifestation of general human capital results in two shortcomings. First: Occupations provide employers with important information about the suitability of candidates for job vacancies and thereby foster the fragmentation of the labor market. This fragmentation follows the lines of different occupation-specific skills. Second: Depending on the requirements of a specific job, the supply of employees with the required occupation-specific skills might be scarce and processes of occupational closure may additionally alter the equilibrium between supply and demand to improve the position of the occupations' incumbents (e.g., Weeden 2002). Hence, an employer's decision whether to use permanent or temporary employment contracts is not merely based on the amount of specific human capital individuals possess and the monitoring costs employers face; the decision is also based on the availability/scarcity of the occupation-specific labor supply. This section provides insights into the importance of both occupation-specific features of general human capital, which is usually neglected by research that addresses the determinants of temporary employment.

1) Although I initially indicated that the bulk of research on the determinants of temporary employment turn a blind eye to occupations, most studies at least mention occupations in passing but treat them superficially; they only control for crude occupational categories like "technical", "sales", or "operative", or they aggregate occupations in social classes like "skilled manual workers" or "professionals, administrators, and managers" (e.g., Goldthorpe

---

12 Some researchers argue that upper-secondary level occupational qualifications can be equated with firm-specific human capital (Giesecke and Groß 2002; Giesecke and Groß 2003; Giesecke and Groß 2004; Giesecke 2006; Giesecke and Groß 2007). However, they ignore the fact that these qualifications are not specific to one organization. I follow Becker's original definition of general human capital, which is applicable to a broad range of employers, in contrast to specific human capital, which is ideally applicable only to one employer (Becker 1964).

2000; McGinnity et al. 2005; Gundert 2007). These kinds of generalized occupational categories

> are merely linguistic proxies for an uncharted population of distinct occupational pursuits. [...] It allows stereotypes to masquerade as knowledgeable descriptions (Van Maanen and Barley 1984, p. 297).

Research that utilizes such an aggregated view of occupations is likely to find no effects or only weak effects of occupations, because this view obscures the enormous heterogeneity within each of these "occupational" categories (see Freidson 1994, pp. 76-80; Hauser and Warren 1997; Grusky and Sørensen 1998, Grusky and Weeden 2001, 2002; Weeden and Grusky 2005a, 2005b, 2012; Kambourov and Manovskii 2009, p. 74).

Other conventional human capital-based measures usually include individuals' education or their skills. Employers rarely use general human capital—in the sense of, for example, a university degree or technical skill—as a source of information when hiring new employees. The reason for this is that some individuals—for example, biomedical engineers and environmental engineers—have similar technical skills and university degrees, but these skills and degrees are related to entirely different task fields. The skills are thus not easily transferable from one task field to the other (e.g., Lazear 2003; Gibbons and Waldman 2006; Gathmann and Schönberg 2007; Kambourov and Manovskii 2009). Task field-based obstacles in the transferability of employees' skills result in the fragmentation of the labor market.

> What the perfectly free market is for classical economics (see Kerr, 1950, p. 279) and perhaps for conventional stratification theory, and what the stratified market is for class theory (see Edwards, 1975), a 'balkanized' labor market composed of occupationally differentiated shelters is for occupational theory (Freidson 1994, p. 82).

However, researchers almost never consider occupations as an important source of labor market fragmentation. This omission is regrettable for a number of reasons. First, employers use occupations as predefined templates that signal proficiency in certain occupation-specific tasks (e.g., Kerr 1954, pp. 92-96; Hall 1975, p. 71; Stolzenberg 1975, pp. 648-649; Mortimer and Lorence 1979; Tolbert 1996, p. 338; Grusky and Sørensen 1998, pp. 1210-1212)[13]. Second, occupations mediate between employers' demands for specific task-field

---

13 Post-occupationalists suggest (e.g., Casey 1995; Sennet 2000; Baetghe 2004) that specialization has limits and most firms will have a greater need for generalists in the future. Though it may be true that specialization has its limits, most firms will fall back on prepackaged solutions provided by the occupational division of labor instead of creating an independent system of job categories with their own in-house staffing and training system.

related skills and employees who have these task field-specific skills (e.g., Dostal et al. 1998, pp. 440; Abraham et al. 2011, p. 5). Third, employers may benefit from occupation-based signals of proficiency because they reduce search costs (Spence 1973). Fourth, employees also benefit from the template function of occupations: Employers who are in need of the occupation-specific skills now compete with other employers who also rely on occupations as prepackaged solutions and who are in need of these occupation-specific skills. It follows that employees are exchangeable depending on the supply of their occupation-specific skills, while employers also become exchangeable depending on their demand for the occupation-specific skills. Thus, there is a strong quasi-natural tendency of labor markets to become segmented along the borders of occupations (Stolzenberg 1975, pp. 648-649; see also Kerr 1954, pp. 92-96, Grusky and Sørensen 1998, pp. 1210-1212).

> 2) "Organizational theorists, in particular, have almost completely ignored occupational phenomena, even though the interplay between occupation and organization clearly constitutes a central dynamic in the work lives of many individuals (Van Maanen and Barley 1984) (Barley and Tolbert 1991, p. 3)."

However, the occupational fragmentation of the labor market has important consequences for the scarcity or abundance of the supply of occupation-specific skills. The fact that occupation-specific skills are both discretionary in character and transferable from one employer to another has a considerable impact on the bargaining power of employees (Freidson 1994, p. 42)[14]. This impact is particularly positive when the supply of occupation-specific skills is limited and the demand is high. The use of long-term employment relationships is therefore not only a result of the investments in firm-specific human capital and does not only stem from problems of control and work complexity (e.g., Struck 2006, pp. 96-97). Long-term employment contracts are also a human resources strategy used by employers to manage and secure scarce commodities like occupation-specific skills (e.g., Althauser 1989, pp. 154-156; Bridges and Villemez 1991; Masters and Miles 2002; Hohendanner and Gerner 2010). Conventional human capital theory allows for the scarcity of skills, but only in the short run. Skill scarcity generates high wages and thereby increases the mobility of employees, who will acquire the scarce skills in response to the market signals of high wages. However, there might be barriers established around occupations that prevent the restoration of an equilibrium between occupation-specific labor supply and labor demand. Hence, short-term rents are

---

14 Kambourov et al. (2009) present empirical evidence that occupational experience (general human capital) is a major determinant of earnings while firm tenure (specific human capital) is only a minor determinant (see also Althauser 1989, p. 153).

converted into long-term rents by preventing workers from responding to the market signal of high wages (Bol and Weeden 2014; Weeden and Grusky 2014, pp. 482-483).

Conceptualizing employment "in terms of occupations sets off a different train of thought" than the conventional theoretical approaches described above (Standing 2009, p. 28). On the one hand, it is important for employers to secure scarce occupation-specific skills. On the other hand, occupations are surrounded by social and legal boundaries that might contribute to the development or preservation of this scarcity by reducing the occupation-specific labor supply and increasing/maintaining the demand for occupation-specific labor (e.g., Parkin 1979, p. 48; Van Maanen and Barley 1984, p. 290; Tolbert 1996; Weeden 2002). These social and legal boundaries might be (un-)intentionally established or reinforced by processes of occupational closure, which are therefore an important and additional determinant of temporary employment (Kerr 1954; Hall 1975, p. 70; Beck et al. 1980, pp. 38-44; Murphy 1988; Weeden 2002, p. 59-60; Weeden and Grusky 2014;). Starting with a conceptual discussion of occupations, the following section will discuss the mechanisms and institutionalized sources of occupational closure and their theoretical impact on individuals' risks of holding temporary employment contracts.

2.3 Occupations—An Elusive Concept

Occupation is a loosely defined concept with a number of meanings[15].

> Sometimes we oppose occupations to guilds, construing occupations as a simpler form of identification with work. Sometimes we oppose occupations in the broad sense to professions, which specialize in certain kinds of expert work, and to crafts, which specialize in expert physical skills. Sometimes we think of occupations as grouped around common organizational positions, as in the occupation of foreman; sometimes we imagine them in terms of common physical capital, as in the occupation of drill press operator. Indeed, when we once begin to face the concept, it comes apart in our hands (Abbott 1989, p. 274).

For my purposes, I will define occupations as collective and competitive enterprises with specific tasks and skills. They compete with other occupations over the differentiation and combination of these tasks and skills (task niches) that

---

15 For the German discussion on the multitude of definitions see Henninges et al. 1976; Stooß and Saterdag 1979; Beck et al. 1980; Dostal et al. 1998; Fürstenberg 2000; Kupka 2005; Matthes et al. 2008, p. 6.

are provided by occupational education and training programs[16]. There are three elements in this definition that are central for the purpose of my research: the tasks, the provision of occupation-specific skills in occupational education and training programs, and the social dimension of occupations.

1) While there is little argument about seeing occupations as task bundles, there is a lot of disagreement on whether these are a mere product of an efficient and rational (technical) division of labor, or whether the division of labor is socially created (see for example Freidson 1994, pp. 49-54, Grusky and Sørensen 1998, pp. 1192-1196). I follow Freidson (1994) and Grusky and Sørensen (1998), who argue that occupation-specific work roles are the result of occupational attempts to establish measures of collective control (Freidson 1994, p. 58)[17]. Occupations are collective enterprises that compete over their specific tasks and actively defend or extend their claims on these tasks (Brint 1994, pp. 30-31; Grusky and Sørensen 1998, pp. 1192-1196). Occupations that successfully claim and secure task niches in the social division of labor improve the labor market chances of their incumbents (at the expense of related occupations) (Kerr 1954; Hall 1975, p. 70; Beck and Brater 1978, pp. 249-252; Beck et al. 1980, pp. 38-44;Murphy 1988; Weeden 2002, pp. 59-60).

2) Occupations are rarely defined by tasks alone. Most researchers also emphasize the relevance of education and training programs that provide occu-

---

16 Even if tasks and jobs are not occupational in nature, individuals who engage in similar activities have the potential to organize and initiate, or further advance a process of occupationalization (Krause 1971, pp. 86-88; Freidson 1994, pp. 58, 76-78, 91; Weeden 2002, p. 58). Hughes sees a quasi-automatic psychological mechanism at work: Even those doing the least rewarding work are bound to develop collective pretensions about their given work tasks (Hughes 1994, p. 59; see also Pavalko 1971, pp. 193-194). Sennett specifies Hughes' claim, adding that all forms of work provide people with an identity as long as the tasks are challenging or difficult (Sennett 1998, p. 72). It should therefore "come as no surprise that detailed occupations continue to be one of the main social identities for contemporary workers" (Grusky and Weeden 2001, p. 204; see also: Krause 1971, p. 87; Kohn and Schooler 1978; Mortimer and Simmons 1978, pp. 440-443; Mortimer and Lorence 1979; VanMaanen and Barley 1984, pp. 298-303; Grusky and Sørensen 1998, pp. 1192-1196; Kohn 2001, pp. 539-540). Accordingly, the term occupation does not describe a fixed destination but a continuum that spans the ideal-type extremes of "job" versus "professional occupations." Depending on the historical point in time at which specific patterns of manpower are considered, they can tend more towards one pole or the other. Yet this limitation is in keeping with the definition of occupations as collective enterprises that were, are, or may become sociologically meaningful or institutionalized (Freidson 1994, p. 76-78).

17 "Indeed, insofar as the division of labor is represented as the outcome of interoccupational conflict and competition, the resulting occupations must perforce be taken as sociologically meaningful rather than nominal" (Grusky and Sørensen 1998, p. 1195; see also: Simpson et al. 1982; Freidson 1994, pp. 64-66).

pation-specific skills[18]. The relevance of education and training programs for the conception of occupations relies strongly on classical sociological authors like Max Weber. Weber defines occupations as follows:

> The term 'occupation' (*Beruf*) will be applied to the mode of specialization, specification, and combination of the functions of an individual so far as it constitutes for him the basis of a continuous opportunity for income and earnings (Weber 1978, p. 140).

The degree of access to valued resources within a society depends on the individuals' combination of functions or tasks. Yet in Weber's view, occupations only constitute continuous opportunities for income and earnings if they are based on formal education and training programs.

> It is only functions which require a certain minimum of training and for which opportunity of continuous remuneration is available which become the objects of independent and stable occupations (Weber 1978, pp. 141-142)[19].

---

18 There are some researchers that define occupations solely through their education and training programs (e.g., Dunkmann 1922; Baethge and Baethge-Kinsky 1998; Baethge 2004). They usually emphasize the mismatch between occupational education and training programs and the tasks and skills employers' actually need. They claim this mismatch is constantly growing because of the increasing speed of technological and social change, and that it erodes the basis of traditional (industrial) occupations, which are the tasks and skills education and training programs provide. However, this perspective ignores the simultaneous emergence of new occupations (Beck et al. 1980, p. 19; Mayer and Blossfeld 1990; Müller and Shavit 1998, p. 185; Fuchs 1999; Kupka 2005, p. 30; Brückner and Mayer 2005; Erlinghagen 2005; Kurz et al. 2005; Mayer et al. 2010).
This strand of thought first came up during the Industrial Revolution in Germany, where the traditional crafts and professions were displaced by new industrial occupations (see Fischer 1918; Dunkmann 1922; Scharmann 1956; Schelsky 1965, Beck et al. 1980, pp. 15-19). Given this (repeating) history, it is ironic that the current post-occupational discussion sees the industrial occupations as the ideal type of occupations. This ideal type of industrial occupation is considered to be under constant threat because of the shift from an industrial to a service economy (again without considering the emergence of new service occupations) (Baethge and Baethge-Kinsky 1998; Baethge 2001; Berger et al. 2001; Daheim 2001; Baethge 2004; a similar line of post-occupational discussions is presented by Rifkin 1995, Casey 1995, Sennett 1998, Doherty 2009).

19 Because of Weber's notions about continuity and stability, short term and discontinuous employment relations are often seen as contradicting his definition of occupations. But Weber explains further that "occupational specialization does not necessarily imply continuous rendering of services [...]. Other forms are not only possible but common: (1) Propertyless occupationally specialized workers may be employed on an occasional basis as needed in the service of either consumers in household units or employers in profit-making enterprises" (Weber 1978, p. 142). Continuous employment is not an essential element of occupations.

Occupational education and training programs are crucial to enable occupational incumbents to perform a complex of occupation-specific tasks, which creates a fragmentation of the labor supply and labor demand. As a consequence, boundaries between occupations emerge (Kerr 1954; Stolzenberg 1975). Employers rely on occupations as a source of information about the suitability of employees for vacant positions that demand certain combinations of tasks and skills. They also provide individuals with information about what work conditions and earnings they can expect.

3) Occupational education and training also has an important impact on the formation of occupational identities (Durkheim 1988, 1991; Hughes and Coser 1994)[20] and the employability of the occupational incumbents. Only occupations whose members share the same values and a sense of identity can become collective enterprises (see: Caplow 1954; Braude 1975, pp. 83-87; Collins 1979, p. 59; Van Maanen and Barley 1984, p. 291; Corsten 1995, pp. 41-42; Rothmann 1998, pp. 5-6; Grusky and Sørensen 1998, pp. 1196-1198; Kupka 2005, p. 24).

2.4 No Trespassing—The Mechanisms and Sources of Occupational Closure

The existence of occupation-specific sets of tasks and skills results in an occupational fragmentation of the labor market, which may be reinforced by institutionalized barriers (Kerr 1954, Stolzenberg 1975, Beck et al. 1980; Sengenberger 1987, Grusky and Sørensen 1998, pp. 1210-1212). These barriers are created by legal and normative provisions that limit access to occupations to a small circle of qualified individuals (Parkin 1979, p. 3). Max Weber (1978) refers to this process as social closure. "Social closure, according to Weber (1978, pp. 43-46, 339-48, 926-55), occurs wherever the competition for a liveli-

---

Essential elements of occupations are the specialization, specification, and combination of tasks or functions that are attained through education.

20 For some authors, occupational identity is a key element that defines occupations. For example, Van Maanen and Barley describe an occupation as a group of individuals "who consider themselves to be engaged in the same sort of work [...]" (Van Maanen and Barley 1984, p. 295; see also: Hall 1975, p. 3-5; Mortimer and Lorence 1979; Statistisches Bundesamt 1992, p. 15; Freidson 1994, p. 86; Hughes 1994, pp. 59-63; Biersack and Parmentier 2002, pp. 480-481; Standing 2009, p. 11). The minimum requirement for a shared identity (or character as Sennett puts it) is a shared narrative of difficulties (Sennett 1998, p. 147).

hood creates groups interested in reducing that competition" (Weeden 2002, p. 58). It is an important basis for unequal labor market opportunities[21].

Analogous to Weber's (1978) concept of social closure, occupational closure refers to mechanisms that continuously establish, contest, or reinforce institutional boundaries around occupations (e.g., Kerr 1954; Hall 1975, p. 70; Parkin 1979, p. 48; Beck et al. 1980, pp. 38-44; Van Maanen and Barley 1984, p. 290; Murphy 1988; Hughes 1994; Weber 1978, 2001, pp. 83-87; Brint 1994, p. 23; Freidson 1994; Tolbert 1996; Weeden 2002;). These boundaries affect employees' negotiating power, their labor market opportunities, and thus, their labor market-related risks, like the employee's risk of holding a temporary employment contract (Freedman 1976; Beck et al. 1980, pp. 77-78; Weeden 2002; Haupt 2012)[22]. Kim Weeden (2002) identifies four different mechanisms of occupational closure that create and reinforce these boundaries: restricting the occupation-specific labor supply, increasing the diffuse demand, channeling the demand for tasks and services to an occupation, and signaling of quality (Weeden 2002, p. 60).

The restriction of the occupation-specific labor supply (hereinafter referred to as the "restricting supply mechanism") is the primary closure mechanism researchers usually consider, if they account for occupational closure at all. They take this mechanism into consideration to analyze inequalities in the distribution of earnings (e.g., Weeden 2002; Kleiner 2006; Weeden et al. 2007; Kleiner and Krüger 2010; Abraham et al. 2011; Groß 2012; Haupt 2012; Bol and Weeden 2014). These studies use the concept of rents to explain the impact of this closure mechanism on inequalities in earnings. Rents exist where demand for an asset exceeds the supply and where the supply is fixed, for example, through political barriers that artificially restrict supply (e.g., Sørensen 1996; 2000; Congleton et al. 2008, 2010; Weeden and Grusky 2014)[23]. The artificially restricted supply of the asset prevents the adjustment of demand and supply that would occur in a free market and thus guarantees higher earnings (Berlant 1975, p. 54). Even if rents explicitly refer to wages, the underlying logic is also applicable to temporary employment. Barriers to entering the labor market create a disjuncture between the labor supply and

---

21 "Usually one group of competitors takes some externally identifiable characteristic of another group of (actual or potential) competitors – race, language, local or social origin, descent, residence, etc. – as a pretext for attempting their exclusion"(Weber 1978, p. 342).

22 This does not mean that all members of an occupation benefit equally from closure. However, the overall labor market chances that are provided by occupations will benefit or harm all its members, but not all to the same degree (Weeden 2002, p. 59).

23 Weeden and Grusky define rent "as returns on an asset (e.g., labor) in excess of what is necessary to keep that asset in production in a fully competitive market" (2014, p. 474)

employer demand for a particular type of labor. This improves working conditions within the occupations—whether in the form of higher pay or in the form of greater job stability through permanent employment contracts.

An increase in diffuse demand (hereinafter referred to as the "increasing diffuse demand mechanism") ensures that the benefits produced by the restrictions in the labor supply can be obtained. A constant demand for occupation-specific tasks and skills is necessary or the restriction of the labor supply will have no effect (e.g., Brint 1994, pp. 76-77). Maintaining constant demand for occupation-specific work or services is thereby essential for occupations that want to avoid ending up in the "dustbin of history with railroad dispatchers, dancing masters, and psychological mediums (Abbott 1988, pp. 29-30)" (Weeden 2002, p. 65).

The channeling of demand to occupations (hereinafter referred to as the "channeling demand mechanism") reduces the competition with other occupations over their profitable task niches (Beck and Brater 1976, p. 246; Abbott 1988). The beneficiaries need to have tools at their disposal that allow them to restrict competition with other occupations. If they do not restrict the competition with other occupations, employers will alternatively choose employees from related occupations with similar sets of tasks and skills. Consequently, the demand for specific tasks and skills has to be channeled to the specific occupation to prevent other occupations from cashing in and thereby driving the closure rent down (Berlant 1975, p. 48; Weeden and Grusky 2014, pp. 482-483).

Signals of quality indicate the appropriateness of individuals for positions that demand certain tasks and skills. They are based on occupations as labels, which instantly invoke stereotypes about the set of skills the occupational members are known to have or believed to have. Employers can rely on these stereotypical templates to assess which individuals are (believed to be) best trained to perform a vacant position effectively, efficiently, and at a particular level of quality (e.g., Hall 1975, p. 71; Stolzenberg 1975; Abbott 1988; Tolbert 1996, p. 338; Weeden 2002, pp. 66-67).

According to Weeden (2002, p. 67), successful signaling of quality has the effect that consumers are willing to pay more for occupational services. However, this mechanism of occupational closure works differently when applied to temporary employment. Successful signaling increases the employer's general willingness to choose members of one occupation above members of other occupations. This is because the signal of quality promises a guaranteed minimum level of quality (skills and knowledge) and thereby a minimum level of productivity. Members of other occupations may have signals that also promise a certain level of productivity, but the signal quality may be lower or there may be no signals at all. In the latter case, employers would have to rely on ineffective and costly trial-and-error procedures to determine the suitability and productivity of these individuals for vacant positions (Arrow 1972; Spence 1973; Thurow 1975; Solga and Konietzka 1999; Haupt 2012; Stuth and Hennig 2014).

If successful signaling increases employers' willingness to choose members of one occupation rather than members of other occupations, then signaling does not constitute a closure mechanism on its own. The true mechanism underlying signaling is the channeling mechanism—signaling channels demand to occupations. In contrast to Weeden (2002), I will therefore subsume the signaling of quality mechanism into the channeling demand mechanism.

Weeden (2002) introduces institutionalized sources of closure as proxies for closure mechanisms because closure mechanisms (e.g., supply side restrictions) are not directly measurable. Yet it is possible to measure the strength of institutions through closure sources that create, for example, supply-side restrictions. Closure sources are institutionalized occupational practices that trigger one or more closure mechanisms and thereby help to create or ensure that occupations remain labor market shelters (Freidson 1994, pp. 83-84; see also Parkin 1979; Weeden 2002). However, closure sources differ in their social and economic payoff because each institutionalized closure source triggers different closure mechanisms. The more closure mechanisms are triggered by an occupation, the lower the risk that its incumbents will hold temporary employment contracts should be.

At this point, it is worth noting why the term "source" is used here and not "strategy". In fact, Weeden (2002) originally used the term "closure strategies" instead of "closure sources". However, the term "strategy" implies some degree of intentional occupation-based collective action. To account for the fact that occupational closure may exist without occupations actively pursuing closure strategies, Weeden suggested using the term "closure source" instead.

In the following sections I introduce five closure sources (credentialism, licensing, preserving occupational specificity, representation by occupational associations, and unionization) and elucidate their impact on the individual's risk of holding a temporary employment contract.

2.4.1 Credentialism

Social closure can be based on virtually any group attribute, like race, religion, regional origin, or social origin etc. (Weber 1978, p. 342), but credentials are the main sources of social closure in modern societies because they make it possible "to control and monitor entry to key positions in the division of labor" (Parkin 1979, p. 48). Credentials provide a signal that certain characteristics have been acquired in formal training or education programs. Credentials persist for a number of reasons—for one, they are important for guaranteeing efficient performance—but the primary interest of credential-providing bodies is in limiting the supply of candidates for the benefit of a given occupation (Weber 1978, p. 344)[24].

> If we hear from all sides demands for introduction of regulated curricula culminating in specialized examinations, the reason behind this is, of course, not a suddenly awakened "thirst for education," but rather the desire to limit the supply of candidates for these positions and monopolize them for the holders of educational patents (Weber 1978, p. 1000; also see: Larson 1977; Collins 1979)[25].

The supply of candidates can be formally controlled by recruiting people into education and training tracks, training them, and requiring them to sit examinations. The examination and training processes that candidates must complete are often challenging, and thus, they give the occupations direct control over the supply of (successful) candidates (Weber 1978, pp. 999-1000; 2001, p. 87; also see: Berlant 1975, p. 182; Larson 1977, p. 55; Parkin 1979, p. 60-64; Beck et al. 1980, pp. 43-48; Murphy 1988, p. 9; Sørensen 1996, pp. 1346-1347; Weeden 2002, p. 62). The occupations may also exert indirect control by defining necessary preconditions for entering the education and training programs (Caplow 1954, p. 105; Parkin 1971, p. 21). If the number of potential candidates increases, training or examination standards may be raised to ensure or maintain the scarcity of the credentials (Caplow 1954, p. 105; Larson 1977, p. 52; Freidson 1994, p. 83-84;), because "[...] it is the degree of scarcity relative to demand which largely determines occupational reward" (Parkin 1971, p. 21, also see: Larson 1977, p. 48; Collins 1979, p. 27; Beck et al. 1980, p. 79; Müller and Shavit 1998).

Weber argues that examinations are a means of selection by qualification. He also notes that formal training dispenses with the need for talent (charisma) and replaces it with the need for economic capital because formal training and education requires considerable investments of time and capital. Occupational candidates also have to comply with cultural requirements. Occupations may have minimum prerequisites that are necessary to get access to their education and training programs; they demand prestigious school-leaving certificates. The problem is that the educational system that grants the school leaving certificates is biased in favor of the culture of the middle class and discriminates "against

---

24 "The smaller and the more exclusive such a circle is, the higher will be both the economic value and the social prestige of membership" (Weber 1978, p. 347).

25 "Even in so modest a form as a letter of reference, credentialism is intrinsically exclusionary, for if one person has a letter and the other has not, the other may not be able to gain the opportunity to work" (Freidson 1994, p. 160; see also Parkin 1979, p. 58).

those who do not use its vocabulary and do not refer to the same literary classics or technicist ideals" (Collins 1975, p. 87; also see: Bourdieu and Passeron 1970; Collins 1971, 1979; Bourdieu 1987, Murphy 1988)[26].

Raising the entry requirements by requiring school-leaving certificates has a selective effect on the composition of potential candidates. However, this kind of social closure does not reduce the absolute number of candidates but ensures that their habitus matches the habitus of the occupational group members (Collins 1971, 1975, p. 87, 1979; Beck et al. 1980)[27]. Any occupation seeking to control or reduce the number of their credentialed members would instead restrict the supply of education and training opportunities or make it more difficult to successfully complete the education and examination processes (e.g., Larson 1977, p. 52).

> *Hypothesis 1:* A worker's risk of holding a temporary employment contract is not only based on his/her individual skills, but on the competitive supply of their credentialed occupation-specific skills[28]. Occupations with a low supply of individuals with occupation-specific credentials reduce competition between their members and simultaneously increase competition between employers, who have to rely on the reduced occupation-specific workforce. Employers may now decide to use permanent employment contracts more often to secure the scarce occupation-specific skills. In contrast, incumbents of occupations with a high supply of occupation-specific credentials should face a high risk of holding temporary employment contracts.

Credentials also have to represent a common standard regarding the commodity occupational incumbents provide to employers. Employers will always choose individuals who have credentials of known value above individuals with credentials of unknown value. Therefore, it is not enough for the various

---

26   The argument Weber makes regarding the need for economic capital also holds true for cultural capital. Setting minimum schooling requirements to enter an occupational training track replaces the individual's talent with the cultural and/or economic capital of his/her parents (Weber 1978, p. 999-1000; 2001, p. 87). However, Murphy stresses the point that these exclusionary rules are set up for protective purposes and that inter-generational (im)mobility is not a foregone conclusion (1988, p. 12; also see Parkin 1979, pp. 60-64). "In other words, although the typical bourgeois family will certainly be better equipped than most to cope with the closure system on its children's behalf, it must still approach the task more in the manner of a challenge with serious risks attached than as a foregone conclusion" (Parkin 1979, p. 63).

27   "A large and widely dispersed supply of cultural currency makes resources available to many groups in the population for organizing themselves in this struggle, which may then result in the proliferation of monopolized occupational enclaves" (Collins 1979, p. 65).

28   "[...] the worker gets his security not from the individual employer but from his skill, the competitive supply of which is controlled by the occupational group" (Kalleberg and Sørensen 1979, p. 359).

training and education tracks to provide occupational incumbents with adequate training and socialization. These skills have "to be standardized in order to clearly differentiate their identity and connect them, in the minds of consumers, with stable criteria of evaluation" (Larson 1977, p. 14). In order to create a common standard on what the occupation's commodity is, occupational education and training programs have to follow standardized curricula and examinations (e.g., Larson 1977, pp. 9-18; Allmendinger 1989; Müller and Shavit 1998, p. 6; Brzsinky-Fay 2012; Ebner 2013). Occupational incumbents' intangible skills and knowledge become more tangible the more standardized formal education and training is. Standardized credentials represent recognizable and distinguishable occupation-specific skills and signal a well-defined use value[29]. They provide employers with information they can utilize to determine the potential productivity of future employees (Spence 1973; Thurow 1975; Barley and Tolbert 1991; Tolbert 1996, pp. 338-339; Solga and Konietzka 1999; Vicari 2014, p. 5). Standardized occupational credentials are thus unambiguous signals of craftsmanship and provide holders with an advantage over individuals whose credentials are unstandardized.

> *Hypothesis 2:* Incumbents from occupations whose credentials are standardized should face a low risk of holding temporary employment contracts because the demand for their tasks and skills is more likely to be channeled to their occupation. Incumbents from occupations without standardized credentials should not benefit from the channeling demand mechanism and face a higher risk of holding temporary employment contracts.

2.4.2 Licensing

Whereas credentialism is often considered to be the most important source of control of the supply of occupational candidates, licensure is viewed as the most significant closure source. It channels the demand to an occupation by restricting employers in their hiring decisions. Legal regulations of occupation-specific tasks require employers to hire only licensed workers for these tasks. Licensing is therefore, theoretically, much more powerful than credentialism because employers are usually not restricted to only recruiting, for example, credentialed carpenters for vacant carpenter positions[30]—they are free to fill positions with anyone they deem fit. Yet if state agencies grant licenses for

---

29 Occupations establish social credit for their sets of tasks and skills through the claim that their members are subject to rigorous evaluations and their credentials thereby life-long guarantors of competence (Murphy 1988, pp. 155-158).

30 For an extensive list of benefits or risks related to licensing of occupations, see Bryson and Kleiner (2010, pp. 670-671) or Haupt (2014, pp. 106-107).

occupation-specific tasks, true monopolizing power is established[31]. Licensing provides occupational incumbents with an exclusive patent on specific tasks and forbids members of other occupations from fulfilling these tasks under threat of legal prosecution (Braude 1975, p. 15; Larson 1977, pp. 14-18; Parkin 1979, pp. 54-60; Beck et al. 1980; Brater and Beck 1982, p. 113f.; Freidson 1994, pp. 80-84; Hughes and Coser 1994, p. 25; Weeden 2002, p. 62)[32]. Licensing in the form of protected titles rather than tasks should signal quality and hence channelthe demand to the occupations in question (Weeden 2002, p. 66).

> *Hypothesis 3*: Licensing should reduce the risk of employees holding temporary employment contracts because it channels the demand to licensed occupations.

2.4.3 Occupational Specificity

The composition of occupation-specific tasks and skills may be wide or narrow. This determines the marketability of these tasks and skills (Beck et al. 1980, pp. 75-90; Rotolo and McPherson 2001). Occupations that have managed to occupy task niches that are highly marketable trigger the "increasing diffuse demand" closure mechanism. Beck et al. (1980, p. 90) argue that the marketability of an occupation's tasks and skills is best described using an ideal-typical continuum that ranges from a very narrow set of tasks and skills to a very wide set of tasks and skills. Occupations with a wide range of tasks and skills can grant access to a multitude of different positions. They guarantee basic employability (Beck et al. 1980, p. 82; Witte and Kalleberg 1995; Hoffmann et al. 2011; Streeck 2011, pp. 4-5) and provide a constant demand for occupation-specific services. Occupational incumbents with narrow sets of tasks and skills are not as mobile as occupational incumbents with a wide range of tasks and skills (Iversen and Soskice 2001, p. 875). If the position of an individual with narrow tasks and skills is no longer required, employers will have very limited options to reassign these employees to jobs within the organization where they would be equally productive. Hence, according to this logic, belonging to an occupation with a narrow set of tasks increases the probability of temporary employment for these individuals.

However, proponents of signaling theory would argue that the opposite is the case. An occupation is highly marketable when its range of tasks and skills

---

31 This monopolizing effect of licensing has been extensively analyzed with regard to occupation's earnings (e.g., Weeden 2002; Kleiner and Morris 2002; Bryson and Kleiner 2010; Kleiner and Krueger 2010; Haupt 2012a; Bol and Weeden 2014; Bol 2014).

32 "The possession of the license implies propriety in activity associated with the work specialty" (Braude 1975, p. 15).

is narrow, and less marketable when this range is wide. The reasons for this are as follows: Signaling theory (Arrow 1972; Spence 1973; Thurow 1979; Williamson 1981) argues that employers need information about the suitability of applicants for available positions, their potential productivity, and the induction costs to decide with whom to fill vacant positions. It is not possible for employers to estimate with certainty how potential employees will perform. To fill positions with suitable employees despite this uncertainty while also minimizing recruitment and headhunting costs, employers use a variety of information sources—*signals*—to evaluate the potential suitability of applicants. The occupation of a potential employee provides employers with information, but the value of the information varies across occupations (Haupt 2012; Stuth and Hennig 2014). The signaling value of an occupation depends on the narrowness or wideness of the occupation in question. Narrow occupational task profiles send strong and clear signals to potential employers as to whether and how well applicants are suited for available positions (Hall 1975, pp. 71; Stolzenberg 1975; Larson 1977, pp. 9-18, 40-48; Mortimer and Lorence 1979, Allmendinger 1989; Tolbert 1996, p. 338; Müller and Shavit 1998, p. 6). Employers will therefore prefer incumbents of occupations with narrow task profiles to fill vacant positions (channeling demand). Occupations with wide task profiles can be widely deployed (Beck et al. 1980, p. 90; Abraham et al. 2011, pp. 8-9.), but they only have a limited signaling function for employers as it remains unclear whether wide task profiles match specific job requirements.

According to the mobility perspective of Iversen and Soskice (2001), occupations with a wide range of tasks should trigger the "increasing diffuse demand" mechanism, whereas the signaling perspective assumes that incumbents of occupations with a narrow range of tasks should trigger the "channeling demand" mechanism. Both theoretical approaches have valid arguments. I will therefore assume that there is an association between narrow and wide sets of tasks and temporary employment. However, because it is not possible to theoretically determine the direction of this association, I propose a bidirectional hypothesis.

Hypothesis 4: The lower mobility of employees with a narrow range of tasks should increase their risk of temporary employment because employers will be reluctant to grant permanent employment contracts to individuals who cannot be efficiently reassigned within their organization.

Hypothesis 5: Employers will use temporary employment contracts more often when the fit between job requirements and the individuals' task profiles is uncertain, which is the case for occupations with a wide range of tasks and skills.

The tasks and skills that occupations provide also differ in their degree of uniqueness. Occupations that provide employers with unique tasks and skills guarantee their members exclusivity (Beck et al. 1980, p. 872; Van Maanen and Barley 1984). Occupations with exclusive sets of tasks and skills trigger the channeling demand closure mechanism. The intersection between occupations' relatively unique task niches and the task niches of other occupations is small. Hence, there is little competition between occupational incumbents with incumbents of other occupations for vacant positions that require these unique tasks and skills. Employers have to rely on the occupational workforce if they require their specific skills. Members of occupations with common sets of tasks and skills share a lot of their tasks and skills with other occupations and thus face an increased level of competition (e.g., Rotolo and McPherson 2001; Abraham et al. 2011, p. 9; Streeck 2011, pp. 22-23). The segmentation of the labor markets for these occupations is imperfect, and the barriers between the occupation-specific labor markets are low. However, unique tasks and skills should be a relatively rare phenomenon because other occupations will encroach on exclusive tasks and skills and try to integrate them into their inventories of tasks and skills so that they can cash in on and profit from their exclusivity (Freidson 1994, p. 85).

> *Hypothesis 6:* Temporary employment contracts will be rare in occupations with unique tasks because employers strongly rely on the workforce of these occupations and do not have the possibility to substitute these individuals with incumbents from other occupations.

2.4.4 Occupational Associations

There is little empirical evidence on whether occupational associations are an important source of occupational closure or not[33], but there are ample theoretical arguments proposing that occupational associations are important organizational actors that represent occupations in their upward mobility project (Pavalko 1971; Braude 1975; Larson 1977; Van Maanen and Barley 1984; Abbott 1988; Weeden 2002). I will consider two features of occupational associations that allow associations to further the interests of the occupations they represent: First, occupational associations act as lobby groups, and second, they attempt to establish or maintain social credit and professional ethics[34].

---

33 Weeden, for example, found no association between occupational associations and wages, net of other sources of occupational closure (Weeden 2002), while a study on closure in Germany found an association between occupational associations and occupational mobility, also net of other sources of occupational closure (Hoffmann et al. 2011).

34 I present only a very narrow set of functions occupational associations perform because my theoretical approach focuses on occupational closure. For a more comprehensive review of

The baseline function of each occupational association is to lobby on behalf of the occupations they represent by engaging in PR campaigns on behalf of their occupational incumbents (Weeden 2002, p. 65). Lobbying is an attempt to trigger the "increasing diffuse demand" closure mechanism. Occupational associations address the general public through advertisements, or lobby the government on the federal or state level for regulations to maintain or increase demand for occupation-specific goods or services (see Weeden 2002, pp. 65-66). Lobbying attempts on the part of occupational associations may aim to increase state or federal expenditure on public services (e.g., increased education spending affects all education related occupations) or introduce laws that oblige the public to make use of certain occupational services (for example: In Germany, house owners have to hire a chimney sweeper at legally defined intervals). They may also aim to increase the demand for occupational services or products using advertisements to address the general public. For example, in 2010, the chambers of crafts in Germany decided to spend 50 million euros over five years on an advertising campaign to emphasize the importance of the crafts. They tried to increase the willingness of consumers to rely on their services and goods because of their tradition of providing skilled services and high quality goods[35].

> *Hypothesis 7*: The lobbying activities of occupational associations may trigger the "increasing diffuse demand" mechanism, which in turn may change the equilibrium between occupation-specific labor demand and supply to the benefit of the occupational incumbents, who should thus face a low risk of holding temporary employment contracts.

Occupational associations also attempt to establish/maintain social credit and to promote the public's belief in the professional and ethical conduct of their members (e.g., Plant 2000; Haynes and Gazley 2011, pp. 60-61). For occupations that wish to improve their public standing, it is important to improve and maintain occupational ethics and standards because it enhances the marketability of their incumbents' tasks and skills. I have already pointed out that occupational training and education establishes standards that render occupation-specific sets of tasks and skills distinctive, recognizable, and, in other words, marketable (Larson 1977, p. 14). Occupation-specific standards may be violated by individual members that wish to maximize their individual chances and profit, and who thereby threaten the social credit and ethics of their occupa-

---

functions occupational associations may perform, see Caplow (1954), Millerson (1964), and Daheim (1967).

35 See, for example, this advertisement, which emphasizes the civilizing function of the crafts: https://www.youtube.com/watch?v=1TwIUgd7eb0.

tion. Yet it will only be possible for occupations to ensure their tasks and skills are very marketable if their individual members obey the occupational standards (Larson 1977, p. 63)[36]. Hence, occupations have to ensure that occupation-specific standards are upheld. Individuals with their own inclinations and ambitions must be subjected to the rule of the occupation's ethics and standards (Larson 1977, p. 58). Occupational associations provide the necessary organizational means to establish a sense of occupational consciousness. They develop social networks that become a means of informal control between the members of occupations and reinforce occupational standards and ethics (Lipset et al. 1956, pp. 106-139; Pavalko 1971, pp. 103-107; Braude 1975, pp. 83-87; Van Maanen and Barley 1984, pp. 331-333; Tolbert 1996, p. 339).

> Thus, persons who may in their normal work activities be in competition with one another (businessmen), or physically and spatially separated (physicians, academicians in different universities, bricklayers working on different construction sites) are brought together under the aegis of the occupational association in such a way as to minimize their differences and maximize their sense of common interest, concern, and destiny (Pavalko 1971, p. 106).

Occupational associations also establish formal sets of sanctions and rules that are used to reinforce occupational identity and standards on formal occasions like conferences or rallies (Pavalko 1971, pp. 105-107)[37]. Standards of performance and conduct are reviewed, the catalogue of relevant work activities and techniques revised, and behavior that contravenes the occupational paradigm is formally or informally sanctioned, including by expelling members (Braude 1975; Van Maanen and Barley 1984; Abbott 1988). Hence, occupational associations use social control to reinforce occupational standards and ethics. Social control is a prerequisite to establishing social credit and furthering the public's belief in the professional ethics of the occupations' incumbents.

> *Hypothesis 8:* Occupations' social credit and professional ethics may trigger the "channeling demand" closure mechanism and thereby reduce the risk of their members holding temporary employment contracts.

---

36 Occupational associations ideally transform loosely connected occupational incumbents into a Weberian-style status group. Status groups make effective claims on social esteem and social honor, and are often able to translate these claims into the monopolization of ideal and material goods and opportunities (Murphy 1988, p. 8).

37 "Here the formality and dignity of ceremony can be combined with the repetition, rhythm, and emotional contagion of ritual to make of any occasion for interaction a situation in which loyalty to occupational norms and views may be further inculcated." (Braude 1975, p. 85).

2.4.5 Unionization

Unions are sometimes conceptualized as a source of occupational closure because unions may affect the supply of labor and thereby generate rents (Weeden 2002; Bol and Weeden 2014). The most direct way unions might affect the supply of labor is through closed-shop agreements, wherein employers are only allowed to hire union members. Unions can also limit the supply of labor through union-run apprenticeship programs, which limit access to training, or through collective bargaining and the threat of strikes (Weeden 2002, pp. 63-64; Bol and Weeden 2014). The ability of unions to collectively bargain may allow occupations to negotiate a greater share of firm profits or improved working conditions like permanent employment contracts (e.g., Morgan and Tang 2007, p. 276; Eichhorst and Marx 2012, p. 85; Weeden and Grusky 2014, p. 482).

> *Hypothesis 9*: Unions may trigger the restricting supply mechanism and thereby decrease their clients' risk of temporary employment.

There is also the theoretical possibility that unions might contribute to the dualization of the workforce (Polavieja 2006; Hipp et al. 2015). Unions may indirectly support a flexibilization at the margins if they concentrate on their traditional core workforce, which would put labor market entrants or low-skilled workers at a disadvantage (Lindbeck and Snower 1988; Rubery 1989; Kahn 2007; Baranowska and Gebel 2010; Hevenstone 2010; Palier and Thelen 2010).

> *Hypothesis 10*: Based on the aforementioned theories, I expect that non-core workforce populations (youths or low skilled workers) are at a higher risk of temporary employment within unionized occupations than within nonunionized occupations.

2.4.6 Human Capital, Internal Labor Markets, and Occupational Closure

Human capital theory stresses the fact that employees differ in their productivity due to training and education (Becker 1962, 1964, Mincer 1974). I expand the standard predictions of human capital and internal labor market theories by incorporating closure theory arguments. Shifting the analytical focus to occupational closure does not mean that I will abandon well-established knowledge regarding human capital and internal labor markets. In the following paragraphs, I will address human capital theory and the internal labor market approach and formulate hypotheses about how they theoretically interrelate with the credentialism and specificity closure sources with regard to temporary employment[38].

My exploration in this regard will not just be theoretical. In the empirical section, I will also check for possible interactions between the complexity of work tasks (monitoring costs) and the occupational closure, and whether occupational closure works differently within occupations with regard to two socio-demographic groups that almost always have the highest risk of temporary employment: poorly qualified individuals and young adults (e.g., Giesecke and Groß 2003; Mertens and McGinnity 2004; McGinnity et al. 2005; DiPrete et al. 2006; Gundert 2007, pp. 276-278). These analyses, however, will be exploratory in nature[39].

Werfhorst (2011, pp. 526-528) describes how the theoretical relationship between skills, human capital, firm-internal labor markets, and temporary/permanent employment might relate to additional education and training. He points out that employers might offer additional training for employees whose productive value is uncertain in order to improve their initial qualifications and to increase their productivity. For employers, the uncertainty associated with occupational incumbents' productive value may be indicated by the standardization of their credentials. If employers require instant productivity, they rely on individuals with highly standardized credentials. Additional education and training of individuals with highly standardized credentials might not increase their productivity much further and should have little effect on their risk of temporary employment. However, with regard to members of unstandardized occupations, additional training might substantially increase their productivity (Werfhorst 2011, p. 526).

> *Hypothesis 11*: The standardization of occupational credentials is theoretically interconnected with additional education and training. The higher initial risk of temporary employment for occupational incumbents with unstandardized credentials (as proposed in hypothesis 2) might be offset by additional education and training courses. Both the investment in further education and the resulting increase in productivity should decrease the risk of temporary employment. This offsetting feature of further education should be much weaker for occupations with highly standardized credentials, as these occupations already have a high level of productivity.

---

38 The other sources of occupational closure, licensing, associations, and trade unions do not theoretically intersect with human capital theory, and licensing and associations do not theoretically intersect with the internal labor market approach.

39 It is not possible to align the ample knowledge on task complexity with my skill complexity measure. Conventional skill measures normally use one measure for each skill, whereas I have to use several measures to capture the skill-level of tasks (see section 5.3.6).

   Because no analysis has been done on the determinants of temporary employment that also includes detailed occupations and various sources of occupational closure, it is not possible to deduce hypotheses for both of these high-risk groups that are based on known facts or theories.

Regarding the skill composition of occupations (narrow or wide sets of skills), additional education and training should positively impact both occupations with narrow and occupations with wide ranges of skills. However, when we take the role of additional education and training into consideration, this makes it necessary to modify the argument that narrow skill sets might more easily become redundant with changing technologies or markets (and therefore should be more often affected by temporary employment contracts). Allowing for an effect of education and training on the relationship between narrow sets of skills and temporary employment might seriously change this predicted outcome because these skill sets would change in line with the changing circumstances. In this context, the initial argument (hypothesis 4 – Iversen and Soskice's (2001) mobility perspective) that employers will reluctantly grant permanent employment contracts to individuals who cannot be efficiently reassigned within their organization, would become obsolete.

> *Hypothesis 12*: Additional education and training may offset the low flexibility employers experience when reassigning occupational incumbents with narrow skill sets. Given this possibility, the incumbents' risk of temporary employment should converge between occupations with wide and narrow sets of skills as their participation in additional education and training courses increases, if hypothesis 5 (signaling perspective) is false.

> *Hypothesis 13*: Alternatively, the risk of temporary employment may diverge even more for incumbents of occupations with wide and narrow skill sets as their participation in additional education and training courses increases. That would be the case if both hypotheses, hypothesis 4 (mobility) and hypothesis 5 (signaling), are true. In this particular setting, the mobility argument would predict a strong decrease in the risk of temporary employment mainly for incumbents of occupations with narrow sets of skills who participate in additional education and training courses.

Occupational incumbents with relatively unique skills might not benefit at all from the uniqueness of their skills if employers can provide these unique skills through additional education and training courses. The positive aspects of an occupation inhabiting a specific task niche (low competition) would cease to exist, but the negative aspects would remain. Incumbents of occupations with relatively unique skills are restricted to a relatively fixed sample of possible jobs. Hence, they cannot easily avoid increasing competition within their niche by choosing other types of jobs.

> *Hypothesis 14*: If additional education and training courses grant access to relatively unique occupational niches, the advantage held by individuals in these niches would deteriorate, while at the same time, the unique character of their skills would tie the incumbents to their niche. The risk of temporary employment should increase steeply for incumbents of these occupations.

A similar argument can be made for scarce credentials. However, only the first half of the argument (increasing competition) also applies to the scarcity of credentials. If employers have the option to provide scarce skills through additional education and training courses, incumbents of occupations whose credentials are scarce might not benefit from the scarcity of their credentials and the occupation-specific skills they signify.

Hypothesis 15: Further education might neutralize the benefits of scarce credentials.

Organizations with internal labor markets are usually also large organizations, which incur lower marginal costs for additional training of employees than small organizations (Knoke and Kalleberg 1994, p. 538; Werfhorst 2011). As a result, the use of temporary employees is more cost effective for large organizations than for small organizations (see Uzzi and Barsness 1998, p. 973). Assuming that hypothesis 15 is not true and, on the contrary, employers try to secure scarce occupation-specific skills (hypothesis 1), they might alternatively use the more cost-efficient temporary employment contracts for incumbents of occupations whose credentials are awarded in an inflationary manner. The ample supply of individuals with such credentials on the labor market means organizations do not have to rely on long-term employment contracts to secure their occupation-specific skills.

Hypothesis 16: Incumbents of occupations with credentials awarded in an inflationary manner may face an increased risk of temporary employment in large organizations.

Temporary employment contracts may be used by the management of large organizations as a critical resource to assert dominance over organizational labor practices. Occupational incumbents who are represented by occupation-specific trade unions might thus be temporarily employed more often in order to weaken the union's power because temporary employees are harder to unionize and remind permanent employees of their substitutability (e.g., Pfeffer and Baron 1988; Uzzi and Barsness 1998).

Hypothesis 17: Incumbents of occupations that are represented by trade unions might face an increased risk of temporary employment in large organizations.

2.5 Summary on Occupational Closure and Temporary Employment

I defined occupations by addressing three major occupational features: their sets of tasks and skills, which are based on occupational education and training programs, and their social dimension. Vocational education and training tracks establish occupation-specific sets of tasks, which differ in their scarcity or abundance. Furthermore, occupations are social groups, which may (un)intentionally improve the labor market chances of their incumbents. I introduced three different closure mechanisms that serve this purpose and thereby might reduce employees' risk of holding temporary employment contracts: restricting labor supply, increasing diffuse demand, and channeling demand to occupations. Since it is not possible to observe these mechanisms directly, I adopt Kim Weeden's (2002) analytical approach and introduce observable closure sources that trigger these closure mechanisms: credentialism, licensing, occupational specificity, and occupational associations.

Credentials may trigger the restricting supply mechanism insofar as the credentialing institutions limit the supply of occupation-specific credentials. Credentials may additionally trigger the channeling demand mechanism, depending on their degree of standardization. Some tasks are legally protected by licenses, which triggers the channeling demand mechanism. The tasks of occupations are structured in very different ways and thereby might trigger the increasing diffuse demand mechanism and/or the channeling demand mechanism, depending on their degree of task specialization or the unique nature of their tasks. Occupations that organize themselves in associations might also trigger the increasing diffuse demand mechanism and the channeling demand mechanism. Unionization also possibly triggers the restricting supply mechanism.

Human capital theory, the internal labor market approach, and task complexity may be interrelated with the previously mentioned closure sources. Additionally, there might be intra-occupational differences in the effects of the various closure sources on an individual's risk of temporary employment.

3   Case Selection

There are various reasons why Germany is an ideal-typical case for studying the interrelationship between occupational closure and temporary employment. First, Germany is renowned for its occupational labor market and the associated upper-secondary apprenticeship training system. Second, in Germany, the normative framework for employment relations is firmly based on standard work arrangements: Almost no employees want to have temporary employment contracts. Third, the institutional setting in Germany is characterized by relatively strict employment protection legislation, which incentivizes employers to use temporary employment contracts to increase their external, numerical flexibility.

Germany therefore represents an ideal setting for the analysis of the association between occupational closure and temporary employment. Occupations are a fixed part of the labor market and the education system. Employers have a constant demand for external and numerical flexibility due to the institutional setting. Since there is almost no voluntary temporary employment in Germany, it is correct to assume that employees would always choose permanent contracts over temporary employment contracts. If the various sources of occupational closure improve the bargaining position of employees, then their risk of temporary employment should be systematically associated with their respective occupations.

3.1 Germany as a Textbook Example of an Occupational Labor Market

In the German labor market, occupations have an important influence on employees' labor-market chances in terms of (un-)employment, income, and promotions (e.g., Blossfeld 1985, 1990; Krüger et al. 1989; Büchtemann et al. 1994; Corsten 1995; Witte and Kalleberg 1995; Dostal et al. 1998; Berger et al. 2001; DiPrete 2002; Mayer et al. 2010; Hoffmann et al. 2011; Haupt 2014; Stuth and Hennig 2014). Occupations relate to specific fields of activity, regulate the social allocation of recognition and prestige, and integrate individuals into the labor market and society (e.g., Dunkmann 1922; Beck et.al. 1976; Stooß 1982; Voß 1994; Kurtz 2001). An important characteristic of the German labor market is that occupations structure both the education/training system and the labor market: Occupational credentials are the key to accessing vacant positions (e.g., Marsden 1992, p. 415; Müller et al. 1998; Solga and Konietzka 1999; Kurtz 2001; Ebner 2013; Heisig and Solga 2014). These credentials are characterized by more vocational than general skills and are constitutive of the German occupational labor market (Marsden 1992; Hall and Soskice 2001). Additionally, Germany is renowned for its highly effective apprenticeship training as part of the upper-secondary education and training system. It provides apprentices with standardized, high-level qualifications that are specialized but not narrow. Employers benefit from the apprenticeship system because it provides relatively large numbers of highly skilled workers (*Facharbeiter*) that are easy to retrain and to redeploy in firm-internal labor markets. *Facharbeiter* are also highly mobile in external labor markets due to their standardized vocational credentials (Marsden 1992; Müller and Shavit 1998; Streeck 2011, pp. 4-5). In sum, *Facharbeiter* with upper-secondary educational credentials are the backbone of the German occupational labor market.

It is important not to confuse the craft workers of Anglophone societies with *Facharbeiter* in Germany. Especially the German apprenticeship system is organized around sets of tasks and skills that are continuously broadened and updated[40] to increase employees' professionalism, versatility, and mobility (Streeck 2011, p. 24). Craft work regimes, on the other hand, are organized around union-imposed job territories that are defined by narrow task specializations, which are also necessary requirements for employment. Although craft occupations (*Handwerk*) may be held in low regard in Anglophone societies, this is not the case in Germany.

> In this context it is interesting to remember that in the 1980s, an English industrial sociologist, who had studied the small-firm Handwerk sector in Germany, expressed his admiration for the high levels of competence he had seen by referring to German *Handwerksberufe* as 'professions for the people'(Streeck 2011, p. 25).

Unlike the English language, the German language does not distinguish between professions and craft occupations. The German word *Beruf* covers carpenters, automobile repairmen, and hairdressers as well as physicians, lawyers, or teachers. Therefore, when I use the term occupation, I refer to the whole spectrum of vocations, crafts, and professions that are practiced in Germany.

---

40 The process of constructing and updating training occupations in Germany occurs through cooperation among a wide range of actors: the federal government, the governments of the *Länder* (states), the employers' associations, the unions, and the Institute for Occupational Research (Bundesinstitut für Berufsbildung (BIBB)).

3.2 The Norm of Standard Work Arrangements and the Deregulation of Employment Protection Legislation in Germany

In Germany, temporary employment is involuntary. Census data show that nearly 99 percent of all workers with temporary employment contracts in Germany would rather have permanent employment contracts (German Microcensus 2008: own calculations; Bellmann et al. 2009, p. 379). This very high percentage confirms that employment relations are firmly based on the normative framework of standard work arrangements. This is an important precondition for the analyses, which are based on the assumption that employees will always choose permanent employment contracts over temporary employment contracts.

Despite the established norm of standard work arrangements, temporary employment is moderately increasing (see figure 1). The share of employees with temporary employment contracts (in comparison to all employees between 15-64 years) increased from 6 percent in 1993 to 10 percent in 2008[41].

Figure 1: Temporary employment in Germany, 1993 to 2008

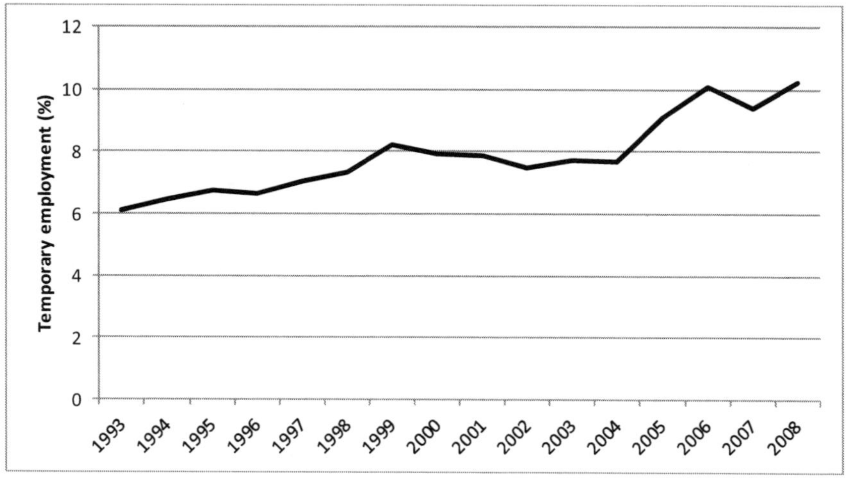

Source: RDC of the Federal Statistical Office and the Statistical Offices of the Länder, Microcensus, survey years 1993-2008, own calculations

---

41 See Allmendinger et al. (2013) for a comprehensive description of the trends in temporary employment (and various other kinds of nonstandard work arrangements) in Germany and another 20 European countries over a period of 16 years.

These changes are due to the relaxation of the legislation on temporary employment, which has allowed employers to circumvent the relatively strict employment-protection legislation. German employment-protection legislation presents employers with three principal challenges when they start dismissal processes: procedural inconveniences, notice periods, and severance payments[42]. The law also restricts the reasons for which employees can get dismissed to reasons of conduct (e.g., absenteeism) or capacity (e.g., illness)[43]. Insufficient business is also valid grounds for laying employees off, but additional restrictions apply[44]. However, employment protection is not relevant for all employees. There are three categories of employees that are not eligible for employment protection: (1) newly hired employees (for the first six months of employment), (2) employees in organizations with less than ten full-time equivalent employees[45], and (3) employees with temporary employment contracts.

Even if temporary employment contracts present employers with a legal opportunity to circumvent the employment protection legislation, labor courts require companies to have "objective reasons" (*sachliche Gründe*) for using temporary employment contracts (§§ 620-628 BGB). Until the introduction of the Employment Promotion Act in 1985 (*Beschäftigungsförderungsgesetz*), it was illegal to employ workers without "objective reasons" on a temporary basis. Legally valid "objective reasons" were, for example, the need for substitutes for unavailable employees, or extra workers for seasonal or (scientific)

---

42 For the impact of legislation on the individual's risk of holding a temporary employment contract see Goux et al. (2001), Blanchard and Landier (2002), Cahuc and Postel-Vinay (2002), Kahn (2007, 2010), Gebel and Giesecke (2011). For information on how the deregulation of employment protection for permanent and temporary employees ambiguously affects the individual's labor market chances and risks, see Bentolila and Saint-Paul (1992), Bentolila and Dolado (1994), Cabrales and Hopenhayn (1997), Smith (1997, p. 327), Boeri (1999), Goux and Maurin (2000), Güell (2000a,b), Korpi and Levin (2001), Blanchard and Landier (2002), Cahuc and Postel-Vinay (2002), Polavieja (2003), Boockmann and Hagen (2005a,b), Kurz et al. (2005), Boockmann and Hagen (2006), Giesecke (2009), Hohendanner and Gerner (2010), Kahn (2010).

43 In situations of gross misconduct (e.g., persistent disobedience, theft), permanent illness and misuse of confidential information, employers are allowed to dismiss employees without notice (extraordinary dismissal) (Schömann et al. 1998, pp. 38-40).

44 Layoffs of this nature are not permitted if alternative and equivalent positions are available, and layoffs have to follow social criteria (seniority, age, disability, support of dependent relatives). There are also groups of persons to whom special protection applies (for example: it is not permitted to dismiss mothers-to-be until the fourth month after birth or members of the works council (see Zimmermann 1997, p. 65)).

45 This special regulation for small organizations has changed repeatedly in the last 20 years between thresholds of five or ten full-time equivalent employees.

project work, etc.[46]. Chains of temporary employment contracts were possible. The Employment Promotion Act from 1985 deregulated the use of temporary employment contracts by removing the requirement to provide "objective reasons" for new employees or apprentices who had just finished training within their organization[47]. The act did not replace the old regulations, which allowed temporary employment for "objective reasons," but complemented the regulations by providing the possibility of time-restricted temporary employment without reason.

The Employment Promotion Act, whose validity was originally limited to five years, was renewed twice (1989 and 1994). It was modified in 1996 and was valid until 2000. The amendment in 1996 made it possible to use temporary employment without objective reasons for all employees; it was no longer restricted to new employees or apprentices who finished their training. Additionally, the maximum duration of temporary employment contracts was increased to two years and employers no longer faced any duration restrictions if they wanted to employ older workers (those aged 60 years or older) on a temporary basis.

As a result of an EU directive[48], in the year 2000, the previous legislation on temporary employment was replaced with a new act on part-time work and temporary employment contracts (TzBfG). There are still no time restrictions on temporary employment with valid reasons. The duration of these contracts is determined by the reason itself (e.g., substitution of employees on sick leave is for the time the sick leave actually takes). There are three exceptions regarding the use of temporary employment without valid reasons (Schaub et al. 2009, pp. 300-350):

(1) For new employees[49], temporary employment contracts may be renewed three times in a row but with an overall maximum duration of two years. (2) New corporations that are not older than four years are allowed to use

---

46 For an extended list of valid reasons see Schömann et al. (1998, p.41), Schaub (1992, pp. 196-202); Rudolph (1987, p. 290) or Walwei (1990, p. 52).

47 The Employment Promotion Act only applies if there was no previous fixed-term contract between the parties in the preceding four months (Schömann et al. 1998, p. 42). It also restricts the duration of temporary employment contracts without "objective reasons" to a maximum of 18 months. Newly founded organizations that were not older than six months were allowed a maximum duration of these kinds of temporary employment contracts of 24 months.

48 Council Directive 1999/70/EC of 28 June 1999 concerning the framework agreement on fixed-term work concluded by ETUC, UNICE and CEEP (OJ 1999 L 175, p. 43)

49 New employees are defined as employees that were never previously employed (permanently or temporarily) by the employer.

temporary employment contracts for up to four years[50]. (3) Employers do not face any restrictions in using temporary employment contracts without valid reasons when the employees are 52 years old or older[51].

There is an additional regulation that applies only for small subpopulations of the workforce—academic and artistic staff as well as doctors. Introduced in the year 1985, it enables universities and (partially) publically financed research facilities to use temporary employment contracts almost without restrictions[52]. Only administrative staff, junior professors, and professors are exempted. Since the introduction of the regulations, there have been changes that have led to more rigidly defined thresholds of the maximum duration of temporary employment contracts (six years for PhD students, six additional years for postdocs and nine years for doctors).

---

50 This passage was not part of the original act on part-time work and temporary employment contracts and was added in 2003 (BGBl part 1, year 2003 nr. 67).

51 The original law included an age threshold of 58 years of age. After two years it was changed to 52 years of age (BGBl part 1, year 2002 nr. 87). However, after this legislation was introduced, the European Court of Justice interpreted this procedure as age discrimination. As a result, the act on part-time work and temporary employment contracts was changed. Since 2007, temporary employment without valid reasons has been possible up to a maximum duration of five years for individuals aged 52 or older, if they have been unemployed for at least four months or are part of a publicly financed employability measure (BGBl part 1, year 2007 nr. 15). The motivation behind these changes was to improve the employability of older workers.

52 HRG §§ 57a-57f, ÄArbVtrG (BGBl part 1, year 1986 nr. 21), WissZeitVG (BGBl part 1, year 2007 no. 13), see also Giesecke (2006, p. 124) or Schaub et al. (2009, pp. 326-330).

4 The Theoretical and Methodological Challenges of Operationalizing Closure Measures for Germany

This chapter will critically discuss established measures of occupational closure and explain why some of them are not a good fit for the German labor market. Research about occupational closure in Germany usually draws on Weeden's (2002) seminal work on occupational closure in the US, without considering national differences between the institutions of Germany and the US (Giesecke and Verwiebe 2009, p. 537; Groß 2009, p. 508; Abraham et al. 2011; Hofmann et al. 2011; Groß 2012, p. 466; Bol and Weeden 2014; Stuth and Hennig 2014). However, these institutional differences between Germany and the USA make it necessary to modify Weeden's (2002) operationalization of occupational closure to fit the German labor market. I will also discuss theoretical as well as methodological issues associated with measures that have not been used in the context of occupational closure.

4.1 Credentialism—An Unbalanced Concept

Research on credentialism as a closure source in Germany typically leans on Weeden's (2002) operationalization of credentialism: the proportion of occupational incumbents with tertiary degrees (e.g., Giesecke and Verwiebe 2009, p. 537; Groß 2009, p. 508; Groß 2012, p. 466)[53]. Weeden (2002, p. 79) argues that occupations successfully establish occupational closure based on credentials if they require their incumbents to hold tertiary degrees. However, there are several reasons why the proportion of occupational incumbents with tertiary degrees may not be the best proxy for the credentialism closure source, which theoretically should trigger the restricting supply mechanism as well as the channeling demand mechanism.

Weeden's (2002, p. 79) argument—that any link between an occupation and academic knowledge is sufficient to activate the mechanisms of occupational closure—is not true with regard to the restricting supply mechanism. There are a number of occupations that require tertiary degrees. However, the degrees required for these occupations are not specified, which has substantial

---

53 Abraham et al. (2011) base their credentialism measure on the percentage of occupational incumbents who only completed their basic schooling.

consequences for the degree of closure of these occupations. For example, executive consultants and management consultants have often studied subjects with very different sets of skills and knowledge (e.g., philosophy, history, literature, linguistics, economics, journalism, psychology, social science, industrial engineering, general physics, etc.). The approach to occupational closure through academic credentials proposed by Weeden (2002) would indicate that the consultant occupation is closed because of the high proportion of employees with tertiary degrees. However, an approach that does not rely on coarse qualification levels but on subject-of-study-specific credentials would show that the executive and management consultant occupation is not closed at all. Employers do not require candidates to have studied a particular academic subject to fill vacant consultant positions. The executive consultants and management consultants therefore fail to establish an occupation-specific credential on which employers mainly or at least partially rely. Hence, given that employers do not require subject-specific credentials to fill vacant consultant positions, we cannot say that credentialism triggers the restricting labor supply mechanism—after all, individuals with tertiary degrees are hardly scarce in most modern industrialized societies[54]. Hence, in terms of their credentials, executive consultants and management consultants are easily exchangeable owing to the fact that employers have access to a large pool of employees with tertiary degrees[55]. The fact that some occupations require tertiary degrees should nevertheless be interpreted as a process of closure in the sense of restricted intergenerational mobility (see Hauser and Warren 1997).

The question remains of how one might alternatively capture the link between the credentialism closure source and the restricting labor supply mechanism. I propose to utilize the German education and training system, which awards occupational credentials to the majority of the German population. I will determine whether the supply of occupation-specific credentials is restricted or not by analyzing the supply of newly credentialed incumbents for each occupation per year. Relating the number of newly credentialed occupational incumbents to the number of employed incumbents should provide a clear picture: If we see a low ratio, it would indicate that an occupation's workforce is modestly reproducing itself and is thereby relatively small, and if we see a high ratio, it would indicate an occupation that awards its credentials in an

---

54 In the US, 42 percent of the population between 25 and 64 years of age has a tertiary degree, whereas in Germany, 27 percent of this population has a tertiary education degree (OECD 2012a, p. 1; Allmendinger and Driesch 2014, p. 9).

55 The critique also applies to attempts to measure closure through apprenticeship training programs by using the percentage of employees within occupations holding vocational qualifications (Stuth et al. 2009, p. 21; Bol and Weeden 2014; Stuth and Hennig 2014).

inflationary manner and the supply of the occupation's workforce is therefore not restricted at all.

The link between credentialism and the channeling supply mechanism is based on the assumption that tertiary degrees are superior to other credentials and thereby signal quality. However, this assumption does not apply in the German labor market (Streeck 2011, pp. 22-26). In Germany, closure is also—and even to a greater extent—established at the level of upper-secondary (apprenticeship) qualifications (see also Bol and Weeden 2014[56]). Although there are some recent publications that seek to avoid such an unbalanced approach by addressing various levels of qualifications on which occupational closure might be established (Konietzka 1999; Solga and Konietzka 1999; Stuth et al. 2009, p. 21; Haupt 2012; Bol and Weeden 2014; DiPrete et al. 2014; Stuth and Hennig 2014)[57], it is nevertheless important to bear this feature of the German labor market in mind. Additionally, there are vast differences between tertiary level degrees (but also between upper-secondary level qualifications, etc.) with respect to the contents of their curricula, quality of education, and the skills obtained, etc. (Streeck 2011, p. 23; Allmendinger and Driesch 2014, p. 14). Therefore, it remains unclear how such a heterogeneous population of credentialed individuals might signal distinctiveness or quality and thereby trigger the channeling demand closure mechanism.

In this respect, there is another plausible mechanism. In the theory section, I introduced an additional dimension of credentialism that should trigger the channeling demand mechanism: standardization. Standardization is most commonly defined as "the degree to which the quality of education meets the same standards nationwide" (Allmendinger 1989, p. 233). This concept is usually used in international comparisons (e.g., Allmendinger 1989; Shavit and Müller 1998; Breen 2005; Ebner 2013). Scholars of occupational closure use the same concept to measure the varying signals of quality given by different credentials in Germany (Hoffmann et al. 2011; Vicari 2014). Hoffmann et al. (2011) and Vicari (2014) conceptualize standardization in terms of the regu-

---

56 Bol and Weeden (2014) point out that apprenticeship training in Germany is special and stands out from other forms of credentials. Therefore, they raise apprenticeship training credentials to the status of a source of occupational closure on their own. However, they do fail to establish why apprenticeships constitute a closure source that is distinct from the credentialism closure source, since underlying functions of both closure sources are similar (Bol and Weeden 2014, pp. 2-4).

57 Haupt (2012b) and Bol and Weeden (2014) use a "subjective" variable where the individuals were asked what kind of credential their position usually requires. The other researchers (Konietzka 1999; Solga and Konietzka 1999; Stuth et al. 2009, p. 21; Stuth and Hennig 2014; DiPrete et al. 2014) use "objective" variables that capture the empirical heterogeneity of different levels of education and training within the occupations.

lation of examinations. I follow Gamoran (1996), who argues that standardized examinations may guarantee a minimum level of skills and knowledge. However, standardized curricula provide even stronger signals for employers because the whole process of training and education (and not only the final examinations) is standardized. Put another way, school pupils, students, and apprentices all receive the same education and training independent of their school, university, or training organization if the curricula are standardized (Horn 2009, p. 346). This differentiation may seem unimportant and superficial, yet for many credentials, a different degree of standardization applies for the examinations and the curriculum.

I will link credentialism to the channeling demand closure mechanism by assessing the degree of standardization of the curricula studied by individual credential holders—these curricula might be standardized on the federal level, the *Länder* (state) level, and the school/university level (Abraham et al. 2011, p. 11)[58].

4.2 Licensing—Two Definitions, Two Worlds of Licensed Occupations

In Germany, the term licensure is used to refer to the protection of occupational tasks and to describe the protection of occupational titles. Licensing in the form of protected occupational titles might have an impact on employers' hiring decisions by signaling quality and hence channeling demand to the occupations in question (Weeden 2002). Licensing as the protection of specific tasks exclusively channels demand to licensed occupations. In Germany, only a small number of occupations are licensed this way. The reason for the low number of licensed tasks lies in the German constitution (Art. 12), which grants every citizen the right to practice an occupation of his or her choosing. The licensing of tasks therefore represents a massive violation of this constitutional right and is only granted if basic necessities (*Grundgüter*) (e.g., health and education) are at stake (see Haupt 2014, pp. 106-116).

Both forms of licensing are fundamentally different. The licensing of occupational titles works on the individual level—i.e., employers might prefer to hire individuals with protected titles. Yet employers might also decide to hire individuals without licensed titles. Hence, the proportion of employees with licensed and nonlicensed titles may vary greatly from occupation to occupation. The second form of licensing, the protection of tasks, is located at the occupa-

---

58 However, Hoffmann et al. (2011) and Vicari (2014) oversimplify their measurement of standardization by mixing credentials that are standardized on the *Länder* level with credentials that are standardized on the federal level.

tional level. All incumbents have to have licenses to be allowed to work in an occupation with legally protected tasks. There is no variation—all incumbents of a task-protected occupation have licenses[59].

Despite these differences, most researchers combine both types of licenses into one measure, even if the theoretical argument that a license is a legal patent on practice does not apply to licensed occupational titles (Hoffmann 2011; Bol and Weeden 2014; Stuth and Hennig 2014; Vicari 2014). Additionally, these authors use incomplete data. Due to omissions in the data provided by the Federal Labor Office (Bundesagentur für Arbeit) they do not include the majority of protected occupational titles that are awarded through the apprenticeship training system and by universities[60]. However, occupational titles that are awarded by apprenticeship training and by universities are protected by law, as are all master craftsman titles, all public service job titles and grades (*Beamte*), all military ranks used in the armed forces and police, and all occupations with licensed tasks[61].

Both forms of licensure theoretically constitute occupational closure, and both trigger the channeling demand closure mechanism. However, they differ in power and reach: There are very few occupations with the more powerful form of licensure, the licensure of tasks, whereas the licensure of titles is less powerful but covers a wide range of occupations. I will therefore test whether licensed titles and licensed tasks are both empirically linked to the occupation members' risk of holding temporary employment contracts.

4.3 Specificity—An Underexplored Niche

Empirical research on occupational specificity, in the sense of uniqueness, is very rare. Rotolo and McPherson (2001) use an ecological concept of niches

---

59 Deviations from the law are nevertheless possible.

60 The data provided by the Federal Labor Office (*Bundesagentur für Arbeit*) on licensed occupations in Germany is inconsistent. The data include occupations with protected tasks and occupations with protected titles. The data on protected tasks is complete while the data on protected titles is fragmentary. The list does not include occupations that are part of the apprenticeship training system and only a selection of protected academic titles.

61 The protection of occupational titles that are part of the apprenticeship system is based on the Vocational Training Act (*Berufsbildungsgesetz* (BBiG)) and the Crafts Code (*Handwerksordnung* (HwO)). The protection of tertiary degrees, all public service job titles and grades, and military ranks in armed forces and police forces are regulated in § 132a Criminal Code (*Strafgesetzbuch*). The protection of master-craftsman occupations is based on § 51 of the Crafts Code (HwO). Haupt (2012a, pp. 330-332) gives a comprehensive overview over the legislation aimed on single occupations and the protection of their tasks or titles.

that differentiates occupations by the presence or absence of competitors within their niche. Hoffmann et al. (2011) address the uniqueness of occupational tasks using an occupational task-similarity matrix that is based on an unpublished database from the Federal Labor Office of Germany. Since the data Hoffmann et al. (2011) draw on are not available, I will use Rotolo and McPherson's (2001, p. 1101) innovative concept of occupational niches instead. It allows me to distinguish between occupations that share their tasks with a lot of other occupations—these occupations will not trigger the channeling demand mechanism—and occupations that share their tasks with only a few other occupations and thereby trigger the channeling demand mechanism.

Occupational specificity in the sense of narrowness is not a new concept in the research on labor market inequalities. However, the established measures of this kind of occupational specificity are not appropriate for analyzing occupational closure. Two major concepts address occupational specificity in the sense of narrowness and its potential consequences for the mobility of employees: asset theory and human capital theory (Iversen and Soskice 2001, p. 875; Becker 1964). Becker (1964) defines narrow/specific skills by the structure of the (monopsonistic) demand for given skills, whereas Iversen and Soskice (2001) focus on the content of the skills, which might be broad in the case of unspecialized skills or narrow in the case of specialized skills (Streeck 2011, p. 15).

The human capital approach cannot easily be used because it is not possible to determine the (monopsonistic) demand for skills directly. Iversen and Soskice (2001) develop their own measure of skill specificity, but it has a number of serious methodological problems. First, they operationalize skill specificity as a function of the size of occupations (Kitschelt and Rehm 2006). It follows that incumbents of small occupations tend to have highly specialized/ narrow sets of skills, whereas incumbents of large occupations tend to have very general/broad sets of skills. Second, they base their measurement of occupational specificity on the artificial structure of the ISCO88 classification and count the number of minor occupational groupings within each major occupational grouping (Kitschelt/Rehm 2006). However, the ISCO88 classification does not represent a real-time map of occupations but a skewed reflection that depicts industrial occupations in great detail and service occupations very crudely[62]. Hence, the degree of specificity might be completely determined by the artificially structured ISCO classification.

62　For example, the major ISCO group "craft and related trade workers" is divided into 70 minor groups whereas the major ISCO group "clerks and service workers" is only divided into 23 minor groups.

I will adopt an alternative approach, which was proposed by Stuth and Hennig (2014). This allows me to model Iversen's and Soskice's (2001) differentiation of specialized/narrow skills and unspecialized/broad skills. Stuth and Hennig (2014, p. 16) measure the dispersion of the main tasks performed in occupations, which allows them to determine whether an occupation does not focus on specific tasks (if so, the occupation is broad) or whether the occupation concentrates on few tasks (and is thus narrow).

4.4 Associations—Two Different Measurement Strategies

In Germany, research on associations as a closure source is based on the presence or absence of occupational associations (Hoffmann et al. 2011, p. 31). Weeden (2002, p. 78) measures associations differently, using the proportion of occupational members who belong to an occupational association instead. Both measures have their merits. Weeden's (2002) approach allows for various degrees of association-based closure. Yet this approach comes with a weakness. The number of occupational members an association represents is a kind of currency that associations use to try to achieve their lobbying goals. Hence, there is a strong possibility that the reported membership numbers are not necessarily correct. Additionally, the power of an association does not so much rely on a simple membership count but on the effective organization of their members' interests, which is a function of the diversity of interests within the association (Schroeder et al. 2011, p. 30). By contrast, Hoffmann et al. (2011) propose a simple dichotomous measurement to determine whether an occupation is represented by an association or not. This is a robust measure, and does not have the problems associated with Weeden's (2002) continuous measure. However, it turns a blind eye to the heterogeneity of association-based closure.

I will adopt the simplistic but robust approach proposed by Hoffman et al. (2011), but will try to improve it to capture some of the various degrees of association-based closure. I differentiate associations by their diversity of interests and identify two different kinds of occupational associations: associations that only represent one occupation or associations that represent incumbents from more than one occupation. Associations that represent only one occupation may have a stronger power base. They should be more able to organize the interests of their members effectively because their members will be relatively homogenous. The relatively homogenous interests of the associations' members should also allow a higher degree of social cohesion, which might result in the successful establishment and maintenance of professional ethics.

4.5 Unionization—Industry-Level versus Occupational-Level Unions

In Germany, there is nearly no research on occupational closure that takes unionization into consideration. The only exception is an article by Bol and Weeden (2014) that measures unionization by taking the proportion of union members per occupation[63]. One reason for this reluctance to measure unionization might be that unions mainly operate at industry level in Germany (e.g., Ebbinghaus 2000, p. 286; Hipp et al. 2015)[64]. The outcome of collective bargaining negotiations is applied to entire industries. Whether individuals benefit from collective bargaining agreements or not is thus dependent on the industry they are employed in and not their occupation[65]. These industries may perfectly overlap with some occupations, but the majority of occupations are distributed across a variety of industries. Thus, the link between the proportion of occupational incumbents who are union members and the unionization closure source is weak at best. However, there are some exceptions: Even if the majority of unions do not operate on the occupational level, there are some unions that do (e.g., Greef and Speth 2013, pp. 13-14). Germany has occupation-specific trade unions that bargain only for the occupations they represent (e.g., aircraft pilots, medical doctors). Hence, I will measure unionization-based closure by assessing whether occupations are represented by occupation-specific trade unions or not. Additionally, I will account for the possible impact of collective bargaining agreements on employees' risk of temporary employment by controlling industries.

4.6 Additional Distinctive Features of the German Labor Market

As previously noted, the institutional differences between the German and the US labor markets make it necessary to carefully adapt the established occupational closure measures to the German labor market. We should also test whether they are interrelated with two distinctive characteristics of the German labor market.

---

63 This measure was originally proposed by Weeden (2002) to analyze the US labor market.

64 Another reason is that unions in Germany were never allowed to use closed-shop agreements. Additionally, apprenticeship programs are not run by unions and thus cannot be utilized to restrict the labor supply. However, they have their say on the design of the apprenticeship programs and use this influence to continuously push for a broadened and updated tasks-and-skills base for the apprenticeship programs (Streeck 2011).

65 The trade union ver.di (United Service Union), for example, represents employees from the whole service sector and claims to represent employees from over 1000 different occupations.

First: The gender composition of occupations is a frequently discussed and well-known precursor of inequalities in pay, working conditions, etc. (e.g., England 1992; Kilbourne et al. 1994; Weeden 1998; England und Folbre 2005; Gartner and Hinz 2009; Haupt 2012). In Germany, the gender composition of the occupations has its structural roots in the occupational education and training system, which is closely linked to the labor market (e.g., Willms-Herget 1985; Krüger 1996, 2003; Solga and Konietzka 2000; Achatz 2005). For example, men dominate the highly standardized apprenticeship training track, whereas women dominate the less standardized vocational full-time schooling track. Additionally, women are concentrated in a few detailed occupations, whereas men are broadly distributed over a very wide range of occupations, which might affect how vigorous the competition for vacant positions is. Because the link between the education and training system and the labor market is not gender neutral, it may affect the credentialism closure source. Hence, I will test for gender differences in the impact of the closure sources on temporary employment.

Second: The general economic conditions are very different between the old and new German *Länder*[66]. These great differences have their roots in the reunification of the formerly socialist German Democratic Republic with the Federal Republic of Germany. Within months of reunification in 1990, the unprepared planned economy of the German Democratic Republic (GDR) was integrated into the West German economy and hence into the world market. As a result, the majority of factories were shut down (the employment volume in the industrial sector decreased by 70 percent) and unemployment skyrocketed (from 1989 to 1992, 3.5 million jobs out of previous 9.7 million jobs were lost) (Lutz et al. 2007, p. 1077). In contrast to the situation in the "old" (western) *Länder*, in the new *Länder*, the industrial sector is now of minor importance in overall employment and most employees are employed in the service sector. Gross wages, collective bargaining coverage, and pensions are considerably lower in the new *Länder* and the competition for vacant positions is very high because of the consistently high level of unemployment. In sum, there are great differences between the two parts of Germany in terms of their economic situation, and hence, there might also be differences in the association between occupational closure and temporary employment. I will therefore check whether occupational closure differs between the old and new *Länder* with regard to temporary employment or not.

---

66 While the socialist German Democratic Republic was a planned economy, it nevertheless continued the long-standing pre-war tradition of the occupational education and training system.

5 Data, Methods, Sample Selection, and Variables

In this study, I will rely on a repeated cross-sectional survey that combines a large sample with information on detailed occupations: the German Microcensus. The German Microcensus meets two essential requirements that allow me to analyze the risk of employees of holding temporary employment contracts and the association of this risk with occupational closure. 1) The first of these requirements is the requirement for information on detailed occupations. Many surveys only provide aggregated information on employees' occupational fields, which are defined by a range of related detailed occupations. Related occupations are grouped according to the degree of similarity of the tasks usually done in the occupations. However, mechanisms of occupational closure operate on the level of detailed occupations. The Microcensus provides information on detailed occupations, and thus fulfills this requirement. 2) The second requirement is that the data set be sufficiently large to generate reliable estimates for each detailed occupation. Many surveys that include information on detailed occupations, for example the German socio economic panel (Gsoep) or BIBB/BAuA, are too small to estimate reliable occupation-level parameters for several hundreds of detailed occupations or even general occupational fields[67]. However, the Microcensus is sufficiently large to generate reliable estimates for detailed occupations. Although ideally one might also want a longitudinal survey that allows for within-person comparisons, longitudinal surveys of this sort do not meet these two essential requirements.

The German Microcensus is a nationally representative, annual survey that provides official statistics on the population and the labor market in Germany. The Microcensus samples 1 percent of the residential population in Germany and includes all persons with the right to reside in Germany living in private or collective households[68]. The primary sampling units are delimited areas consisting of residential buildings or, in the case of large buildings, subsets of units within these buildings. The secondary sampling units are persons, households, and dwellings within the sampling areas. The sampling method used is

---

67 This might not be such a problem if these parameters are used as dependent variables in multi-level models because these correct unreliable measures using partial-pooling (Bayes) estimates (e.g., Gelman and Hill 2007, p. 276; Rabe-Hesketh and Skrondal 2012, p. 213). However, if these parameters are used as independent variables no such correction applies and these potentially unreliable estimates will introduce a lot of noise into the models.

68 Homeless persons are therefore excluded from the Microcensus.

single-stage stratified cluster sampling with a systematic random selection sampling technique.

The Microcensus provides information about detailed occupations[69], temporary employment, and the socio-demographic characteristics of the employed working population. The Microcensus also includes some information on the individual level, which can be aggregated at the occupational level. It provides, for example, the information that I need in order to operationalize occupational specificity. Still, much data that are necessary to measure occupational closure thoroughly are not provided by the Microcensus. Therefore, I have gathered additional data and matched this information with the Microcensus data using the German Dictionary of Occupational Titles (*Klassifikation der Berufe* (KldB 1992))[70].

5.1 Methods

To distinguish between individual-level effects and occupational-level effects, I will use a two-step multilevel strategy[71] because for my purposes, it provides several advantages over the one-step (partial-pooling) multilevel strategy: First, a two-step multilevel approach is based on less demanding assumptions than partial-pooling multi-level approaches, which assume a multivariate normal distribution of the error terms (Gebel and Giesecke 2011, p. 27). Second, one-step strategies become progressively more complicated with stochastic model

---

69 Due to confidentiality and privacy legislation, the Federal Statistical Office of Germany provides scientific-use files of the Microcensus with a reduced sample size (a 70 percent sub-sample) and coarsened information on occupations. These scientific-use data files do not provide information on detailed occupations but on general occupational fields. To nevertheless be able to work with the full 1 percent population sample and with detailed occupations, I had to analyze the Microcensus in the Federal Statistical Office's research data centers and in the statistical offices of the *Länder*. The research data centers (RDC) provide access to special versions of micro data of official statistics in a secure working environment to comply with confidentiality and privacy legislation.

70 The dictionary of occupational titles identifies 2,287 detailed occupations (*Berufsklassen*), which are identified by a four-digit number. The digits do not provide additional information on, for example, required skills or physical demands. However, the last digit has some informative value. For example, a seven as the last digit describes laborer occupations (*Helferberufe*) with simple occupation-specific assistant/helping tasks.

71 Irrespective of the differences between both analytical strategies, a two-step (no-pooling) multilevel approach is basically the same as a partial-pooling multilevel model, but with group-level variance parameters set to infinity (Gelman 2005, p. 459). Both estimation procedures produce similar results (Achen 2005, pp. 450-451) but have different advantages, which are dependent on the data structure (Franzese 2005).

specifications that differ across levels, which is true for binary outcomes like temporary employment (Franzese 2005, pp. 431-432). The third advantage is also linked to the binary nature of the dependent variable: The analysis of binary outcome variables requires a minimum number of events because conventional logistic regression models rely on asymptotic methods, and asymptotic methods suffer from small-sample bias (e.g., Mehta and Pathel 1995; King and Zeng 2001; Kin and Ryan 2002; Agresti 2007, pp. 152-160; Hosmer et al. 2013, pp. 387-395)[72].

In this context, it is important to note that the "performance of model-based estimates may be determined more by the number of events rather than the total sample size" (Hosmer et al. 2013, p. 408). This is a serious issue even for large occupations with a low number of temporarily employed incumbents. In order to avoid specification errors and biased, unreliable estimation results (Peduzzi et al. 1996; Vittinghof and McCulloch 2006), I might have to drop such occupations and would thereby compromise the aim of the analyses. However, relying on a two-step approach allows me to use exact logistic regressions for occupations where conventional logistic regression models would produce small-n-biased estimates, and to use conventional regression models for occupations with a sufficiently high cell count on temporary employment[73]. (See online appendix[74] 11.1 for a comparison between exact and conventional logistic regressions for a sample occupation.) Exact logistic regression derives its regression parameters by relying on conditional maximum likelihood estimates and uses test statistics that are based on permutational distributions of sufficient statistics[75] (Hirji et al. 1987; Hirji et al. 1989; Mehta and Pahtel 1995, p. 2143; King and Zeng 2001; Agresti 2007, p. 158). The exact inference of parameters makes it possible to analyze small samples (few occupational incumbents),

---

72 The degree of this bias depends on the number of observations in the less frequent of the two categories of the dependent variable.

73 Exact logistic regression requires extensive, time-consuming computations, which easily become too complex to be solved, even with fast computers. Hence, I restrict the use of the exact method to those settings where sample sizes are small enough to call into question the use of the large sample assumption (Hosmer et al. 2013, p. 393). Where large sample assumptions apply, I use the conventional logistic regression technique.

74 Link to the online appendix: http://www.nomos-shop.de/Stuth-Closing-on-Closure/productvie w.aspx?product=28864&pac=weco

75 "The central idea behind the theory of exact methods for logistic regression is to construct a statistical distribution that can, with efficient algorithms, be completely enumerated" (Hosmer et al. 2013, p. 388).

samples with very few events (few temporary employees), and even models with empty cells (sparse or unbalanced data)[76].

The fourth advantage also relates to a shortcoming of one-step multilevel models with binary dependent variables. These models would drop all occupations where the incumbents have no temporary employment contracts at all because on the micro level they do not vary across the dependent variable. Yet these occupations might be especially important to determine the association between occupational closure and temporary employment. The complete absence of temporary employees might be an outcome of occupational closure. A two-step approach also drops these occupations in the first stage of the analysis but allows them to be reintroduced into the analyses on the second stage.

The general form of the two-step multilevel model is given in the following two equations:

Equation 1: The general form of the first step of the two-step multilevel model

$$Y_{mot} = \beta_{0ot} + \beta' X_{mot} + v_{mot}$$

The first step consists of a series of separate regression analyses, where Y_{mot} is the permanent or temporary employment contract of each member m of occupation o in the year t. β' is the vector of coefficients that estimates the association between individual-level characteristics, X_{mot}, and permanent or temporary employment[77]. V_{mot} is an individual-level disturbance term. To avoid small-sample bias, I use conventional logistic regression for occupations with at least 50 incumbents with temporary contracts[78], and exact logistic regression for occupations with fewer temporarily employed incumbents. The asymptotic methods of conventional logistic regression are based on the assumption of a random sample. Hence, I had to adjust the conventional logistic regression analyses to account for the fact that the German Microcensus is not a random

---

76 The last problem is especially prevalent if occupations are the objects of interest because occupations often have incumbents with relatively homogeneous characteristics. For example, in many occupations all the incumbents have the same qualification level, so the other qualification levels are either not populated or sparsely populated.

77 As a byproduct of two-step multilevel analyses, the intercepts and the slopes of individual-level coefficients are allowed to vary across occupations.

78 I determined this threshold by comparing the results of exact and conventional logistic regressions for occupations that had between 30 and 80 temporary employees. The differences between both logistic methods converged for occupations with 50 or more temporarily employed incumbents.

sample of individuals but a random sample of areas with 100 percent of all individuals within this area being sampled[79]. To account for the survey design, I use clustered standard errors, with the clusters being defined by the random sample of areas (e.g., Deaton 1997, pp. 74-78; Schimpl-Neimanns 2009, pp. 51-54).

Equation 2: The general form of the second step of the two-step multilevel model

$$\sqrt{\widehat{Y_{ot}}} = \gamma_{00} + \gamma'\left(Z_{ot} - \overline{Z}_{..}\right) + \varepsilon_{ot}$$

$$\text{with } \widehat{Y_{ot}} = \frac{1}{n} \cdot \sum_{m=1}^{n} \widehat{Y_{mot}}$$

I calculate the mean of the predicted probabilities of the occupational members $\widehat{Y_{mot}}$ for each occupation o and year t and thereby transform Y_{mot} into the continuous occupational-level variable $\widehat{Y_{ot}}$, which I use as the dependent variable in the second step (means as outcomes). I also include occupations without any temporary employees at this level of the analyses by replacing their missing value on $\widehat{Y_{ot}}$ with a zero[80]. The second step consists of linear regression analyses, where the coefficients γ' estimate the linear association between the grand-mean centered occupational characteristics, $\left(Z_{ot} - \overline{Z}_{..}\right)$, and the mean (square-rooted) predicted probability $(\sqrt{\widehat{Y_{ot}}})$ of temporary employment in occupation o in the year t. ε_{ot} is an occupational-level disturbance term. The square root of $\widehat{Y_{ot}}$ ensures an approximate normal distribution of the variable. All second-stage analyses use heteroscedastic consistent Huber-White standard errors (see Wooldridge 2002, pp. 55-58)[81]. These analyses also consist of pooled time-series cross-sectional data. However, I cannot model time, given

---

79 The individuals within each area are thereby not independent from each other.

80 It does not seem to be too bold to assume that in occupations without any temporary employment, all incumbents enjoy a zero probability of temporary employment.

81 Using estimated parameters as dependent variables might induce heteroscedasticity because the uncertainty of these parameters may vary across occupations (Lewis and Linzer 2005). Lewis and Linzer (2005) propose the use of two different methods to estimate heteroscedastic consistent standard errors: the Huber-White standard errors (see Wooldridge 2002, pp. 55-58 for a comprehensive overview) and the feasible generalized least squares estimator (Lewis and Linzer 2005). Both methods perform equally well. The Huber-White standard error is more reliable than the feasible generalized least squares estimator (FGLS), whereas the FGLS is

that I have only three cross sections available (see next section). Instead, I apply a complete pooling strategy for the second stage, control for time on the occupational level, and assume that the association between temporary employment and occupational closure is approximately identical for each cross section (Gelman and Hill 2007, p. 251; Firebaugh 1997, p. 4).

I will also use the coefficients $\beta\,'X_{mot}$ (from equation 1) as a dependent variable for the second-step analyses (slopes as outcomes). This allows me to check whether the relationship between individual-level characteristics and temporary employment changes as a function of the occupational-level closure sources. This is equal to cross-level interactions in standard multilevel models.

5.2 Sample selection

As with any repeated cross-sectional design, the challenge of the Microcensus is that not all the variables are available in all years, and that their wording, response categories, or coding schemes change. The availability of comparable variables, which are required for operationalizing the various closure sources, restricts the number of repeated cross sections to the years 2000, 2004, and 2007[82].

The sample of individual-level cases will be limited to individuals between 15 und 64 years of age[83]. I exclude individuals who were questioned at their second home, who are in compulsory military service or compulsory civil service, and individuals who are apprentices. Because the primary sampling units of the German Microcensus are housing units in artificially delimited areas and not individuals, it is possible that a small fraction of individuals with

---

more efficient than Huber-White standard error "if a sufficiently high fraction of the total regression error variance is due to sampling error" (Lewis and Linzer 2005, p. 363).

Lewis and Linzer originally introduced a third heteroscedastic consistent standard error (Efron or HC3 standard errors (Efron 1982)), but I will not refer to this measure because it is only an alternative to the Huber-White standard error when the sample size is small (<=250) (Long and Ervin 2000). However, my analyses are based on a large sample, where the Huber-White standard error outperforms the Efron standard error (Lewis and Linzer 2005, p. 356).

82 In order to operationalize the credentialism closure sources I need detailed information about the individuals' qualifications. This information is available at the necessary level of detail only from the year 2000 onwards (with regard to the level of qualification) and only for the years 2000, 2004, and 2007 (with regard to the field of study of individuals with tertiary degrees).

83 The lowest boundary of 15 years and the highest boundary of 64 years of age are based on standard age thresholds used for labor market analyses by the Federal Statistical Office of Germany (e.g., Eisenmenger et al. 2014, p. 546).

a second home could be interviewed twice in the same year. According to their legal status, it is not possible for apprentices and individuals in military or civil service to have permanent employment contracts. I also omit unpaid family workers, unemployed and economically inactive individuals, and self-employed individuals because they are not at risk of holding temporary employment contracts. Individuals who live in collective housing units, such as asylums or monasteries, are also excluded.

Some individuals did not state their current occupations as specifically as necessary to map them properly into their detailed occupations. Those individuals were assigned to generalized occupational categories, which serve as catch-all categories. For example, the general occupational category "engineer" replaces 59 detailed engineer occupations. Therefore, I had to exclude those general occupations from my sample of detailed occupations[84]. Very few occupations primarily consist of unqualified individuals. For these occupations, the credentialism closure source cannot be meaningfully operationalized[85]. Hence, I dropped those few occupations from my sample[86].

In light of Hosmer's et al. (2013) cautionary tale that the performance of model-based estimates may be determined more by the number of events rather than the sample size, I use a two-step approach, which allows me to address the number-of-events problem. However, as a result of this decision, I will not benefit from the borrowing-strength effect and the shrinkage effect of a one-step (partial-pooling) multilevel approach, which would have allowed me to address the sample size problem[87]. The absence of this advantage means that the standard requirements for the number of observations per occupation apply[88]. Hence, I need to ensure I have enough observations to run a separate regression analysis for each detailed occupation and year[89]. The Federal Statis-

---

84 I also had to exclude the occupation "soldier" because it is so general that it allows neither the differentiation between army, navy and air force, nor the differentiation between the various military ranks.

85 I tested various specifications that included unqualified occupations, but, not surprisingly, they all played havoc with the credentialism measures.

86 The number of unqualified occupations is very small. In the pooled three years, I classified only 24 occupations as unqualified occupations.

87 Using a one-stage (partial-pooling) multilevel model would allow me to include occupations into the analysis that only consist of very few incumbents or even one incumbent (e.g., Gelman and Hill 2007, p. 276; Rabe-Hesketh and Skrondal 2012, p. 213).

88 These conventional requirements are necessary because potentially unreliable measures through low case numbers will not be replaced by more plausible partial-pooling (Bayes) estimates.

89 Haupt (2014) tries to avoid the small-N problem by merging similar occupations until they are sufficiently large. However, a new problem emerges: In order to aggregate occupations,

tical Office of Germany provides a binding guideline for the minimum number of observations for researchers using their data. To guarantee stable and reliable estimates, the Federal Statistical Office of Germany requires researchers to only report estimates of units of interest, like occupations, that have at least 50 observations each (Mikrozensus-Referenten/-innen des Bundes und der Länder 2013, p. 1)[90]. The authors of the guideline specify that units with fewer observations have relative sampling errors above 15 percent and are thereby not representative for the populations of these units. Therefore, I defined a minimum threshold of 50 or more occupational incumbents per occupation. I drop occupations below that threshold from the sample.

Starting from a full sample of 2,364 detailed occupations[91] with 702,002 incumbents, my final sample consists of 1,118 occupations with 677,080 incumbents after applying the threshold of 50 incumbents per occupation (see table 1). My analytical sample still represents more than 96 percent of the employed individual-level population. The considerable reduction of the number of occupations is mainly due to the large number of occupations that have zero temporary employment and that also have less than 50 incumbents.

Table 1:   Description of individual-level and occupational-level sample sizes of the full sample and the final sample (pooled for the years 2000, 2004, and 2007)

	Full sample	Final sample
Number of occupations	2.364	1.118
Number of individuals	702.002	677.080
Number of occupations with more than 0 and less than 50 events	1242	818
Number of members of occupations with more than 0 and less than 50 events	248.019	229.017
Number of occupations with zero temporary employment	880	58
Number of members of occupations with zero temporary employment	11.735	5.815

Although the sample represents nearly all employed individuals and the majority of occupations that have temporarily employed incumbents, the threshold of 50 employees per occupation may introduce a bias against very

---

assumptions have to be made about the identifiers of similarity. These assumptions are always arbitrary to a certain degree and have to be uncorrelated with the dependent and independent variables.

90 The contractual obligations of the researcher are also stated under the following link under bullet point seven:
http://www.gesis.org/missy/en/studie/erhebung/rechtliche-und-allgemeine-informationen/leit-faden-zur-faktischen-anonymisierung/.(Date of last access: January 2014)

91 The full sample does not contain generalized catch-all occupations; however, it does contain some unqualified occupations.

small occupations. This bias would occur if the incumbents of small occupations are temporarily employed more often than employees in larger occupations. To test for this possible bias, I correlated the size of the occupations with their proportion of temporarily employed incumbents and did not find a statistically significant correlation[92].

5.3 Variables

The dependent variable—temporary employment—is based on a binary variable in the Microcensus[93]. I will measure occupational closure, addressing five different closure sources—credentialism, licensing, occupational specificity, occupational associations, and unionization. The operationalization of these closure sources will be described in the following sections. I first discuss my measures of occupational credentialism at some length, then proceed to licensure, followed by the relatively unknown concept of occupational specificity, and finally address occupational associations and unionization. The discussion of the measures of credentialism will necessarily be somewhat lengthy because these measures are deeply rooted in the German education and training system.

5.3.1 The Credential Inflation Index—A New Approach to Capture the Supply of Occupation-Specific Credentials

To capture the credentialism closure source, I follow Müller and Shavit (1998), who argued that the value of credentials for individuals derives not only from the specific skills these credentials represent, but also from their scarcity, i.e., the number of individuals who hold the same credential (also see: Parkin 1971, p. 21, Larson 1977, p. 48; Collins 1979, p. 27; Beck et al. 1980, p. 79). To capture the scarcity of occupation-specific credentials, I have developed the credential inflation index. Occupational credentials are highly institutionalized in Germany. As scholars of comparative inequality have long noted, the German labor market and the education and training system are closely linked (e.g., Allmendinger 1989; Shavit and Müller 1998; Konietzka 1999; Solga and Konietzka 1999; Kurtz 2005; Brzinsky-Fay 2007; Brzinsky-Fay 2011, pp. 26-27; Bol and Weeden 2014; Bol 2014). This linkage is reflected in the German Dictionary of Occupational Titles, which is not only used to classify occupations, but also the corresponding credentials. Utilizing this uniformity, I

---

92 Based on the full sample, the correlation is -0.06.
93 The variable is based on the question: "Is your employment contract permanent or temporary?"

conceptualize the credential inflation index (CIX) as the number of all freshly awarded occupation-specific credentials, divided by the number of employees in the respective occupation in a given year.

The task of developing the measure is complicated by a specific feature of the German education and training system: It is possible for individuals to acquire credentials for one occupation in different institutionalized education and training tracks[94]. There are six different education and training tracks that provide occupational credentials: *Apprenticeship training* combines work-based training in private businesses with education in vocational schools[95]; hence, it is described as the dual system[96]. The second track is the *vocational full-time schooling track with recognized credentials*—the credentials here are similar to the credentials awarded through apprenticeship training[97]. This schooling track awards very few credentials in comparison to the other five education and training tracks and is a rarely used alternative for young adults who did not find an apprentice position in the apprenticeship system. The third education and training track is the *vocational full-time schooling* track with nonrecognized credentials[98]. It covers a very wide range of credentials that correspond with current demand for qualifications that are not covered by the apprenticeship training system. This track awards credentials for occupations that operate, for example, in the social service, foreign language, health care, or information technology sectors. The fourth education and training track consists of *schools of the healthcare sector*. This type of vocational school trains its students for various healthcare occupations (for example nurses, midwifes or physiotherapists) and cooperates closely with hospitals, where practical training usually occurs. The fifth education and training track consists of trade, technical, and master's schools, which provide credentials at a tertiary education level[99]. These schools prepare the occupational incumbents for executive tasks and

---

94　A count of the various education and training tracks that award credentials for the same occupation is shown in online appendix 11.2.

95　Because the training is conducted in two different places (in private businesses and vocational schools) the apprenticeship training system is called the dual system (*duales System*).

96　For a more exhaustive description of the vocational education and training system in Germany in general, see Ebner (2013) or Hippach-Schneider et al. (2011). For a detailed description of the organization of a training program that awards bricklayer credentials, see Clarke et al. (2013, pp. 941-945).

97　They are also recognized by the Vocational Training Act (BBiG) and the Crafts Code (HwO).

98　These credentials are called nonrecognized because they are not regulated by the Vocational Training Act (BBiG) and the Crafts Code (HwO) (In German: *berufliche Abschlüsse in Berufen die keine Ausbildungsberufe sind*).

99　The International Standard Classification of Education (ISCED) classifies trade, technical, and master's-school-based credentials as ISCED 5B.

self-employment and award, for example, master-craftsman credentials (*Meister*)[100]. The sixth education and training track is publicly financed[101] *higher education at universities*[102], which allows students to acquire credentials in a wide range of academic subjects.

I count all occupation-specific credentials that are awarded by the different education and training tracks by combining various data sources[103]. Based on these combined data sources, I derive a total count of occupation-specific credentials[104] awarded annually, which I relate to the Microcensus-based number of employees in the respective occupation (see equation 3).

---

100 The trade, technical, and master's schools do not provide initial occupational training but provide further intermediate training and hence require their pupils to have relevant occupational credentials and work experience to gain access to their training programs.

101 There are also private but state-recognized universities run by the Catholic or Lutheran churches or private institutions.

102 There are three types of higher education institutions in Germany: the universities of applied sciences, which place a strong emphasis on practical work and application, the universities, which are research oriented, and the Colleges of Art and Colleges of Music, which are of equivalent status to universities.

103 The Federal Statistical Office of Germany provides data on the yearly number of successfully acquired occupation-specific credentials of the university students, school pupils, and apprentices in the various education and training tracks. Data for the apprenticeship system are to be found in Fachserie 11, Reihe 3 (vocational training). Data are available as Excel files for the years 1999-2008, except 2002. I had to rely on the printed edition for the year 2002, which I scanned and edited with special software to avoid and check for errors due to the scanning process (For example the number 7 is often misread as 1, lines shifts, etc.). Due to changes in the survey methodology, no data on graduates are available for the year 2007.

Data for vocational full-time schools (recognized), vocational full-time schools (not recognized), schools of the healthcare sector, and trade, technical and master's schools are to be found in Fachserie 11, Reihe 2 (Vocational schools). Data are available as Excel files for the years 2000 to 2009. Due to a time lag in the official publications, data on graduates are released with a delay of one year. For example: The number of graduates in the year 2000 is to be found in the release of 2001.

Data for tertiary education at universities are to be found in Fachserie 11, Reihe 4.2. (Examinations at universities) and were made available by the Federal Statistical Office of Germany in a special edited Excel file that contained all years from 1999 to 2008.

104 To smooth out short-term fluctuations and to emphasize longer-term trends, I use a central moving average of three years to calculate the total count of yearly issued occupation-specific credentials. This procedure also allows me to impute the missing data for the apprenticeship system in the year 2007.

Equation 3: The credential inflation index

$$\mathrm{CIX}\!\left(\mathrm{o}_t\right) = \frac{\sum_{i=1}^{6} C(o_{it})}{N(o_t)}$$

$\mathrm{CIX}(o_t)$: Credential inflation index of the occupation o in the year t

$N(o_t)$: Number of the occupational incumbents of the occupation o in the year t

$\sum_{i=1}^{6} C(o_{it})$: Count of all newly awarded credentials through the six education and training tracks i for the occupation o in the year t

The occupation-specific credential count and the number of occupational incumbents are matched using the German Dictionary of Occupational Titles (KldB 1992). However, the continuous upgrading and broadening of the apprenticeship training system[105] and its corresponding credentials creates a mismatch because new credentials that combine formerly distinct credentials are introduced[106]. For example, in the year 2004, a new credential was introduced—the construction-mechanic credential—which replaced four credentials that were no longer awarded: the construction-mechanic (equipment engineering) credential, the construction-mechanic (sheet-metal construction technology) credential, the construction-mechanic (metal-construction and ship-building technology) credential, and the construction-mechanic (welding technology) credential. I adapt the raw data on the credentials to take account of the fact that, for example, each of the four construction-mechanic occupations still exists, but they now share the same credential[107].

There is an important difference between the tertiary education track and the other five education and training tracks: Many degrees do not obviously track into a particular occupation—for example, German studies (*Germanistik*).

---

105   This process dates back to the 1960s and has resulted in a continuously decreasing number of apprenticeship-training-based credentials and a simultaneously broadened skills base for the remaining credentials (Busemeyer 2009).

106   There were more changes in the apprenticeship training system, but these changes do not negatively affect the matching of the credential count with the number of employees. These changes consisted of the modernization of the curricula, the discontinuation of old training programs, or the establishment of new ones. Curriculum changes have no impact on the data structure at all. The decision to discontinue old or establish new training programs causes marked changes in the number of credentials (the number of credentials rises from zero or falls to zero), but the organizing principle of the data remains the same.

107   Starting with the year 2004, I assigned the new credential to the four detailed occupations. However, a simple reassignment would bias the number of awarded credentials by multiplying the number of credentials with the number of occupations they are assigned to. Therefore, I divided the absolute number of awarded credentials by the number of occupations this credential was assigned to.

Instead, tertiary education at universities provides generalist training (see, e.g., Abraham et al. 2011; Bol and Weeden 2014), which results in an imperfect match between field-of-study-specific credentials and occupations[108]. The problem is easily solved by calculating the weighted sum of the awarded fields-of-study-specific degrees that grant access to the same occupation. The weight allows me to account for the fact that most field-of-study-specific credentials correspond to more than one occupation (see equation 4).

Equation 4: The computation of the number of occupation-specific credentials that are awarded by the tertiary education track

$$C(o_t) = \sum_{j=1}^{74} C(o_{jt}) \bullet weight(o_{ij}),$$

$$\text{with } weight\left(o_{jt}\right) = \frac{N(o_{jt})}{\sum_{o=1}^{O} N(o_{jt})}$$

$C(o_t)$: Number of new credentials for the occupation o awarded by the tertiary education track in the year t

$C(o_{jt})$: The number of new credentials for the occupation o corresponding to the 74 fields of study j of the tertiary education track[109] in the year t

Weight(o_{jt}): The relative weight or importance of the field of study j in occupation o in the year t

$N(o_{jt})$: Number of the incumbents of the occupation o with credentials corresponding to the field of study j in the year t

$\sum_{o=1}^{O} N(o_{jt})$: Count of all employees of all occupations o who have a credential corresponding to the field of study j in the year t

---

108 The data on tertiary-level credentials are available at a detailed level of aggregation that differentiates between approximately 300 different subjects of study *(Studienfach)*. This detailed level allows for the matching of the number of awarded degrees to the Microcensus' 74 fields of study *(Studienbereich)*. I matched the 300 subjects of study to the 74 fields of study using a coding system provided by GESIS. GESIS is an organization that provides advisory services for social scientists in Germany (http://www.gesis.org/missy/fileadmin/ missy/klassifikationen/Amtliche_Klassifikationen/Hfr/hfr00.pdf (Date of last access: January 2014)). There is one Microcensus field of study that cannot be matched with specific subjects of study—teacher. It is not possible because the term teacher does not refer to a subject of study but a special kind of degree like bachelor's or master's degrees—the *Lehramt*. However, the Federal Statistical Office also provides overall statistics for *Lehramt*, which are used instead. There are two exceptions: teachers in primary schools and special schools (for pupils with disabilities) have specific subjects of study.

109 I have merged the number of new credentials of the various fields of study j with each occupation o and all years t with the Microcensus using the Microcensus information about the fields of study j the occupational incumbents have majored in.

Some occupations have no occupation-specific credential, yet employers nevertheless require their incumbents to have credentials (e.g., product testers, product inspectors). In these cases, employers usually rely on established credentials that are relatively similar to the occupation in question[110]. However, there are no data available on which occupation-specific credentials employers rely on as an alternative. Instead, I will use an approximation of the credential inflation index for these occupations. This approximation accounts for the broad variety of credentials employers might alternatively rely on and is based on the averaged credential inflation index of the education and training track in which employees acquired their credentials. For each of these occupations, the education-and-training-track-specific credential inflation index is weighted by the frequency of the incumbents with credentials from the respective education and training tracks[111].

Figure 2 illustrates my operationalization strategy for the sample occupation designer/graphic designer in the year 2004. The middle column displays the different education and training tracks that provide credentials for the designer/graphic designer occupation. The majority of new credentials (3,746) were awarded by the vocational full-time school training track (not recognized). The second most important education and training track was the tertiary education track (1,705 credentials) followed by trade, technical, and masters schools (272 credentials) and the dual system (31 credentials).

The credentials awarded through the tertiary education track were awarded in various fields of study. The majority of these credentials are awarded in design-related fields of study (interior designer and audio-visual designer)[112]. The other fields of study (home economics, economics, and German studies) only contribute small numbers of new credentials. There are an additional 14 fields of study (e.g., textile and clothing engineering, biology, computer sciences, etc.) that award even fewer credentials—I subsumed these under the miscellaneous fields-of-study category.

---

110 For example: Product testers in a shoe factory might be required to have a shoemaker credential. In other cases, employers require the employees to have a credential that is relevant for the vacant position, which they complement with additional informal training courses (for example, this could apply to branch managers, sales managers, etc.).

111 The German Microcensus provides information for all six vocational training tracks. However, it is not possible to differentiate between the recognized and nonrecognized vocational fulltime schooling tracks and it is also not possible to differentiate between the schools of the healthcare sector and the trade, technical, and master's schools. In both cases I use a weighted average of the education-and-training-track-specific credential inflation index where the weight of each track is determined by the number of credentials they award in the respective years.

112 I derived the numbers of credentials of the fields of study using equation 4.

Figure 2: The designer/graphic designer occupation as an example of the operationalization of the credential inflation index, in the year 2004

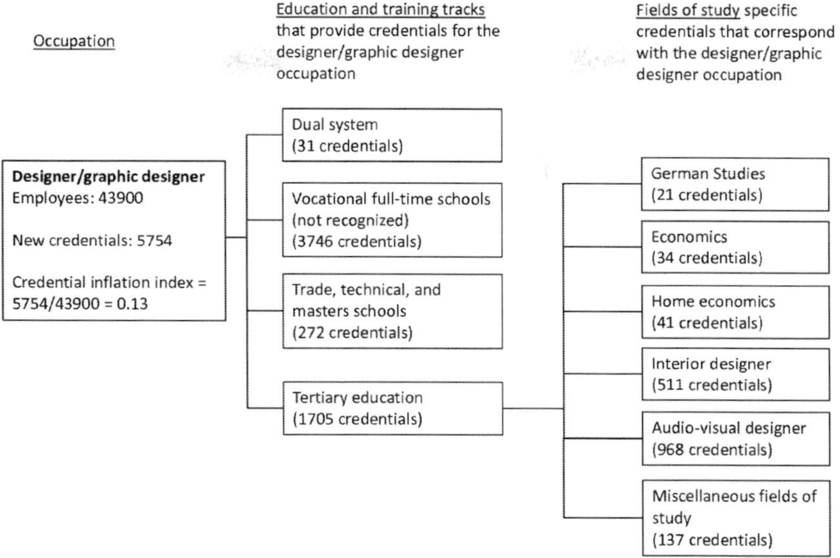

Before I apply equation 3 and divide the total number of credentials for the designer/graphic designer occupation by the number of actual employees within the occupation, I have to make one final adjustment. This is necessary because the count of credentials is not comparable to the count of employees: The number of 439 employees in the designer/graphic designer occupation is based on a 1 percent population sample, whereas the number of 5,754 credentials is based on a complete sample. To account for the different sampling plans, I multiply the overall number of employees by the inverted 1 percent selection probability of the Microcensus.

The designer/graphic designer occupation has a credential saturation ratio of 0.13. This means that, in the year 2004, for approximately every tenth employee in this occupation, a freshly credentialed designer/graphic designer entered the labor market.

5.3.2 The Standardization Index

I operationalize the credentials-level of standardization by relying on the data I described in the last section and by conducting additional research to determine the level of standardization of the curricula for each credential[113]. Curricula may be standardized on the federal level, the *Länder* (state) level, or the school/ university level. All credentials awarded by the apprenticeship training track and the vocational full-time schooling track (recognized) have federal-level standardized curricula[114]. Most training programs of the vocational full-time schooling track (not recognized) and the trade, technical, and master's schools are usually standardized on the *Länder* level[115]. These credentials are comparable within the German *Länder* but not between them. Some credentials awarded through the vocational full-time schooling track (not recognized) are regulated at the federal level or at the school level. Credentials that are awarded by schools of the healthcare sector also vary in their degree of standardization. Most of these credentials are standardized on the federal level, whereas some are standardized on the *Länder* level or even both on the federal level and the level of the *Länder*. Most credentials awarded by the tertiary education system are standardized at the university level[116]. There are few exceptions: Medicine- and pharmacy-related credentials are standardized at the federal level, and law, food chemistry, and teacher training credentials have curricula that are standardized on the *Länder* level.

To create an index of standardization, I assign each credential a value between 1 and 3. Value 1 describes credentials that are standardized on the school/university level, value 2 refers to *Länder*-level standardized credentials, and value 3 relates to credentials that are standardized on the federal level[117]. I have to average the standardization index for occupations where credentials are awarded through more than one education and training track. To account for

---

113 I used the internet database of the Federal Labor Office of Germany (http://berufenet.arbeit-sagentur.de/berufe/).

114 Federal legislation regulates the curricula, duration of training, range of learning fields, basic sectoral skills, and specific occupational skills. The federal legislation consists of the Vocational Training Act (*Berufsbildungsgesetz* (BBiG)) and the Crafts Code (*Handwerksordnung* (HwO)).

115 All credentials awarded by trade, technical, and master's schools, and many credentials awarded by the vocational full-time schooling track (not recognized) are regulated by the Standing Conference of the Ministers of Education and Cultural Affairs of the *Länder*.

116 Despite the fact that tertiary education is formally regulated by the *Länder*, the constitution (*Grundgesetz*) of Germany (Art. 5 (3) GG) guarantees the freedom of science, research, and teaching, and results in quasi autonomous universities. The curriculum taught in one subject of study may not only vary between the *Länder,* but also within the *Länder* between universities.

117 For the very few credentials that are standardized both at the federal and the *Länder* level, I assign the lower of the possible two values. The lower value reflects the leeway schools have in designing the curricula.

differences in the importance of the credentials of the various education and training tracks for the same occupation, I apply weights (see equation 5).

Equation 5: The standardization index

$$\text{Standardization}(o_t) = \sum_{i=1}^{6} standard(o_{it}) \cdot weight(o_{it}),$$

$$\text{with } weight\left(o_{it}\right) = \frac{C(o_{it})}{\sum_{i=1}^{6} C(o_{it})}$$

Standardization(O_t): The average credential standardization of the occupation (*o*) in the year *t*

standard(O_{it}): Value of standardization of the occupation's (*o*) credential awarded by the education and training track *i* in the year *t*. The value is one of the following three:
1 for school/university-level standardized curricula,
2 for *Länder*-level standardized curricula,
3 for federal-level standardized curricula.

weight(O_{it}): Weight of the credential of the occupation *o* awarded by the education and training track *i* in the year *t*

$C(o_{it})$: Number of new credentials for the occupation o awarded by the education and training track *i* in the year *t*

$\sum_{i=1}^{6} C(o_{it})$: Count of all awarded credentials through the six education and training tracks *i* for the occupation *o* in the year *t*

In the section on the credential inflation index, I explained that no specific credentials are awarded for some occupations. For the purposes of approximating the standardization index, I will use the same approximation technique that I used for the credential inflation index. In the first step, I estimate the average standardization of each education and training track. In the second step, I weight the resulting training-track-specific standardization by the density of employees with credentials from the different training tracks within the occupation in question.

5.3.3 The Licensure of Tasks and Titles

I measure the licensure of tasks using a dichotomous variable (licensed occupations versus occupations without a license). Haupt (2014, pp. 330-332) provides a complete list of every occupation for which licensure is available in Germany and also provides a timeline of the enactment of the licensure legislation. A dichotomous measure differs from the established measures, which suffer due to the mismatch between the levels of analyses. This mismatch arises because occupations are addressed at an aggregated level, whereas occupations are licensed at the detailed occupational level. This mismatch causes some slippage and requires continuous licensing measures (e.g., Hoffmann 2011; Haupt 2014; Bol and Weeden 2014; Vicari 2014). Unlike these conventional approaches, I base my analysis on detailed occupations and hence have no slippage. Occupations that are subject to task licensure legally require all their incumbents to have the license. Hence, an occupation, along with all its incumbents, is licensed or not.

I capture the licensure of occupational titles using a continuous measure that reflects the proportion of occupational incumbents with protected titles. The Microcensus makes it possible to identify all individuals who have protected titles: That includes all individuals with titles that were awarded by apprenticeship training tracks or by universities, all individuals with public service job titles and grades (*Beamte*), and master craftsman positions. Additionally, some occupations solely consist of incumbents with licensed titles. For example: policemen, industrial master craftsmen (*Industrie- und Werkmeister*), and all occupations with licensed tasks.

5.3.4 The Specificity of Occupational Tasks

I use data provided by the Microcensus to capture whether occupational tasks and skills are common or unique and narrow or wide. Since the Microcensus does not directly measure skills, I use the "main task" variable as a proxy and assume that the occupational incumbents have the skills that would allow them to perform this main task[118]. The respondents can choose their main task out of a list of 20 tasks. I use the index of qualitative variation (IQV) to determine whether the tasks performed in one occupation are relatively common or relatively unique across all occupations (see equation 6). That means I compare the broadness of the distribution of each task over all occupations with the maximum dispersion that is theoretically possible[119]. Tasks that are relatively similar to the maximum dispersion are common while tasks that are dissimilar are unique. In a second step, I calculated the weighted mean of the IQVs for all tasks in an occupation, where the weights are based on the frequency with which incumbents report performing each main task in the occupation[119].

---

118   The Microcensus asks "Which task do you primarily perform?" (Statistisches Bundesamt and GESIS 2012: p.92).

119   The IQV measure is based on the ratio of the total number of differences in a distribution to the maximum number of possible differences within the same distribution. The specific version of the IQV that I use is based on Klemm (2002, pp. 58-59).

Equation 6: The relative uniqueness of tasks and skills in occupations using the index of qualitative variation

$$\text{Uniqueness}\left(o\right) = \sum_{x=1}^{20} IQV_x * weight(o_x) ,$$

$$\text{with } IQV_x = \frac{s \bullet \left(n_x^2 - \sum_{r=1}^{s} f(x_r)^2\right)}{n_x^2 \bullet (s-1)}$$

$$\text{and weight}\left(o_x\right) = \frac{N(o_x)}{\sum_{x=1}^{20} N(o_x)}$$

Uniqueness(o) = weighted mean of the IQV of all activities mainly exercised in occupation o

IQV_x = The Index of Qualitative Variation of activity x over all occupations

n_x = Number of individuals of all occupations primarily exercising activity x

s = Number of nominal categories (number of occupations)

$\sum_{r=1}^{s} f(x_r)^2$ = Frequency f of empirical pairs with the same value on x_r ($r = 1...s$)

Weight(o_x): Intra-occupational weight of the activity x of occupation o

N(o_x): Number of the incumbents of the occupation o who exercise activity x

$\sum_{x=1}^{20} N(o_x)$: Count of all employees within occupation o

I measure how narrow or wide the range of tasks performed in an occupation is by using the skill-specificity measure proposed by Stuth and Hennig (2014). In this paper, my coauthor and I also use the index of qualitative variation to determine whether all the incumbents of an occupation perform the same main task or if they are distributed over a wide range of main tasks. For example, occupations are deemed to be very narrow when their incumbents all state that they perform the same main task. I will again use the IQV, but in this instance, I will evaluate the dispersion of activities within each detailed occupation (see equation 7).

---

120 The IQV is based on the full sample of occupations and individuals, not the final sample as described in chapter 5.2, in order to ensure an unbiased estimate of the unique or common sets of tasks.

*Equation 7: The relative variety of tasks and skills within occupations using
the index of qualitative variation*

$$\text{Variety}(o) = IQV_o$$

$$\text{with } IQV_o = \frac{s \cdot \left(n_o^2 - \sum_{r=1}^{s} f(o_r)^2\right)}{n_o^2 \cdot (s-1)}$$

$\text{Variety}_o = IQV_o$ = The Index of Qualitative Variation of all activities within the occupations o

n_o = Number of individuals exercising all activities in occupation o

s = Number of nominal categories (number of activities)

$\sum_{r=1}^{s} f(o_r)^2$ = Frequency f of empirical pairs with the same value on O_r (r = 1…s)

Equations 4 and 5 are not indexed for time. However, both measures are calculated separately for each year.

5.3.5 *Occupational Associations and Occupation-Specific Trade Unions*

Measuring the representation of occupations by associations is difficult because no official data on occupational associations exist in Germany. However, Schroeder, Kalass, and Greef conducted a survey on occupational associations in Germany from 2009 to 2010 (Schroeder et al. 2008, pp. 34-38)[121]. I assume that occupational associations are a relatively stable phenomenon and that the data also apply for my occupational sample of the years 2000, 2004, and 2007.

Because the focus of this survey was on associations and not occupations, I had to research what occupation(s) each occupational association represented. I then transposed the focus of the data from occupational associations to occupations[122]. I matched the modified survey to the Microcensus data and was thus

---

121 Using a combined postal/online survey, they were able to obtain a response rate of 84.5 percent of the approximated total number of occupational associations (Schroeder et al. 2011:45). To validate and complete the survey, I conducted extensive internet-based research for those occupations where the survey indicated the nonexistence of occupational associations. (The website http://berufenet.arbeitsagentur.de/berufe/ of the Federal Labor Office (*Bundesagentur für Arbeit*) provides information for occupations on whether there are associations or not.) Due to the high response rate, my research only turned up few additional associations.

122 The resulting data matrix is more complex than the original one because many occupations are represented by more than one occupational association and many associations represent more than one occupation.

able to distinguish occupations that are represented by associations from occupations that are not. The survey on occupational associations also included data on occupation-specific trade unions, which allowed me to code occupations as being represented by occupation-specific trade unions in contrast to occupations that were not represented by an occupation-specific trade union.

To determine whether occupational associations might have a strong powerbase (homogeneity of interests) or not (heterogeneity of interests), I counted the number of occupations each association represented and estimated the minimum value of the represented occupations over all associations that are assigned to one occupation. Occupations with associations that only represent one occupation are coded as having a potentially strong powerbase. Occupations with values above 1 are coded as being represented by occupational associations with a potentially weak powerbase. Occupations without any associations are coded as not being represented by an association at all.

5.3.6 Control Variables

There are a range of additional variables at the occupational level and the individual level that are also associated with temporary employment. I integrate these characteristics into my empirical models to control for their well-known impact.

The first of these relates to further education. Further education affects an individual's risk of holding a temporary employment contract because it increases the amount of human capital possessed (e.g., Booth et al. 2002, Giesecke and Groß 2004, pp. 351-352). It also provides individuals with additional credentials that might increase their labor-market chances by signaling high productivity (e.g., Weeden 2002, p. 68; Haupt 2012)[123]. Therefore, I control for the proportion of individuals per occupation who have engaged in work-related further education in the last 12 months. This measure is based on Microcensus data.

Second, research on the impact of occupational characteristics on wages, working conditions, and promotion chances usually finds net effects for gender composition and racial composition (e.g., England 1992 ; Kilbourne et al. 1994; Weeden 2002; Cohen and Huffman 2003; England und Folbre 2005; Gartner and Hinz 2009; Haupt 2012). Using the Microcensus, I therefore construct measures of the percentage of women within the occupations and the percentage of employees with non-German nationality within the occupations.

---

123 Some occupations mandate their incumbents to engage in further education in fixed time intervals (e.g., commercial and professional drivers, animal keepers, physicians or teachers).

Third, small organizations in Germany are not subject to employment protection legislation. Because they do not face procedural inconveniences, notice periods, and severance payments when they lay off employees, small organizations do not need temporary employment contracts to maintain external flexibility. Incumbents of occupations that are concentrated in small businesses may therefore have a low incidence of temporary employment contracts. The law defines organizations as small when they have less than ten full-time equivalent employees. This definition was true for the years 2004 and onwards. Before 2004, the threshold was set at five full-time equivalent employees. To control for this possible bias, I use the Microcensus to construct a measure of the percentage of occupational incumbents that are employed in organizations with up to five or ten employees.

Fourth, the use of temporary employment contracts might be more cost effective for large organizations than for small organizations because large organizations incur lower marginal costs for additional training of new (temporary) employees than small organizations (e.g., Knoke and Kalleberg 1994; Uzzi and Barsness 1998; Werfhorst 2011). To control for the fact that large organizations use temporary employment contracts more often than small organizations[124], I use the Microcensus to construct a measure of the percentage of occupational incumbents that are employed in organizations with 50 or more employees[125].

Fifth, the general economic conditions differ greatly between the old and new German *Länder* and this might also have an impact on an individual's risk of holding temporary employment contracts. I therefore control for the different economic conditions and construct a Microcensus-based measure of the percentage of occupational incumbents that are employed in the new *Länder*.

Sixth, to account for the human capital approach and its emphasis on the economic value of skills, I will also control for occupational skills. Bol and Weeden (2014) use the BIBB/BAUA data from the year 2006 along with the German Microcensus to compute scales for a broad variety of occupational skills (see also Haupt 2012, 2014; Bol 2014). However, this data source does not have sufficient cases to construct reliable skill measures for detailed occupations[126]. As an alternative, I will use less detailed but more reliable data that are provided by the Microcensus. The Microcensus differentiates between four

---

124 See Fritsch and Schank (2005), Giesecke (2006, pp. 212-213) or Bellmann et al. (2009, pp. 383-384).

125 Unfortunately, the Microcensus only makes it possible to identify organizations with between one and fifty or more employees.

126 Bol and Weeden (2014) based their analyses on general occupational fields rather than detailed occupations. However, for at least one fifth of their sample of general occupational

different skill levels of tasks: routine/labor tasks, skilled tasks, skilled tasks with some managerial responsibilities, and managerial tasks. I construct a density measure for each of the four skill levels of the tasks performed by the incumbents of each occupation. I cannot use a composite measure for the skill level of tasks because each skill level varies in a nonlinear fashion in its association with temporary employment.

Seventh, collective wage bargaining not only affects wages but also employment relations and hence temporary employment. However, German unions mainly operate at a sectoral or industry level (e.g., Ebbinghaus 2000, p. 286). To control for their potential association with temporary employment, I construct ten density measures for the proportion of occupational incumbents within ten industries.

Eighth, nearly all the studies on the individual-level determinants of temporary employment in Germany agree in their assessment of the importance of the individual-level characteristics qualification, age, public service employment, and region (e.g., Rudolph 1987, Hagen 2002; Giesecke and Groß 2002, p. 99; Giesecke and Groß 2003, p. 168; Kim and Kurz 2003; Giesecke and Groß 2004; Mertens and McGinnity 2004; Kurz et al. 2005, pp. 64-65; McGinnity et al. 2005; Boockmann and Hagen 2006, p. 33; Buchholz and Grunow 2006; Giesecke 2006, pp. 210-213; Giesecke and Groß 2007, p. 92; Gundert 2007; Gebel 2009; Gebel and Giesecke 2009; Allmendinger et al. 2013, pp. 32-34). Almost all studies find no effect of gender on temporary employment. However, because I stratify my individual-level analyses using detailed occupations, it is highly probable that gender might nevertheless have an impact.

Therefore, I will control for qualifications, age, public service employment, region, and gender on the individual level. I differentiate qualifications into low, medium, and high education groups (Allmendinger et al. 2013, p. 9). This categorization is based on the International Standard Classification of Education (ISCED). The "low" education group covers ISCED groups 1, 2, and 3c and captures individuals who only completed basic education. The "medium" category (ISCED groups 3 and 4) includes all individuals who completed upper secondary education (e.g., apprenticeship training or vocational full-time schooling) or a program in preparation for tertiary education. The "high" education group (ISCED 5 and 6) includes all individuals with a completed tertiary education. I differentiated age into three categories: "Young" people are those who are between 15 and 29 years old. The "middle" age category contains all people between 30 and 49 years, and the "older" category includes all people between the ages of 50 and 64. Public service employment contains

---

fields, these skill measures are based on less than ten incumbents. Because I use detailed occupations, the reliability of such measures would be significantly lower.

all individuals who are employed in the public sector as opposed to private sector employment. Region differentiates between the old and new *Länder*.

6   Descriptive Statistics

In the following sections, I first present the trends in temporary employment at the individual level, differentiated by the individual characteristics I used in the first step of my two-step multilevel regression analysis. The descriptive trends are based on data from the full 1 percent population sample of the German Microcensus for the years 1993 to 2008. Second, I show descriptive statistics for the dependent and independent variables at the occupational level. Finally, I present an overview of the means and standard deviations of the occupational-level variables and of the bivariate occupational-level correlations between the various closure source variables. I also provide an overview on how the various closure sources are distributed over major occupational groupings.

6.1 The Trends in Temporary Employment in Germany

Figure 3 presents the differences between the old and new German *Länder* (former West and East Germany respectively) as the percentage of employees in temporary employment in order to give a first impression of the rate of temporary employment and its association with the different regions of Germany. The relative prevalence of temporary employment contracts is measured in comparison to the individuals in employment who are at risk of holding temporary employment contracts (see chapter 5). Temporary employment was of relatively low importance for the West German labor market, at least in the 1990s. However, the share of temporary employment contracts rose slowly but continuously in the old *Länder* from 4.8 percent (1993) to 7 percent (1999). Between 1999 and 2004, the share stagnated but it again rose steeply to 9.5 percent in the years 2005 to 2008. In the new East German *Länder,* temporary employment contracts were much more important than in the old West German *Länder*. In the early 1990s, every tenth employee in the new *Länder* had a temporary employment contract. This high initial percentage remained relatively stable until 2004. In 2006, temporary employment peaked (14.3 percent) and then declined to its 2008 value of 13.2 percent.

The sharp increase in both parts of Germany from 2005 onwards is due to profound changes in the unemployment insurance system—the Hartz reforms. The Hartz reforms constituted the most radical change in the welfare tradition of post-war Germany and transformed the unemployment benefit system from an insurance-based system that aimed to preserve status to a system providing flat-rate assistance at a subsistence level (for a short literature overview see

Figure 3:   Temporary employment in the old and new German Länder,
            1993-2008

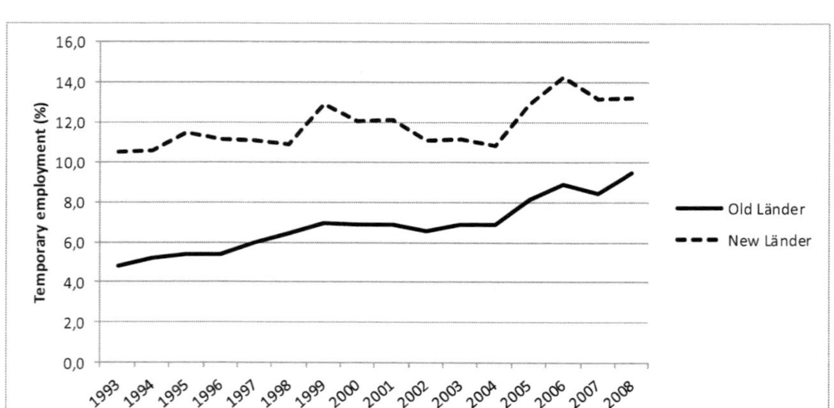

Source: RDC of the Federal Statistical Office and the Statistical Offices of the Länder, Micro-census, survey years 1993-2008, own calculations

Bernhardt 2015). Before 2005, the unemployment insurance system aimed to preserve the newly unemployed person's status. The new flat-rate assistance established as part of the Hartz reforms provides basic, status-independent income support that is only granted if savings are used up beforehand. Long-term unemployment (unemployment that lasts longer than one year) now entails the real threat of downward social mobility particularly for the middle class (Bernhardt forthcoming, p. 7). While the old regulation granted the unemployed the necessary time and money to find a new status-equivalent job, the revised regulation incorporates strong incentives to take jobs that are not status equivalent to avoid long-term unemployment. This pressure may have caused the increase in temporary employment, since more unemployed people may have tried to get back into employment regardless of the status or employment conditions of the new job[127].

---

127   There was also an important change in the sampling technique of the Microcensus. Before 2005 all respondents were surveyed in one week of the second quarter of the year. The survey was changed to a continuous survey in 2005 and the respondents were equally distributed through the year. To avoid measuring errors through design effects I restricted the sample for the Microcensus years 2005-2008 to the second quarter. This reduces the number of observations for these years by three quarters.

Figure 3 shows the share of temporary employment contracts for three age groups[128] and shows a strong association between age and temporary employment. The share of temporary employment contracts increased strongly and continuously for the young age group. In the early 90s, every tenth employee aged below 30 held a temporary employment contract. By 2008 this ratio had increased steeply: One out of four employees held temporary employment contracts. Although older employees have the lowest share of temporary employment contracts, the differences between the 30-49 year olds and the older employees are minimal.

Figure 4: Temporary employment differentiated by age, 1993-2008

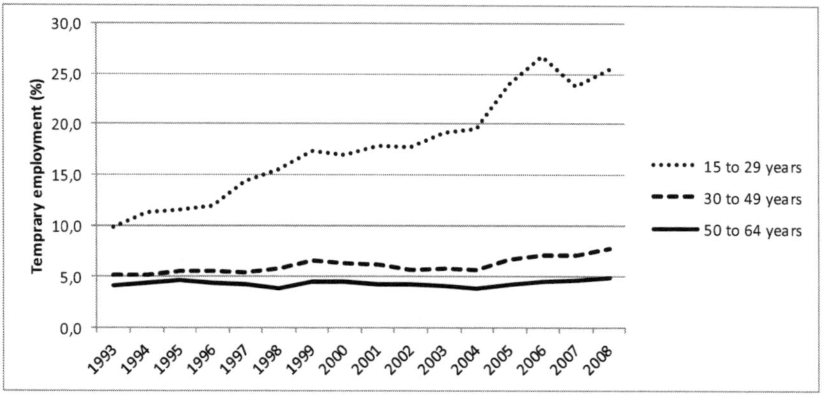

Source: RDC of the Federal Statistical Office and the Statistical Offices of the Länder, Microcensus, survey years 1993-2008, own calculations

In general, an individual's qualification level is an important influence on the risk of holding a temporary employment contract (see figure 4). Most notably, the absence of formal qualifications (no additional formal education beyond basic schooling) is most strongly associated with temporary employment. People without formal qualifications had temporary employment levels that ranged between 8 percent and 19. However, until the middle of the 1990s, the proportions of temporary employment among those who have high levels of vocational qualifications (individuals with master-craftsmen credentials or

---

128 The differentiation of the age categories into three groups (15-29 years, 30-49 years, 50-64 years) is based on Allmendinger et al. (2013, p. 9). The main idea behind this coding is to emphasize the prime working age and contrast it with those age groups that are usually more at risk of being unemployed, economically inactive, or in nonstandard employment.

tertiary degrees) were similar. While the difference in the share of temporary employment for individuals with medium- and high-level qualifications converged, individuals with high-level qualifications were more often temporarily employed than individuals with medium-level qualifications (completed vocational training and education below the tertiary level).

Figure 5: Temporary employment differentiated by qualification, 1993-2008

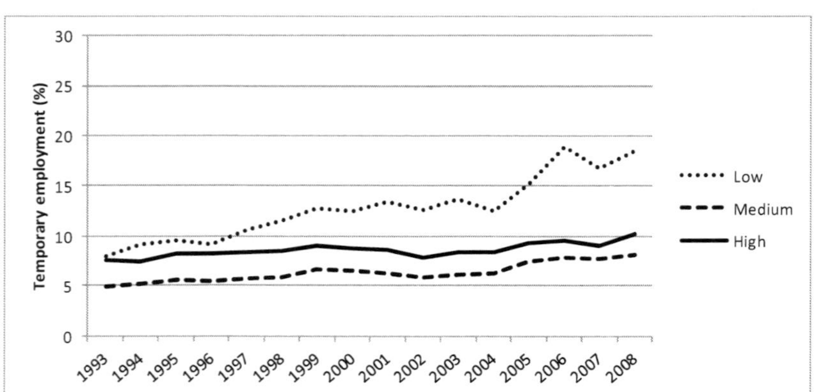

Source: RDC of the Federal Statistical Office and the Statistical Offices of the Länder, Micro-census, survey years 1993-2008, own calculations

The use of temporary employment contracts in the public sector differs from its use in the private sector. Individuals in the public sector were more often temporarily employed than employees in the private sector, but the gap between both sectors was closing. The share of temporary employment was higher in the public sector than in the private sector.

There were no appreciable differences in temporary employment between women and men (see figure 6). In the 1990s, women were temporarily employed slightly more often than men. In the 2000s, the picture changed and even this small difference in men's and women's temporary employment rates vanished almost completely. However, the maximum difference between men's and women's temporary employment rates was very small in any case (1.3 percent in 1994 and 1995).

Figure 6: Temporary employment differentiated by public and private sector, 1993-2008

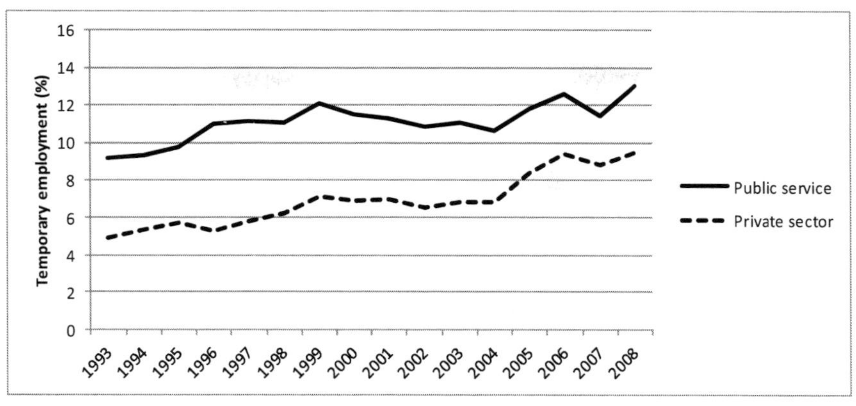

Source: RDC of the Federal Statistical Office and the Statistical Offices of the Länder, Microcensus, survey years 1993-2008, own calculations

Figure 7: Temporary employment differentiated by sex, 1993-2008

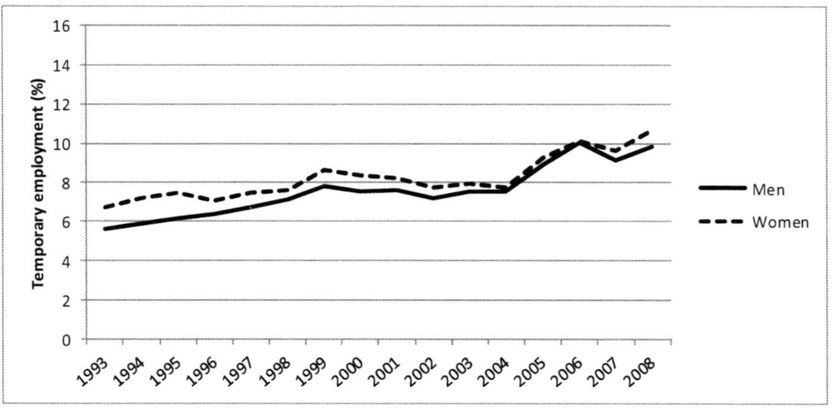

Source: RDC of the Federal Statistical Office and the Statistical Offices of the Länder, Microcensus, survey years 1993-2008, own calculations

6.2 Closure Sources and Their Bivariate Association with Temporary Employment

For the following descriptions of the occupational-level variables, I will use descriptive statistics that are based on deciles. These deciles divide the ordered sample of the occupations into ten essentially equal subsets of occupations. The variable I use for the ordering of the occupations is the variable of interest for the respective section (e.g., standardization). First, I use these deciles to describe the distribution of the variable of interest (e.g., the mean standardization value of each decile). Second, I use the same deciles to assess the potential association between the variable of interest and temporary employment (e.g., the mean proportion of temporary employment for each decile). The style of the descriptions will be necessarily different for categorical/binary variables like associations, unionization, and task-licensure. The descriptive statistics for the credential inflation index will include an additional figure that shows the association between the conventional credentialism measure (proportion of occupational incumbents with tertiary degrees) and the credential inflation index measure. The focus of the descriptive analyses is the pooled total sample (N = 1,118 occupations), but I will also show the distribution of the average values for the years 2000, 2004, and 2007 to check the stability of the closure measures over time.

6.2.1 The Credential Inflation Index

The lower the value of the credential inflation index (CIX), the fewer the numbers of freshly credentialed individuals entering the occupational labor market in comparison to the employees who are already employed in the occupation in question. Lower credential inflation index values thereby indicate more closed occupations.

Figure 8 shows the distribution of the CIX values across the occupations, which were assigned to ten deciles according to their credential inflation index values. The majority of occupations in Germany have low CIX values. Only occupations in the eighth decile exceed the mean CIX value of 0.05. For most of the occupations in the ninth and tenth decile, credentials are awarded in an inflationary manner. Some sample occupations with values around the median of the credential inflation index are bakers (CIX=0.038), HR administrators (CIX=0.04), and field representatives and traveling salesman (CIX=0.044). Occupations with very high values on the credential inflation index include application software developers (CIX=0.29), industrial clerks and business managers (CIX=0.4), and car electricians (CIX=0.69). Examples of occupations

Figure 8:   *The distribution of the mean credential inflation index values over the deciles of the occupations for the years 2000, 2004, and 2007*

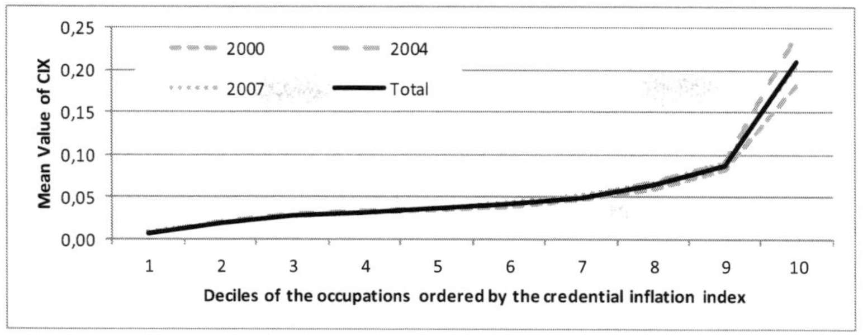

Note: N = 677,080 individuals in 1,118 occupations
Sources: Statistisches Bundesamt a, b, c, d, e, f, g, h, i, j 1999-2008, own calculations; RDC of the Federal Statistical Office and the Statistical Offices of the Länder, Microcensus, survey years 2000, 2004, 2007, own calculations; Berufenet internet data-base of the Federal Labor Office of Germany.

with very low credential inflation index values include shoemakers (CIX=0.007), goods decorators and goods painters (CIX=0.005), and miners (CIX=0.003).

Figure 9 shows the average rate of temporary employment for each decile of occupation-specific values of the credential inflation index. The association between CIX and temporary employment appears to be relatively weak. Occupations within the first two deciles had the lowest shares of temporary employment. Occupations within the third to eigth decile had slightly higher shares of incumbents who are in temporary employment. Occupations within the last two deciles had the highest share of their incumbents in temporary employment. This pattern mirrors the pattern depicted in Figure 8, which shows that credentials were only awarded in an inflationary manner in the occupations in the last two deciles. Even though the mean credential inflation values of occupations within the last decile is very high, the share of temporary employees increases only slightly from the ninth to the tenth decile. The reason for this small increase is that the last decile also contains relatively "new" occupations (e.g., software developers). The number of new employees within these new occupations is still relatively small, but the numbers of freshly credentialed individuals is high.[129]

---

129 "Old" and "dying" occupations are most often to be found in the first deciles. Even if only few incumbents are left working in their occupation, even fewer freshly credentialed individuals enter these occupational labor markets.

Figure 9:   The mean rate of temporary employment differentiated by the deciles of CIX for the years 2000, 2004, and 2007

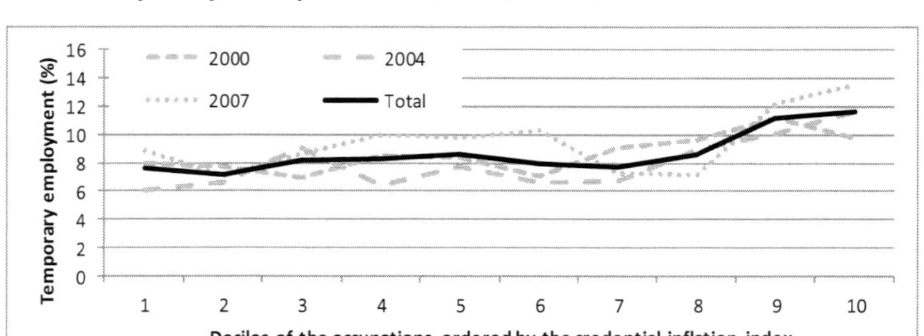

Note: N = 677,080 individuals in 1,118 occupations
Sources: Statistisches Bundesamt a, b, c, d, e, f, g, h, i, j 1999-2008, own calculations; RDC of the Federal Statistical Office and the Statistical Offices of the Länder, Microcensus, survey years 2000, 2004, 2007, own calculations; Berufenet internet database of the Federal Labor Office of Germany.

Figure 10:   The mean rate of occupational incumbents with tertiary degrees differentiated by the deciles of CIX for the years 2000, 2004, and 2007

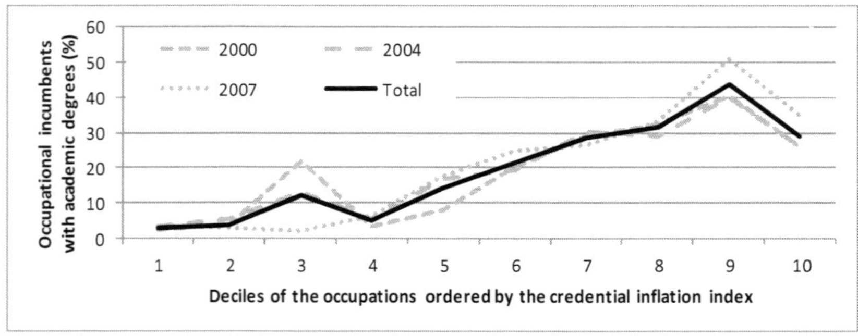

Note: N = 677,080 individuals in 1,118 occupations
Sources: Statistisches Bundesamt a, b, c, d, e, f, g, h, i, j 1999-2008, own calculations; RDC of the Federal Statistical Office and the Statistical Offices of the Länder, Microcensus, survey years 2000, 2004, 2007, own calculations; Berufenet internet database of the Federal Labor Office of Germany.

Figure 10 shows how the credential inflation index is associated with the measure most commonly used to capture the credentialism closure source (see chapter 4.1)—the proportion of occupational incumbents with tertiary degrees. For occupations with low values on the credential inflation index, the proportion of occupational incumbents with tertiary degrees is also low. Starting with the fourth decile up to the ninth decile, this proportion steadily increases as the credential inflation index increases.

6.2.2 The Standardization of Occupational Credentials

The standardization of the curricula of occupational credentials varies between 1 and 3 with a median standardization value of 2.61. The high median value reflects the importance of apprenticeship credentials for the German labor market. The apprenticeship training track only awards credentials that are standardized at the federal level.

Figure 11:   The distribution of the mean standardization index values over the deciles of the occupations for the years 2000, 2004, and 2007

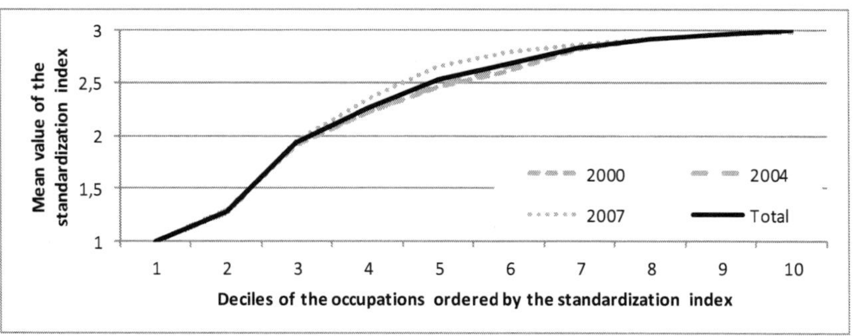

Note: N = 677,080 individuals in 1,118 occupations
Sources: Statistisches Bundesamt a, b, c, d, e, f, g, h, i, j 1999-2008, own calculations; RDC of the Federal Statistical Office and the Statistical Offices of the Länder, Microcensus, survey years 2000, 2004, 2007, own calculations; Berufenet internet database of the Federal Labor Office of Germany.

Figure 11 shows the distribution of the standardization values across the occupations, which were assigned to ten deciles according to their standardization index values. The curricula of the occupations within the first two deciles are mainly regulated on the school/university level and thus had the lowest standardization values. The occupations within the fourth, fifth, and sixth deciles are mainly standardized on the Länder level. Most of these occupations also have incumbents with credentials that are standardized on the federal level. Nearly all incumbents of the occupations within the seventh up to the tenth decile have credentials that are standardized on the federal level. Sample occupations with values around the median of the standardization variable include HR administrators (standardization=2.47), product testers, product inspectors (standardization=2.59), and assistant desk officers (standardization=2.63). Occupations with a very high degree of standardization include plate glass mechanics (standardization=3), tile and mosaic layers (standardization=2.99), and management assistants in data processing (standardization=2.98). Examples of occupations with a very low degree of standardization include all engineering occupations (standardization=1), IT consultants (standardization=1), and singers, actors, and performers (standardization=1).

Figure 12 shows an unambiguous association between temporary employment and the standardization of credentials. Occupations had the lowest share of temporarily employed incumbents when the majority of their incumbents held highly standardized credentials, whereas occupations had the highest shares of temporary employment when the majority of their members held credentials that were not very standardized. However, the occupations with the highest level of standardized credentials, i.e., those in the tenth decile, deviate from the overall pattern. They have a similar share of temporary employment as the occupations in the fourth to the sixth decile.

Figure 12:   The mean rate of temporary employment differentiated by the standardization of vocational credentials in the years 2000, 2004, and 2007

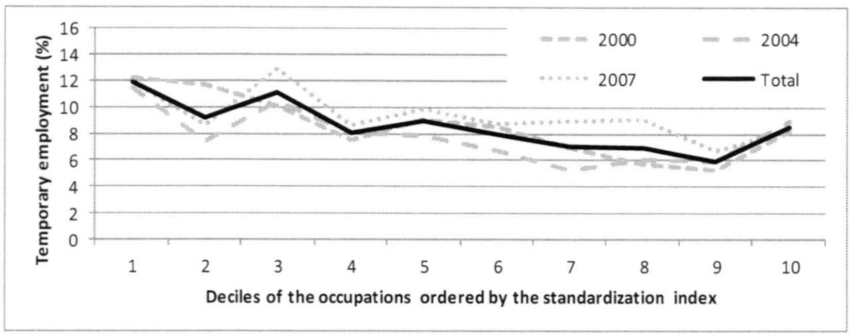

Note: N = 677,080 individuals in 1,118 occupations
Sources: Statistisches Bundesamt a, b, c, d, e, f, g, h, i, j 1999-2008, own calculations; RDC of the Federal Statistical Office and the Statistical Offices of the Länder, Microcensus, survey years 2000, 2004, 2007, own calculations; Berufenet internet database of the Federal Labor Office of Germany.

6.2.3 Occupational Specificity

Occupational specificity measures the composition of tasks within occupations and across occupations. Both measures of occupational specificity range between values of 0 and 1. Low values on the measures of occupational specificity indicate occupations with relatively unique or narrow combinations of tasks, whereas high values indicate occupations with tasks that are common or occupations that have a broad set of tasks and skills.

Figure 13:   The distribution of unique and common sets of tasks over the deciles of the occupations for the years 2000, 2004, and 2007

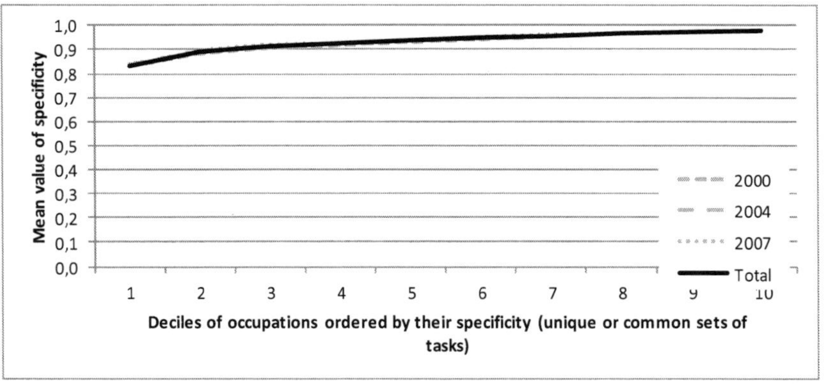

Note: N = 677,080 individuals in 1,118 occupations
Source: RDC of the Federal Statistical Office and the Statistical Offices of the Länder, Micro-census, survey years 2000, 2004, 2007, own calculations

In the theory section I have already argued that occupations with unique tasks should be a relatively rare phenomenon. This assumption is evidently true because most occupations had sets of tasks that were relatively common (see figure 13). The median value of the uniqueness/commonness variable of 0.94 indicates that most occupations share the same tasks[130]. Sample occupations with values around the median of the uniqueness variable include dental laboratory assistants and dental technicians (uniqueness = 0.93), administrative professionals (higher service) (uniqueness = 0.94), and scientific librarians (uniqueness = 0.95). Occupations with very common tasks include milling machine operators (uniqueness = 0.98), screed layers (uniqueness = 0.98), and

---

130   The range of the variable is 0.26.

machine setters and setter operators (uniqueness = 0.98). Examples for occupations with relatively unique tasks are industrial cleaners (uniqueness = 0.73), cooks (uniqueness = 0.8), and animal keepers (uniqueness = 0.83).

Figure 14: *The mean rate of temporary employment differentiated by the deciles of occupational specificity (unique or common sets of tasks) for the years 2000, 2004, and 2007*

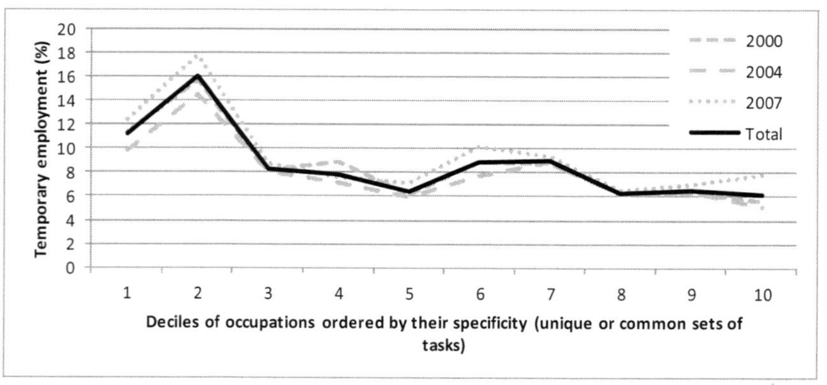

Note: N = 677,080 individuals in 1,118 occupations
Source: RDC of the Federal Statistical Office and the Statistical Offices of the Länder, Microcensus, survey years 2000, 2004, 2007, own calculations

Figure 14 shows the average rate of temporary employment for each decile of the occupations. The association between occupational specificity and temporary employment is ambiguous. Occupations with very unique sets of tasks (those in the first and second decile) had the highest share of incumbents with temporary employment contracts. Occupations in the fourth and fifth decile had similarly low rates of temporary employment as occupations in the eighth, ninth, and tenth decile. This similarity might be caused by the very low variance of this variable, that is, most occupations have relatively common sets of tasks. As figure 13 shows, the differentiation of the occupations into deciles signifies that the differences in the occupational specificity of the occupations are only small after the second decile.

The specificity measure for occupations with narrow or broad sets of tasks is evenly distributed (see figure 15). The median value of this specificity measure is 0.42. Sample occupations with values around the median of the specificity measure include pastry cooks (narrowness = 0.59), gas and water fitters (narrowness = 0.61), and surveying technicians (narrowness = 0.64).

Occupations with very broad sets of tasks include communications electronics technicians (narrowness = 0.88), hydraulic technicians (narrowness = 0.9), and social scientists (narrowness = 0.92). Examples of occupations with narrow sets of tasks include lower secondary school teachers (narrowness = 0.01), judges, attorneys, and public prosecutors (narrowness = 0.1), and food sellers (narrowness = 0.14).

Figure 15:   The distribution of narrow and wide sets of tasks over the deciles of the occupations for the years 2000, 2004, and 2007

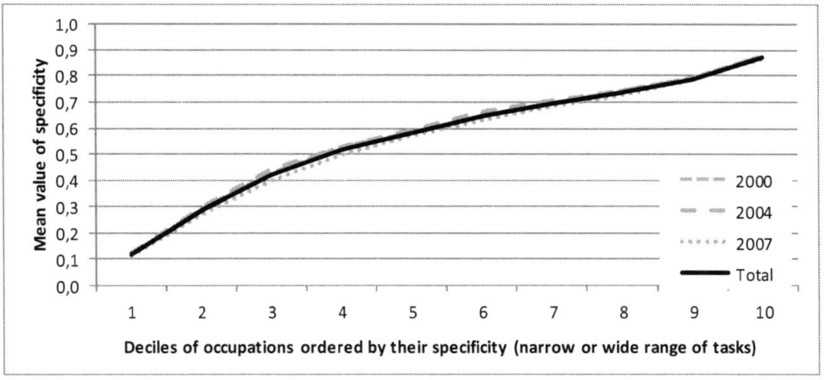

Note: N = 677,080 individuals in 1,118 occupations
Source: RDC of the Federal Statistical Office and the Statistical Offices of the Länder, Microcensus, survey years 2000, 2004, 2007, own calculations

Figure 16 shows the average rate of temporary employment for each decile of the occupations. The association between this measure of occupational specificity and temporary employment was weak. Occupations with a focus on a few skills and tasks had higher levels of temporary employment. The highest shares of temporary employees were found in occupations in the first decile up to occupations in the fourth decile. The share of temporary employment was relatively stable and low for occupations in the fifth up to occupations in the tenth decile. There seems to be an association between occupations with narrow sets of tasks and skills and temporary employment. However, after the range of tasks of occupations becomes relatively wide, further increases in the wideness of the tasks and skills had a visible association with their incumbents' risks of temporary employment.

*Figure 16: The mean rate of temporary employment differentiated by the
             deciles of occupational specificity (narrow or wide range of tasks)
             for years 2000, 2004, and, 2007*

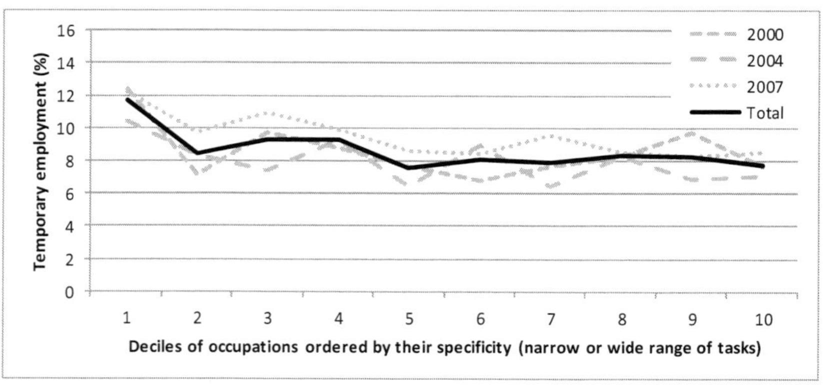

Note: N = 677,080 individuals in 1,118 occupations
Source: RDC of the Federal Statistical Office and the Statistical Offices of the Länder, Micro-census, survey years 2000, 2004, 2007, own calculations

6.2.4 The Licensing of Occupations

My first licensing measure is based on the federal-level legislation regarding the licensure of occupation-specific tasks. I am able to identify 37 licensed occupations. Two occupations were not licensed in the year 2000. The number of licensed occupations is therefore 35 in 2000. As a result, approximately 10 percent of the occupations in my sample were licensed. Sample occupations that are licensed include: nurses, medical doctors, and teachers.

Figure 17 presents the share of temporarily employed incumbents in licensed and nonlicensed occupations, which are differentiated by time. Employees in licensed occupations had a higher rate of temporary employment than occupations that were not licensed. The small increase from 35 licensed occupations in 2000 to 37 licensed occupations in 2004 and 2007 had no visible impact on the mean share of temporary employment of licensed occupations. The differences in temporary employment between licensed and nonlicensed occupations were smallest in 2007 because temporary employment strongly increased in the nonlicensed occupations.

Figure 17:   The mean rate of temporary employment differentiated by licensed and nonlicensed occupations in the years 2000, 2004, and 2007

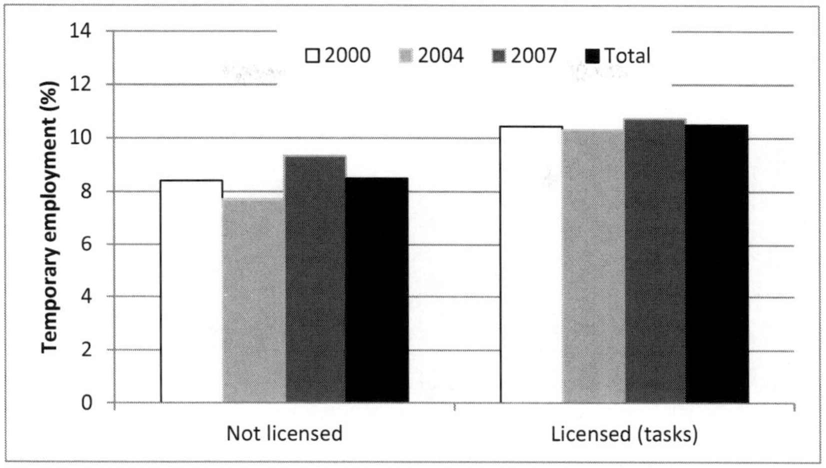

Note: N = 677,080 individuals in 1,118 occupations

Sources: RDC of the Federal Statistical Office and the Statistical Offices of the Länder, Microcensus, survey years 2000, 2004, 2007, own calculations; Berufenet internet data base of the Federal Labor Office of Germany; Haupt (2012a).

My second licensing measure is based on the federal-level legislation regarding the licensure of occupation-specific titles. It measures the proportion of occupational members with protected titles. Hence, the licensing of titles varies between 0 and 100.

*Figure 18:   The distribution of the mean licensure (titles) over the deciles of the
occupations for the years 2000, 2004, and 2007*

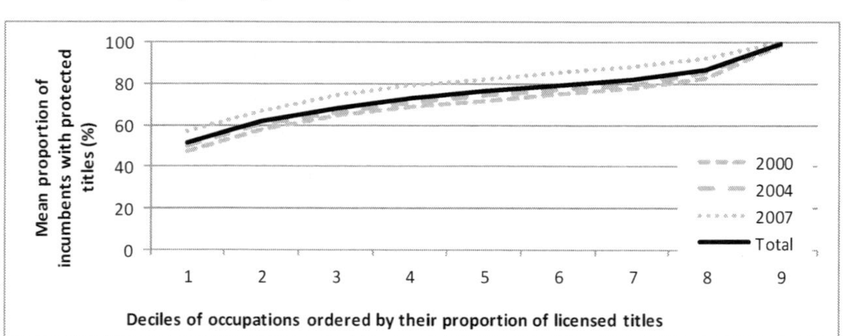

Note: N = 677,080 individuals in 1,118 occupations
Source: RDC of the Federal Statistical Office and the Statistical Offices of the Länder, Microcensus, survey years 2000, 2004, 2007, own calculations.

Figure 18 shows the distribution of protected titles across the occupations,
which were assigned to nine deciles. The ninth and tenth decile could not be
meaningfully distinguished from each other because the majority of occupations within these two deciles had incumbents who all had protected titles. Even
the occupations in the first decile had a relatively high density of incumbents
with protected titles (50 percent). Sample occupations with a median density of
incumbents with protected titles include forestry workers (licensure (titles) =
78%), software developers (licensure (titles) = 76%), and freight forwarding
and logistics services clerks (licensure (titles) = 80%). Occupations with a very
high density of incumbents with protected titles include industrial master
craftsmen (licensure (titles) = 100%), professional fire fighters (licensure (titles
= 100%), and chaplains (licensure (titles) = 100%). Examples for occupations
with a very low density of incumbents with protected titles are therapists (licensure (titles) = 48%), publishing house workers (licensure (titles) = 54%), and
waiters and waitresses (licensure (titles) = 51%).

Figure 19 shows the average rate of temporary employment for each decile
of the occupations. The association between this measure of licensure and the
proportion of temporarily employed individuals is strong for occupations within
the first up to the fifth deciles: A higher density of occupational members with
protected titles is strongly associated with a decrease in the proportion of occupational incumbents who have temporary employment contracts. A further
increase in the density of occupational members with protected titles did not

Figure 19:   The mean rate of temporary employment differentiated by the deciles of title licensure for years 2000, 2004, and, 2007

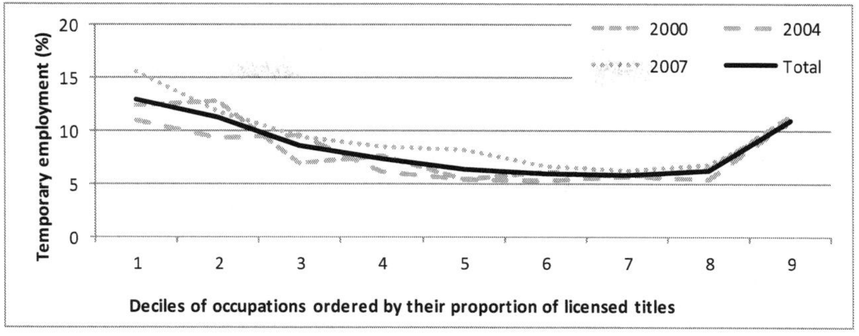

Note: N = 677,080 individuals in 1,118 occupations
Source: RDC of the Federal Statistical Office and the Statistical Offices of the Länder, Micro-census, survey years 2000, 2004, 2007, own calculations.

correspond to a further decrease in their risk of holding temporary employment contracts. The share of incumbents with temporary contracts remains stable for occupations within the fifth up to the eighth decile. However, for occupations where nearly all incumbents have protected titles, the share of temporary employment goes back up.

6.2.5 Occupational Associations

One third of all occupations in my sample were represented by associations. I use the degree of exclusivity to differentiate between occupational associations that represent more than one occupation and occupational associations that represent only one occupation. 17 percent of the occupations were represented by an association that only represented that occupation and no other occupa-tions. I will refer to them as specific associations. 16 percent of the occupations were represented by associations that represented other occupations, too. I will refer to these associations as general associations. The majority of occupations, two thirds, were not represented by any associations. Examples of occupations without representation are butchers, interior decorators, and earth-moving machine drivers. Various engineer, technician, and management occupations are represented by general associations, while commercial and professional drivers, executive consultants and management consultants, and hair stylists are repre-sented by specific occupational associations.

Figure 20 presents the level of temporary employment for occupations without occupational associations, for occupations with general associations, and for occupations with specific associations. Temporary employment was highest for employees in occupations with associations, irrespective of their general or specific character, and was lowest in occupations without associations.

Figure 20: Occupational incumbents' mean rate of temporary employment differentiated by their representation by occupational associations in the years 2000, 2004, and 2007

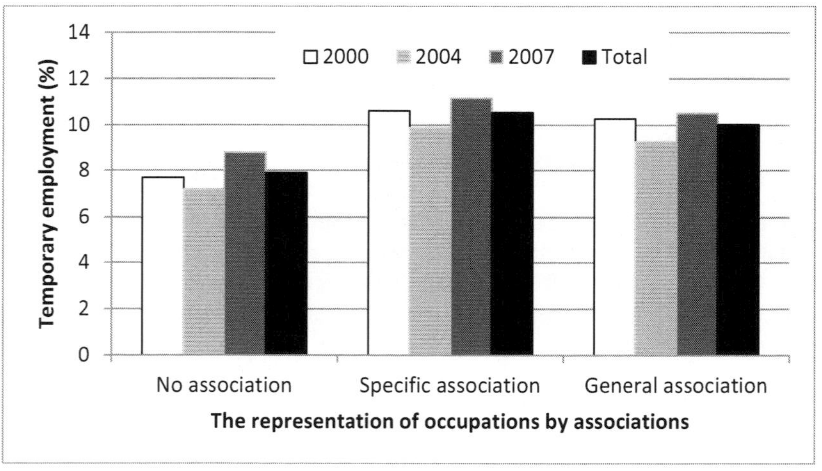

Note: N = 677,080 individuals in 1,118 occupations
Sources: RDC of the Federal Statistical Office and the Statistical Offices of the Länder, Micro-census, survey years 2000, 2004, 2007, own calculations; survey of the total population of occupational associations conducted by Schroeder, Kalass and Greef, own calculations

6.2.6 Occupation-Specific Trade Unions

Thirteen percent of all occupations were represented by trade unions, which were legally permitted to collectively bargain for the interests of the occupational incumbents. Examples of occupations with trade unions include train drivers/rail vehicle operators, medical doctors, and road maintenance workers. Figure 21 presents the level of temporary employment for occupations with and without occupation-specific trade unions. Temporary employment was high for employees in occupations with occupation-specific trade unions and was low in occupations without trade union representation.

Figure 21: *Occupational incumbents' mean rate of temporary employment differentiated by their representation by trade unions in the years 2000, 2004, and 2007*

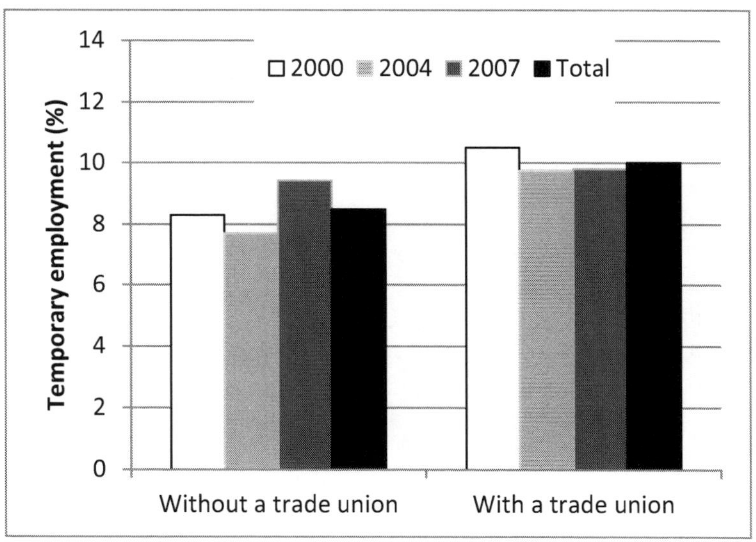

Note: N = 677,080 individuals in 1,118 occupations
Sources: RDC of the Federal Statistical Office and the Statistical Offices of the Länder, Microcensus, survey years 2000, 2004, 2007, own calculations; survey of the total population of occupational associations conducted by Schroeder, Kalass and Greef, own calculations

6.3 Summary of the Descriptive Statistics

Table 2 presents the occupational-level variables' means and standard deviations. The descriptive statistics show that nearly all closure sources were stable over time. There was only one exception: the licensure of occupational titles. In 2007, the mean level of title licensure increased considerably. The association between the credential inflation index and the proportion of occupational incumbents with tertiary degrees seems to support my theoretical concerns: For Germany, the established measure of credentialism does not seem to capture the restricting-supply closure mechanism: Occupations for which credentials are awarded in an inflationary manner have the highest proportions of members with tertiary degrees. However, Bol and Weeden (2014), Giesecke and Verwiebe (2009), and Groß (2009, 2012) found a positive association between occupational closure and tertiary degrees for Germany. I will therefore return to this conundrum in the next chapter.

Table 2: Descriptive statistics of occupational-level measures

Variable	Mean	SD
Closure Sources (omitted categories: no occupational association, no task licensure, no trade union):		
Credential inflation index	0,06	0,07
Standardization	2,33	0,71
Narrow or wide range of tasks	0,57	0,23
Unique of common sets tasks	0,93	0,04
Specific occupational association	0,17	-
General occupational association	0,16	-
Task licensure	0,10	-
Title licensure	0,78	0,15
Occupation-specific trade union	0,13	-
Skill level of tasks (omitted category = skilled functions):		
Routine/labor functions	0,20	0,22
Managerial and skilled functions	0,25	0,20
Managerial functions	0,23	0,25
Establishment size:		
Small organizations	0,11	0,13
Large organizations	0,36	0,22
Region (omitted category = old *Länder*):		
New *Länder*	0,21	0,10
Human Capital:		
Further education	0,10	0,12
Gender Composition:		
% female	0,38	0,30
Time (omitted category = 2004):		
Year 2000	0,33	-
Year 2007	0,33	-

Variable	Mean	SD
Nationality:		
% non-German citizenship	0,06	0,07
Industry (omitted category = manufacturing):		
Agriculture	0,02	0,11
Mining, electricity, gas	0,02	0,07
Construction	0,08	0,22
Distributive trades and repair services	0,10	0,20
Transportation and information services	0,05	0,16
Financial and insurance services	0,03	0,13
Business services	0,09	0,16
Miscellaneous services	0,07	0,18
Non-profit organizations	0,16	0,30
Public service	0,09	0,20
Dependent variable		
Square root (predicted probability of temporary employment)	0,29	0,12
Predicted probability of temporary employment	0,10	0,08

Note: N = 677,080 individuals in 1,118 occupations; standard deviations are not shown for binary or categorical variables

Sources: Statistisches Bundesamt a, b, c, d, e, f, g, h, i, j 1999-2008, own calculations; RDC of the Federal Statistical Office and the Statistical Offices of the Länder, Microcensus, survey years 2000, 2004, 2007, own calculations; Berufenet internet data base of the Federal Labor Office of Germany; Haupt 2012a; survey of the total population of occupational associations conducted by Schroeder, Kalass and Greef, own calculations.

Bivariate correlations between the independent occupational-level variables are presented in table 3[131]. The strongest associations are found between task licensure and title licensure (0.48), and between task licensure and occupation-specific trade unions (0.43). The correlation between task licensure and title licensure comes as no surprise: All occupations with licensed tasks have protected titles. Because of this conceptual intersection between both licensure variables, I will use them separately in the coming multivariate models, even if the statistical relationship between the two measures is not very high. There might be reason to be concerned about multicollinearity between both measures of occupational specificity, given that they use the same basic information but

---

131 A full correlation matrix that also includes the occupational-level control variables and the proportion of incumbents with academic degrees is available in the online appendix (11.3).

process it in different ways. However, there is only a weak mathematical relationship (r=0.32) between them.

Table 3: Bivariate correlations of the occupational-level closure variables

	Variable	1	2	3	4	5	6	7	8	9
1	Credential inflation index	1								
2	Standardization	*-0,01*	1							
3	Narrow or wide range of tasks	-0,07	-0,19	1						
4	Unique or common sets of tasks	-0,07	*0,00*	0,32	1					
5	Specific occup. association	*0,02*	-0,24	-0,08	-0,19	1				
6	General occup. association	0,09	-0,38	-0,10	-0,07	-0,19	1			
7	Task licensure	0,19	-0,16	-0,35	-0,18	0,22	0,23	1		
8	Title licensure	0,11	-0,24	*-0,03*	0,16	0,14	0,15	0,48	1	
9	Occupation-specific trade union	0,14	-0,12	-0,20	-0,25	0,18	0,27	0,43	0,24	1

Note: N = 677,080 individuals in 1,118 occupations; correlations in italic are not significant at the p<0.05 level

Sources: Statistisches Bundesamt a, b, c, d, e, f, g, h, i, j 1999-2008, own calculations; RDC of the Federal Statistical Office and the Statistical Offices of the Länder, Microcensus, survey years 2000, 2004, 2007, own calculations; Berufenet internet data base of the Federal Labor Office of Germany; Haupt 2012a; survey of the total population of occupational associations conducted by Schroeder, Kalass and Greef, own calculations.

To give a more tangible impression of how the closure sources vary in their distribution over the occupations, I aggregated the detailed occupations into major occupational groups. Table 4 shows the mean value of the closure sources for each major occupational group. The credential inflation index does not vary greatly. Service occupations and operative/labor occupations have the highest mean credential inflation index values. The standardization of credentials is lowest in technical and managerial occupations and highest in craft occupations. The sets of tasks are relatively narrow in service occupations and relatively wide in technical and managerial occupations. Agricultural occupations have relatively unique sets of tasks, whereas craft, technical, and managerial occupations have relatively common sets of tasks. Service occupations and managerial occupations are most often represented by specific associations and technical and managerial occupations by general associations.

Table 4: Mean of the various closure sources by major occupation group

Closure sources	Opera-tive/labor	Agri-culature	Sales/clerical	Ser-vice	Crafts	Tech-nical	Mana-gerial
Credential inflation index	0,07	0,05	0,05	0,07	0,05	0,04	0,05
Standardization	2,53	2,40	2,33	2,02	2,88	1,54	1,45
Width of the sets of tasks	0,50	0,53	0,58	0,47	0,58	0,75	0,71
Commonness ofthe tasks	0,92	0,87	0,93	0,90	0,96	0,96	0,95
Specific association	0,04	0,00	0,13	0,40	0,01	0,21	0,31
General association	0,00	0,11	0,14	0,28	0,01	0,38	0,38
Task licensure	0,03	0,00	0,00	0,35	0,00	0,03	0,06
Title licensure	0,63	0,78	0,78	0,84	0,74	0,81	0,81
Trade union	0,00	0,22	0,06	0,32	0,03	0,00	0,44

Note: N = 677,080 individuals in 1,118 occupations
Sources: Statistisches Bundesamt a, b, c, d, e, f, g, h, i, j 1999-2008, own calculations; RDC of the Federal Statistical Office and the Statistical Offices of the Länder, Microcensus, survey years 2000, 2004, 2007, own calculations; Berufenet internet data base of the Federal Labor Office of Germany; Haupt 2012a; survey of the total population of occupational associations conducted by Schroeder, Kalass and Greef, own calculations.

Task licensure is strongly concentrated in service occupations. More than a third of service occupations have licensed tasks. Title licensure is also most common in service occupations and relatively rare in operative/labor occupations. Nearly half of all managerial occupations, a third of service occupations, and a fifth of agricultural occupations are represented by occupation-specific trade unions.

The descriptive analyses show that the bivariate associations between most closure sources and temporary employment are relatively weak. Most of the relationships may be as theoretically predicted, but they are obscured by compositional effects. In the next chapter, I will therefore present multivariate analyses to assess the association between the various closure sources and temporary employment.

7 Closing in on Closure—The Association between Occupational Closure and Temporary Employment

Table 5 displays the distributional characteristics of the estimated logit coefficients resulting from 1,118 stage-one regressions (one regression for each occupation). These coefficients express the occupational incumbents' relative risk of holding temporary employment contracts. Coefficients smaller than zero indicate a lower risk in comparison with the reference group, whereas coefficients greater than zero indicate a higher risk. The table includes the mean of the coefficients over all occupations and years, as well as the standard deviation of these coefficients and their distribution over 5 percentiles of the occupations (the 10 percent percentile (p10), the 25 percent percentile (p25), the median (p50), the 75 percent percentile (p75), and the 90 percent percentile (p90)). Interpreting the distributional characteristics of the individual-level occupation-specific logit coefficients is relatively simple. For example: Each occupation provides one logit coefficient for the relative risk held by women in comparison to men. The overall mean of 0.26 indicates that women have a slightly higher risk of temporary employment than men, when all occupations are considered. To create the percentile measures, the logit coefficients are ordered according to their size. The 10 percent percentile indicates the mean risk of temporary employment for women in the first 10 percent of the occupations after the occupations were ordered. The 90 percent percentile indicates the mean risk of temporary employment when all occupations, except for the last ten percent, were taken into consideration. Positive logit coefficient values indicate a higher risk of temporary employment for women in comparison to men, whereas negative values indicate a lower risk of temporary employment in comparison to the male incumbents of the same occupations.

Table 5 shows that most individual-level variables do not have a fixed positive or negative effect for the incumbents of the various occupations. For example: The 10th and 25th percentile indicate that women face lower risks of temporary employment than men in 25 percent of all occupations. However, the 75th and 90th percentile indicate a reversed and even stronger relationship[132]. There is, however, one exception: Occupational incumbents aged between 15 and 29 seem to always have a higher risk of temporary employment than

---

132 Hence, a multilevel model with fixed random slopes would represent a clearly mis-specified empirical model.

Table 5:   A description of the estimated logit coefficients of the 1,118 separate stage-one regression analyses

Variable	Mean	p10	p25	p50	p75	p90	SD
Demography:							
15 to 29 years	1,32	0,21	0,82	1,32	1,85	2,40	0,88
50 to 64 years	-0,27	-1,36	-0,81	-0,28	0,26	0,86	0,92
Female	0,26	-0,76	-0,30	0,15	0,67	1,40	0,96
"Human capital":							
Low level of qualification	0,83	-0,28	0,14	0,70	1,40	2,18	1,02
High level of qualification	0,81	-0,36	0,00	0,54	1,48	2,55	1,17
Workplace characteristic (ommited variable = private sector employment):							
Public service	0,61	-0,66	-0,02	0,35	1,30	2,34	1,31
Region:							
New *Länder*	0,58	-0,46	0,05	0,56	1,07	1,67	0,83

Note: N = 677,080 individuals in 1,118 occupations
Sources: RDC of the Federal Statistical Office and the Statistical Offices of the Länder, Microcensus, survey years 2000, 2004, 2007, own calculations

incumbents of the same occupation who are between 30 and 49 years old. Members of occupations that are between 50 and 64 years old are the only subpopulation with a negative mean/median risk of temporary employment. Incumbents who have low levels of qualification share a similar risk of temporary employment as incumbents with high levels of qualification (the reference are incumbents with medium levels of qualification). Occupational incumbents that are employed in the new *Länder* or in the public sector also face an increased risk of temporary employment compared to their fellow occupational incumbents who are employed in the old *Länder* or the private sector.

In the next section, I will give a short introduction on how to interpret the results of the second-stage regressions and present stepwise models, a full model with all closure sources, and a full model with standardized coefficients. In section 7.2, I include interaction terms for human capital and for internal labor markets. Section 7.3 includes the exploratory interaction terms for the monitoring costs (transaction cost approach), and section 7.4 includes the exploratory interaction terms that address distinctive features of the German labor market—the different economic situations in the old and new *Länder* and the gender composition of occupations. Section 7.5 shifts the focus of the analyses from the variation between occupations to the variation within occupations, which allows me to check whether the relationship between individual-level characteristics and temporary employment changes as a function of the occupational-level closure sources. In section 7.6, I try to determine the relationship between the conventional credentialism measure (proportion of the incumbents with tertiary degrees) and my closure measures. Section 7.7 gives a short overview of the sensitivity checks I have done.

7.1 Occupational Closure and Temporary Employment—Results

To check whether the theoretical arguments I have drawn from closure theory are supported by empirical evidence, I present stepwise second stage regression results for each closure source and their association with the occupation-specific risk of temporary employment (hypotheses 1 to hypothesis 9)[133]. The dependent variable at the second stage is based on the occupational-level aggregation of the individual-level predicted probabilities of temporary employment (see section 5.1, equation 2). It is relatively straightforward to interpret the regression coefficients with regard to the dependent variable. For example: A mean predicted probability value of 0.4 can roughly be interpreted as 40 percent of the occupational incumbents having temporary employment contracts. Regression coefficients can hence be interpreted as the percentage-point change that occurs in the dependent variable if the independent variable changes by one unit. To ensure an approximately normal distribution of my dependent variable, I take the square root of the occupational mean of the predicted probabilities[134]. To be able to interpret these square rooted coefficients regardless, I retransform the coefficients using the inverse function of the square root. The occupational-level heterogeneity (variance) of the square rooted dependent variable is 0.0137 (standard deviation is 0.1172 and mean is 0.29) with a minimum value of zero and maximum value of 0.801.

Table 6 summarizes the results for the closure sources and their association with the occupation-specific risk of temporary employment. The two licensure measures, task licensure and title licensure, are introduced in separate models because both measures contain task-licensed occupations. The estimates show statistically significant associations for three of the five closure sources: credentialism, occupational specificity, and occupation-specific trade unions. However, the trade unions do not remain significant in the full models (models 6a and 6b). Model 1 introduces the credential inflation index, which is posi-

---

133　Link to the online appendix: http://www.nomos-shop.de/Stuth-Closing-on-Closure/productvi ew.aspx?product=28864&pac=weco

134　The mean predicted probabilities of temporary employment have a mean of 0.098, a median of 0.079, a skewness of 2.67, and a kurtosis of 13.58. Taking the square root of the mean predicted probabilities transforms the distributional characteristics of the dependent variable as follows: mean: 0.29, median: 0.28, skewness: 0.36, kurtosis: 5.59).

tively associated with the occupational incumbents' probability of holding temporary employment contracts. Occupations for which credentials are awarded in an inflationary manner increase their incumbents' risk of holding temporary employment contracts. An increase of CIX by one unit increases the risk of temporary employment by 3.4 percentage points (square[0.185] = 0,034)[135]. The results support hypothesis 1 by indicating that a low supply of occupation-specific credentials reduces the risk of temporary employment. The negative sign of the standardization measure corresponds with my argument that standardized occupation-specific credentials signal craftsmanship and thereby channel the labor demand to the occupation (hypothesis 2). Yet the effect size of standardization is quite small: Temporary employment decreases by 0.03 percentage points (square[-0.016] = 0.0003) with each increase in the degree of standardization[136].

Model 2 introduces measures of occupational specificity. It allows me to test whether occupational task breadth is associated with a lower risk of temporary employment, as implied by the mobility approach, or a higher risk of temporary employment, as implied by signaling. According to the mobility argument of Iversen and Soskice (2001), occupations with wide sets of tasks grant their incumbents access to a multitude of different positions. Employers will thus more frequently offer them permanent employment contracts because they can be effectively reassigned within organizations (hypothesis 4). Proponents of signaling theory argue that employers more frequently offer temporary employment contracts to occupational incumbents when the fit between job requirements and the individuals' task profiles is uncertain, which is the case for occupations with a wide range of tasks and skills (hypothesis 5). The coefficient of model 2 offers support for signaling (hypothesis 5): occupations with narrow task profiles have a lower probability of temporary employment than occupations with a wide range of tasks. The level of temporary employment within occupations increases by 0.2 percentage points (square[0.041] = 0.002) for each unit increase in the breadth of the task range[137]. The second variable for occupational specificity indicates how strong the barriers between the occupation-specific labor markets are. Employers will not be able to easily replace employees from relatively unique occupations with incumbents from other occupations. Hence, the risk of temporary employment should be low (hypothesis 6). Indeed, incumbents of occupations with common sets of tasks are more at risk of holding temporary employment contracts than incumbents of

---

135 The majority of the occupations, at least eight out of ten, had values between 0.004 and 0.1 (see figure 8). The range of the CIX variable is 0.86.

136 The range of the standardization variable is 2.

137 The range of the variable is 0.92.

occupations with unique sets of tasks. The probability of temporary employment increases by 26 percentage points (square[0.508] = 0.258) for each unit increase in the commonness measure[138].

Table 6: Pooled linear regression of temporary employment on the different sources of occupational closure, 2000, 2004, and 2007[139]

	Model 1	Model 2	Model 3	Model 4a
Credential inflation index	0,185***			
	(0,051)			
Standardization	-0,016*			
	(0,007)			
Width of the sets of tasks		0,065**		
		(0,019)		
Commonness of the task sets		0,504***		
		(0,113)		
Associations (omitted category = no association)				
Specific association			-0,014	
			(0,010)	
General association			-0,018	
			(0,011)	
Task licensure (omitted category = not licensed)				
Licensed				-0,030
				(0,017)
Unionization (omitted category = no union)				
Trade union				
Constant	0,281***	0,272***	0,285***	0,281***
	(0,009)	(0,009)	(0,009)	(0,009)
F	14,38***	15,65***	13,99***	14,590***
R squared	0,272	0,286	0,263	0,263
Root MSE	0,101	0,100	0,102	0,102
Mean vif	2,94	3,15	2,86	2,96

---

138 The range the commonness variable is 0.25.

139 The full table with all control variables is shown in the online appendix (11.5).

	Model 4b	Model 5	Model 6a	Model 6b
Credential inflation index			0,172***	0,171***
			(0,048)	(0,048)
Standardization			-0,008	-0,009
			(0,008)	(0,008)
Width of the sets of tasks			0,055**	0,052**
			(0,019)	(0,019)
Commonness of the task sets			0,437***	0,445***
			(0,111)	(0,109)
Associations (omitted category = no association)				
Specific association			-0,002	-0,001
			(0,010)	(0,010)
General association			-0,007	-0,008
			(0,011)	(0,011)
Task licensure (omitted category = not licensed)				
Licensed			-0,002	
			(0,017)	
Title licensure	-0,001			0,000
	(0,000)			(0,000)
Unionization (omitted category = no union)				
Trade union		-0,042**	-0,028	-0,028
		(0,015)	(0,016)	(0,015)
Constant	0,278***	0,283***	0,279***	0,278***
	(0,009)	(0,009)	(0,010)	(0,009)
F	14,62***	14,85***	13,47***	13,59***
R squared	0,263	0,271	0,300	0,301
Root MSE	0,102	0,101	0,099	0,099
Mean vif	3,05	2,92	3,02	3,07

Note: N = 677,080 individuals in 1,118 occupations; Heteroscedastic consistent Huber-White standard errors in parentheses. All models control for time, skill level, small organizations, large organizations, region, further education, %female, %non-German citizens, and industries. *p<0.05, **p<0.01, and ***p<0.001

Sources: Statistisches Bundesamt a, b, c, d, e, f, g, h, i, j 1999-2008, own calculations; RDC of the Federal Statistical Office and the Statistical Offices of the Länder, Microcensus, survey years 2000, 2004, 2007, own calculations; Berufenet internet data base of the Federal Labor Office of Germany; Haupt 2012a; survey of the total population of occupational associations conducted by Schroeder, Kalass and Greef, own calculations.

Model 3 introduces two binary variables for specific and general occupational associations. General associations might trigger the increasing diffuse demand mechanism via lobbying and PR campaigns (hypothesis 7), whereas specific associations might trigger the channeling demand mechanism by reinforcing occupational standards and ethics, and thereby further the public's belief in the professional ethics of the occupations' incumbents (hypothesis 8). The coefficients for both types of associations point in the predicted direction but are not significant. Considering their binary nature, the effect size is also very small. Temporary employment decreases by 0.02 (0.03) percentage points for incumbents in occupations with a specific (general) association in comparison to members of occupations without an association.

Model 4 tests the binary task licensure measure and the continuous title licensure measure. Both task licensure and title licensure trigger the "channeling demand" mechanism (hypothesis 3), either through a legal task monopoly (task licensure), or through the signaling of quality (title licensure). Both have coefficients with the predicted negative signs, but neither is statistically significant, and both have weak effect sizes (hypothesis 3). Incumbents of occupations that are protected by task licensure have a risk of temporary employment that is 0.1 percentage point lower than incumbents of occupations that are not protected by task licensure. The effect of title licensure is also weak: The risk of temporary employment decreases by 0.0001 percentage points for each increase in the degree of title licensure[140].

Model 5 tests the unionization measure. Unionization triggers the "restricting supply" mechanism through collective bargaining and the threat of strikes, which might be used by unions to improve working conditions by restricting the employers' use of temporary employment contracts (hypothesis 9). Unionization is significant and has the predicted negative sign but also has a small effect size. Members of occupations that are represented by occupation-specific trade unions have a lower risk of temporary employment (0.18 percentage points) than incumbents of occupations without trade union representation.

Models 6a (the full model with task licensure) and 6b (the full model with title licensure) show a considerable reduction in the size of the coefficients for most closure source variables. As a result, the measures for standardization and unionization are no longer statistically significant. The width of tasks variable is an exception. Its coefficient increases in comparison with model 2.

I also wanted to test whether licensed titles and licensed tasks are both empirically linked to the occupation members' risk of temporary employment. To compare their contribution to the explanation of the probability of temporary

---

140 The range of the title licensure measure is 0.81

employment, I used model fit statistics. I fitted a full model with all independent and control variables except for the licensure measures. Then I introduced both variables separately into the models and compared their model fit (Wald) statistics. The addition of the binary task licensure measure did not induce any change in R^2 and had an F statistic of 0.01, whereas the addition of the continuous title licensure measure induced a change in R^2 by 0.0012 with an F statistic of 1.89. The model fit statistics from the title licensure measure is far from compelling, but nevertheless indicates a stronger link with the occupational incumbents' risk of temporary employment than the task licensure measure. Hence, I will focus on the title licensure measure in the following analytical sections.

Table 7 again presents the full model with all closure sources. In addition, all control variables and standardized regression coefficients are shown. The standardized coefficients allow a valid comparison of metric variables. The interpretation of these standardized "beta" coefficients is simple: The increase, for example, of CIX by one standard deviation increases the square-rooted probability of temporary employment by 0.1 standard deviations.

The standardized coefficients indicate that, in comparison to the other metric closure sources, the variable measuring the commonness and uniqueness of tasks has the biggest impact, followed by the credential inflation index and the width of the range of tasks, both of which have a similar impact on temporary employment. A variety of control variables also have an impact on the probability of temporary employment. Most important are the different industries and the task complexity measures. Simple routine/labor tasks, as well as complex managerial tasks, increase the risk of temporary employment. The probability of temporary employment also positively corresponds with the proportion of occupational incumbents that were employed in the new *Länder* and the proportion of women within the occupations. The proportions of occupational members who have participated in further education, or who are employed in very small companies, are inversely associated with the probability of temporary employment.

Table 7:   *Pooled linear regression of temporary employment on the different sources of occupational closure—full model with standardized coefficients, 2000, 2004, and 2007*

	Model 6b		
Credential inflation index	0,100	(0,048)	***
Standardization	-0,053	(0,008)	
Width of the sets of tasks	0,100	(0,019)	**
Commonness of the task sets	0,166	(0,109)	***
Associations (omitted category = no association)			

	Model 6b		
Specific association	-	(0,010)	
General association	-	(0,011)	
Task licensure (omitted category = not licensed)			
Licensed			
Title licensure	-0,059	(0,000)	
Unionization (omitted category = no union)			
Trade union	-	(0,015)	
Control variables			
Complexity of work (omitted category = skilled tasks)			
Routine tasks	0,279	(0,035)	***
Skilled/managerial tasks	-0,081	(0,032)	
Managerial tasks	0,173	(0,029)	**
Small organizations	-0,081	(0,001)	
Large organizations	0,045	(0,001)	
New *Länder*	0,110	(0,000)	**
Further education	-0,180	(0,001)	**
% female	0,125	(0,000)	**
Time (omitted category: 2004)			
Year 2000	-	(0,008)	
Year 2007	-	(0,025)	
% non-German citizenship	-0,015	(0,001)	
Industries (omitted category = manufacturing)			
Agriculture	0,141	(0,000)	***
Mining, electricity, gas	-0,077	(0,001)	*
Construction	0,099	(0,000)	**
Distributive trades and repair services	0,099	(0,000)	**
Transportation and information services	0,074	(0,000)	*
Financial and insurance services	-0,013	(0,000)	
Business services	0,153	(0,000)	***
Miscellaneous services	0,229	(0,000)	***
Nonprofit organizations	0,541	(0,000)	***
Public service	0,127	(0,000)	*
Constant	.	(0,009)	***
F	13,59	***	
R squared	0,301		
Root MSE	0,099		
Mean vif	3,07		

Note: N = 677,080 individuals in 1,118 occupations; Heteroscedastic consistent Huber-White standard errors in parentheses. *p<0.05, **p<0.01, and ***p<0.001

Sources: Statistisches Bundesamt a, b, c, d, e, f, g, h, i, j 1999-2008, own calculations; RDC of the Federal Statistical Office and the Statistical Offices of the Länder, Microcensus, survey years 2000, 2004, 2007, own calculations; Berufenet internet data base of the Federal Labor Office of Germany; Haupt 2012a; survey of the total population of occupational associations conducted by Schroeder, Kalass and Greef, own calculations.

7.2 Occupational Closure, Human Capital, and Internal Labor Markets

Having established the main effects of occupational closure, I will use this section to explore the relationship between the various closure sources, specific human capital, and internal labor markets. The aim is to push the boundaries of our knowledge of human capital and internal labor markets by augmenting their standard predictions based on arguments derived from closure theory. In order to do so, I will first address specific human capital by taking the proportion of occupational incumbents who have participated in work-related further education. Secondly, I will add occupational-level interaction terms between the further-education-density measure and all closure sources (see table 8).

Table 8: Pooled linear regression of temporary employment on the different sources of occupational closure—with interactions between further education and the closure sources, 2000, 2004, and 2007[141]

	Model 7		
Credential inflation index	0,152	(0,049)	**
Standardization	-0,014	(0,008)	
Width of the sets of tasks	0,051	(0,019)	**
Commonness of the task sets	0,304	(0,131)	*
Associations (omitted category = no association)			
Specific association	-0,008	(0,010)	
General association	-0,014	(0,011)	
Title licensure	0,000	(0,000)	
Unionization (omitted category = no union)			
Trade union	-0,026	(0,016)	
Further edcuation x closure strategies:			
Further education (FE)	-0,002	(0,001)	*
FE x CIX	0,007	(0,004)	
FE x standardization	0,001	(0,000)	**
FE x narrow/wide tasks	0,003	(0,001)	*
FE x unique/common tasks	-0,023	(0,011)	*
FE x title licensure	0,000	(0,000)	
FE x general association	0,002	(0,001)	**
FE x specific association	0,002	(0,001)	*
FE x trade union	-0,001	(0,001)	
Constant	0,279	(0,010)	***
F	12,54	***	
R squared	0,321		

---

141 The full table with all control variables is shown in the online appendix (11.5).

	Model 7	
Root MSE	0,098	
Mean vif		
F test statistic[a]	3,27	**
df	8	

Note: N = 677,080 individuals in 1,118 occupations; Heteroscedastic consistent Huber-White standard errors in parentheses. All models control for time, skill level, small organizations, large organizations, region, further education, %female, %non-German citizens, and industries. *p<0.05, **p<0.01, and ***p<0.001

[a] The contrast for the model fit statistics is model 6b.

Sources: Statistisches Bundesamt a, b, c, d, e, f, g, h, i, j 1999-2008, own calculations; RDC of the Federal Statistical Office and the Statistical Offices of the Länder, Microcensus, survey years 2000, 2004, 2007, own calculations; Berufenet internet data base of the Federal Labor Office of Germany; Haupt 2012a; survey of the total population of occupational associations conducted by Schroeder, Kalass and Greef, own calculations.

Including the interaction terms between further education and the closure sources does not substantially change the main effects of the closure sources. The effect sizes of CIX and the commonness of the tasks decreases, whereas the effect size of the width-of-task range increases slightly. The interaction of further education with standardization with both occupational specificity measures, and with both association measures is significant.

Because the task of interpreting interaction terms between metric variables is very complex, I provide graphs of the association between the interacting variables and the dependent variable for three scenarios: for occupations that have the minimum, average, and maximum values on the closure variable of interest. The x-axis indicates the percentage of occupation members who participated in further education, and the y-axis refers to the dependent variable (the square root of the mean predicted probability of temporary employment). All other covariates in the model are fixed at their average value and are thus zero (all covariates are grand mean centered).

In hypothesis 11, I argued that the theoretical impact of standardization on temporary employment might be offset by additional education and training. Occupational incumbents with highly standardized credentials should not benefit much from additional training because their productivity is already high. The marginal utility of further education and training for this group is much lower than for occupational incumbents with unstandardized credentials, who should thereby benefit strongly from further education and training because their productivity should substantially increase. Figure 22 lends support to the assumptions of closure theory, as well as to the assumptions of human capital theory. If their occupation has highly standardized credentials,

Figure 22:   The interaction between further education and standardization with regard to the probability of temporary employment

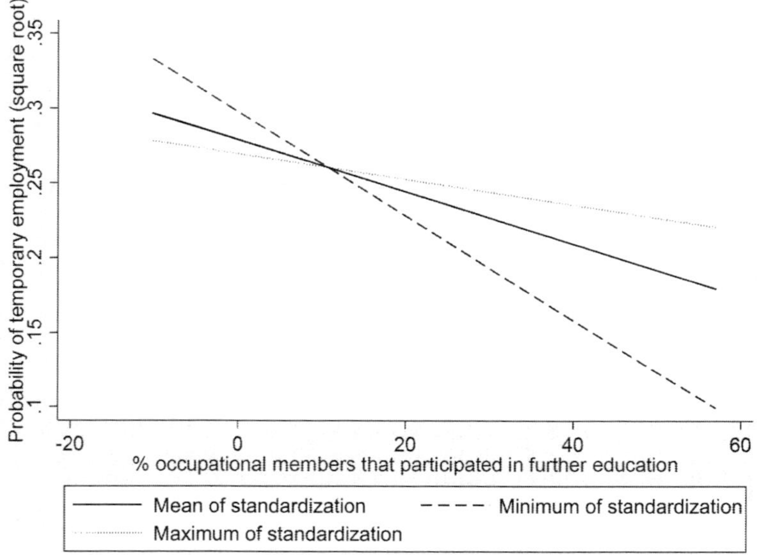

Note: N = 677,080 individuals in 1,118 occupations. All models control for time, skill level, small organizations, large organizations, region, further education, %female, %nonGerman citizens, and industries. Sources: Statistisches Bundesamt a, b, c, d, e, f, g, h, i, j 1999-2008, own calculations; RDC of the Federal Statistical Office and the Statistical Offices of the Länder, Microcensus, survey years 2000, 2004, 2007, own calculations; Berufenet internet data base of the Federal Labor Office of Germany; Haupt 2012a; survey of the total population of occupational associations conducted by Schroeder, Kalass and Greef, own calculations.

occupational incumbents with a below-average participation in further education are subject to a lower probability of temporary employment than incumbents of occupations with unstandardized credentials. However, the story changes if we compare occupations that have above-average further education participation rates, but have minimum standardization values or maximum standardization values respectively. Occupations with minimum values on standardization benefit strongly from further education, and their incumbents face a sharply decreased probability of temporary employment. Occupations with highly standardized credentials also benefit from further education, but not as strongly as occupations with minimally standardized credentials. My initial argument (hypothesis 2) regarding standardization as a closure source (highly standardized credentials equal a low probability of temporary employment and vice versa) is only true for occupations with a below-average participation in further education. The results confirm hypothesis 11: The initially higher risk of temporary employment for occupational incumbents with unstandardized credentials is offset by further education.

When we consider the potential impact of specific human capital on the occupational incumbents' risk of temporary employment, this changes the assumed association between the width of occupation-specific sets of tasks and the probability of temporary employment. The initial findings of the previous section indicate that narrow task profiles have a signaling value for employers because they help employers to evaluate whether and how well applicants are suited for available positions. As a consequence, employers do not have to rely on temporary employment contracts as prolonged probationary periods to assess the fit between job requirements and individuals' task profiles. However, I have also considered the possibility that employers might reluctantly grant permanent employment contracts to individuals with narrow task profiles because they might not be easily reassigned within organizations if their current position should become redundant. Yet employees' mobility within organizations might be improved by further education and training. The initial advantage of incumbents of occupations with narrow task profiles (signaling) might be additionally increased if further education and training increases their potential intra-organizational mobility (hypothesis 13). Figure 23 substantiates the assumptions of hypothesis 13. Occupations with narrow sets of tasks benefit strongly from participation in further education: Their probability of temporary employment decreases steeply the more incumbents participate in further education. Incumbents in occupations with wide sets of tasks always face a higher probability of temporary employment and they hardly benefit at all from further education. Thus, hypothesis 5 (signaling approach) is confirmed and hypothesis 12 is falsified[142].

---

142 In hypothesis 12, I based my argument on the assumption that occupations with narrow sets of tasks and skills do not have a signaling value for employers. In this scenario, occupations with wide sets of tasks should grant their incumbents access to a wide range of positions and a multitude of possible employers and thereby trigger the "increasing diffuse demand" mechanism, which in turn should reduce their risk of temporary employment in comparison to incumbents of occupations with narrow sets of tasks. Hypothesis 12 expanded this argument by assuming that further education and training may offset the initial low flexibility employers experience when reassigning occupational incumbents with narrow sets of skills within their organizations. In this case, the difference in the risk of temporary employment between incumbents of occupations with narrow and wide sets of tasks should converge with increasing further education and training.

*Figure 23:   The interaction between further education and the width of tasks
            with regard to the probability of temporary employment*

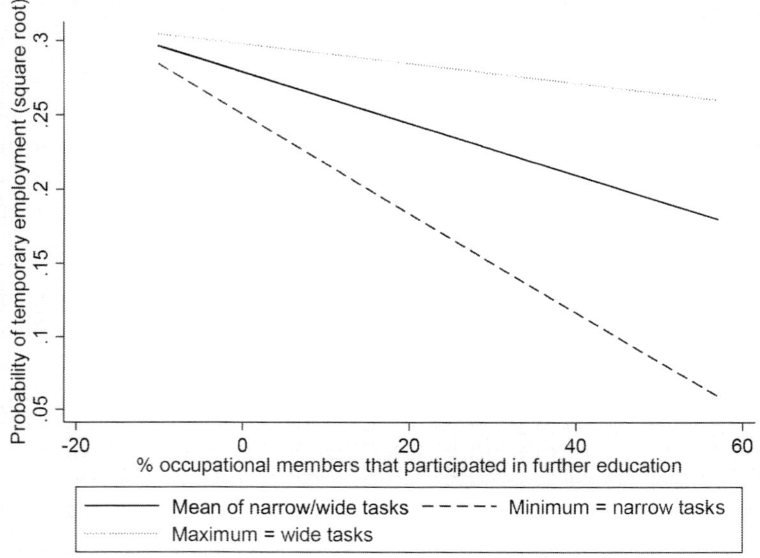

Note: N = 677,080 individuals in 1,118 occupations. All models control for time, skill level, small organizations, large organizations, region, further education, %female, %non-German citizens, and industries.
Sources: Statistisches Bundesamt a, b, c, d, e, f, g, h, i, j 1999-2008, own calculations; RDC of the Federal Statistical Office and the Statistical Offices of the Länder, Microcensus, survey years 2000, 2004, 2007, own calculations; Berufenet internet data base of the Federal Labor Office of Germany; Haupt 2012a; survey of the total population of occupational associations conducted by Schroeder, Kalass and Greef, own calculations.

In hypothesis 14, I argued that employers may circumvent the problem of relatively unique sets of tasks and skills by using additional education and training, and thus break down the barriers to relatively unique occupational niches. The increasing competition within the niche should increase their incumbents' risk of temporary employment.

When we consider the empirical association between occupational specificity, defined as the relative uniqueness or commonness of the occupation-specific sets of tasks, and further education, we find confirmation for the findings of model 6b, but only for occupations with average or below-average further education participation rates (see figure 24). For these occupations, the relative uniqueness of their sets of tasks is clearly associated with a lower probability of temporary employment in comparison to occupations with common sets of tasks. However, this relationship is reversed for occupations with above-average further education participation rates. As greater numbers of incumbents of occupations with relatively unique sets of tasks participate in further education, their risk of temporary employment becomes higher. This result confirms hypothesis 14: Additional education and training may break down the barriers around occupational niches and thereby increase their incumbents' risk of temporary employment. However, incumbents of occupations with common sets of tasks nevertheless benefit from further education. Their risk of temporary employment decreases with increasing participation rates.

Figure 24: The interaction between further education and the commonness of tasks with regard to the probability of temporary employment

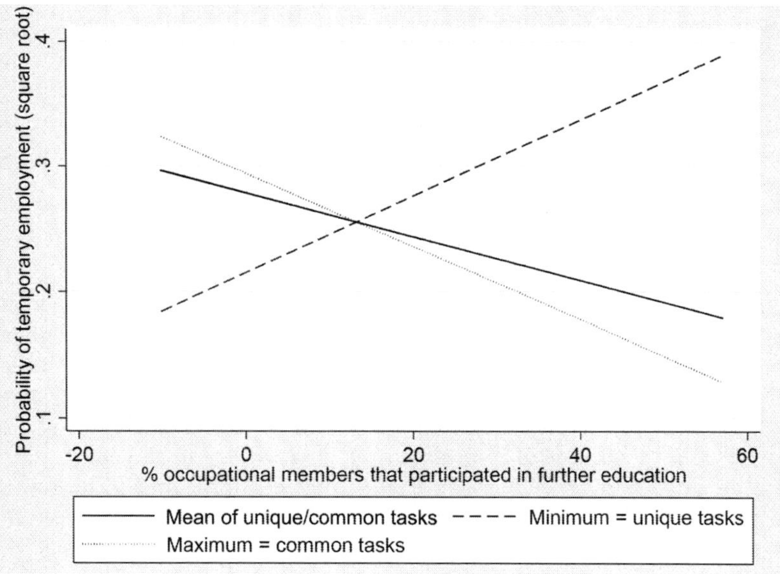

Note: N = 677,080 individuals in 1,118 occupations. All models control for time, skill level, small organizations, large organizations, region, further education, %female, %non-German citizens, and industries.

Sources: Statistisches Bundesamt a, b, c, d, e, f, g, h, i, j 1999-2008, own calculations; RDC of the Federal Statistical Office and the Statistical Offices of the Länder, Microcensus, survey years 2000, 2004, 2007, own calculations; Berufenet internet data base of the Federal Labor Office of Germany; Haupt 2012a; survey of the total population of occupational associations conducted by Schroeder, Kalass and Greef, own calculations.

In hypothesis 15, I argued that additional education and training courses might be used to neutralize the scarcity of occupation-specific credentials. The prediction shows no such association. The credential inflation index remains constant, even if its effect size decreases slightly. This result lends further credence to the closure argument, i.e., that a restricted supply of credentials increases the bargaining power of the occupational incumbents and thereby reduces their risk of temporary employment.

I had not argued that an interaction between further education and association representation might be possible. Nevertheless, the relationship for specific and general associations with regard to further education and temporary employment is statistically significant. However, differentiating between both types of associations might not seem relevant with regard to the interaction with human capital. The slopes for both types of associations are the same, and only the intercepts are slightly different. Because the graph is essentially the same for general and specific associations, figure 25 shows only the graph for specific associations. The result, however, is surprising. Occupational incumbents who are represented by associations face an increasing probability of temporary employment the more they participate in further education. Incumbents of occupations without associational representation have a lower probability of temporary employment if they participate in further education.

To secure investments in human capital and to exclude outside competition, employers rely on firm-internal labor markets. I do not have the means at hand to identify whether occupational incumbents are part of firm-internal or -external labor markets. However, most research on internal labor markets agrees that large organizations are able to partition their labor markets into hierarchical/bureaucratic firm-internal labor markets and market-mediated firm-external labor markets. I will therefore test for additional effects of employment in large organizations on the closure sources. To check for additional effects of large organizations and internal labor markets, table 9 presents the main model, which is supplemented with interaction terms between large organizations and the closure sources. However, the inclusion of the interaction terms between the proportion of occupational incumbents within large organizations and the closure sources does not substantially change the main effects of the closure sources. The coefficient of CIX increases, and the coefficients of the other closure measures remain constant for the most part. Only one interaction term indicates a significant interrelation between closure, internal labor markets, and temporary employment: It is the interaction term for the credential inflation index. Thus, hypothesis 17, the interrelation between trade unions, large organizations, and temporary employment, has to be rejected. I had argued that large organizations may use temporary employment contracts as a human resource practice to weaken the power of occupation-specific trade unions. The lack of

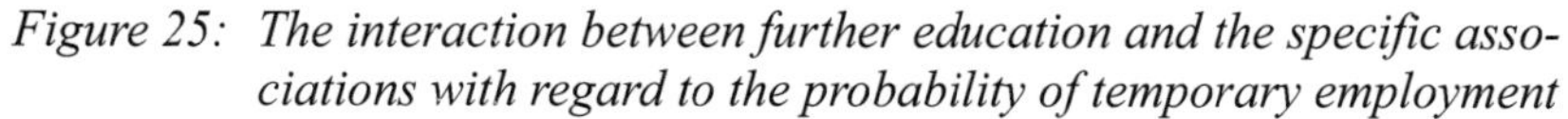

Figure 25: The interaction between further education and the specific associations with regard to the probability of temporary employment

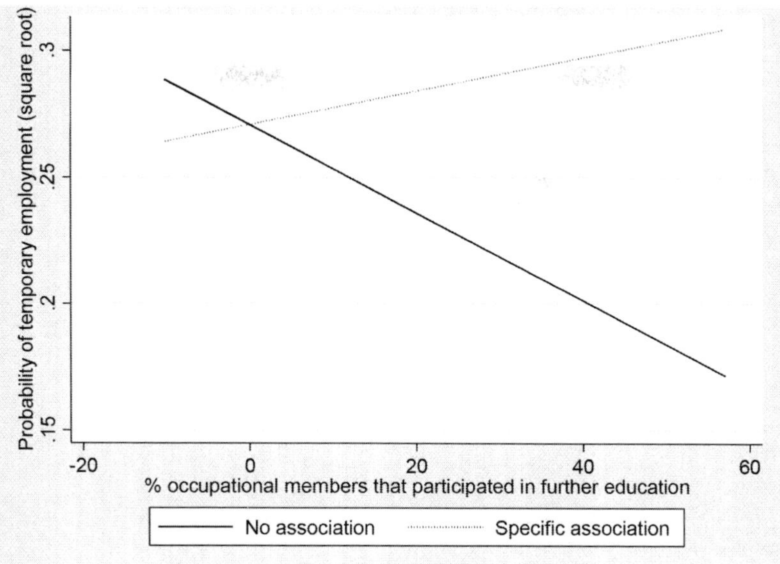

Note: N = 677,080 individuals in 1,118 occupations. All models control for time, skill level, small organizations, large organizations, region, further education, %female, %non-German citizens, and economic sectors.

Sources: Statistisches Bundesamt a, b, c, d, e, f, g, h, i, j 1999-2008, own calculations; RDC of the Federal Statistical Office and the Statistical Offices of the Länder, Microcensus, survey years 2000, 2004, 2007, own calculations; Berufenet internet data base of the Federal Labor Office of Germany; Haupt 2012a; survey of the total population of occupational associations conducted by Schroeder, Kalass and Greef, own calculations.

more significant interactions between organization size and closure might be due to the relatively low threshold that defines large organizations (50 employees).

Table 9: *Pooled linear regression of temporary employment on the different sources of occupational closure—with interactions between firm-internal labor markets (large organizations) and the closure sources, 2000, 2004, and 2007*[143]

	Model 8		
Credential inflation index	0,209	(0,052)	***
Standardization	-0,008	(0,008)	
Width of the sets of tasks	0,054	(0,019)	**
Commonness of the task sets	0,430	(0,106)	***
Associations (omitted category = no association)			
Specific association	-0,002	(0,010)	
General association	-0,007	(0,011)	
Title licensure	-0,001	(0,000)	
Unionization (omitted category = no union)			
Trade union	-0,029	(0,015)	
Large organizations x closure strategies:			
Large organizations (IL)	0,001	(0,001)	
IL x CIX	0,006	(0,003)	*
IL x standardization	0,000	(0,000)	
IL x narrow/wide tasks	0,000	(0,001)	
IL x unique/common tasks	-0,006	(0,004)	
IL x title licensure	0,000	(0,000)	
IL x general association	0,001	(0,000)	
IL x specific association	0,000	(0,001)	
IL x trade union	-0,001	(0,001)	
Constant	0,284	(0,010)	***
F	11,90	***	
R squared	0,310		
Root MSE	0,099		
Mean vif	2,89		
F test statistic[a]	1,52		
df	8		

Note: N = 677,080 individuals in 1,118 occupations; Heteroscedastic consistent Huber-White standard errors in parentheses. All models control for time, skill level, small organizations, large organizations, region, further education, %female, %non-German citizens, and industries. *p<0.05, **p<0.01, and ***p<0.001

[a] The contrast for the model fit statistics is model 6b.

---

143 The full table with all control variables is shown in the online appendix (11.5).

Sources: Statistisches Bundesamt a, b, c, d, e, f, g, h, i, j 1999-2008, own calculations; RDC of the Federal Statistical Office and the Statistical Offices of the Länder, Microcensus, survey years 2000, 2004, 2007, own calculations; Berufenet internet data base of the Federal Labor Office of Germany; Haupt 2012a; survey of the total population of occupational associations conducted by Schroeder, Kalass and Greef, own calculations.

Large organizations incur lower marginal costs for employee training than small organizations. Hence, the use of temporary employment is more cost effective for large organizations. Given that all organizations try to secure scarce occupation-specific skills, I argued that large organizations may use temporary employment contracts primarily for occupational incumbents whose credentials are in ample supply (hypothesis 16). The empirical results indicate that whether or not incumbents of an occupation are employed in large organizations is irrelevant for occupations with a minimum value or a mean value on the credential inflation index (see figure 26). However, occupations whose incumbents are often employed in large organizations face a steep increase in their risk of temporary employment if the credentials for their occupation are awarded in an inflationary manner. This association confirms hypothesis 16. Employers especially use temporary employment contracts for incumbents of occupations that have a large supply of credential holders. This association is most detrimental for occupational incumbents in large organizations because large organizations incur lower marginal costs for the repeated training of new temporary employees than small organizations.

*Figure 26:   The interaction between large companies and the credential infla-
tion index with regard to the probability of temporary employment*

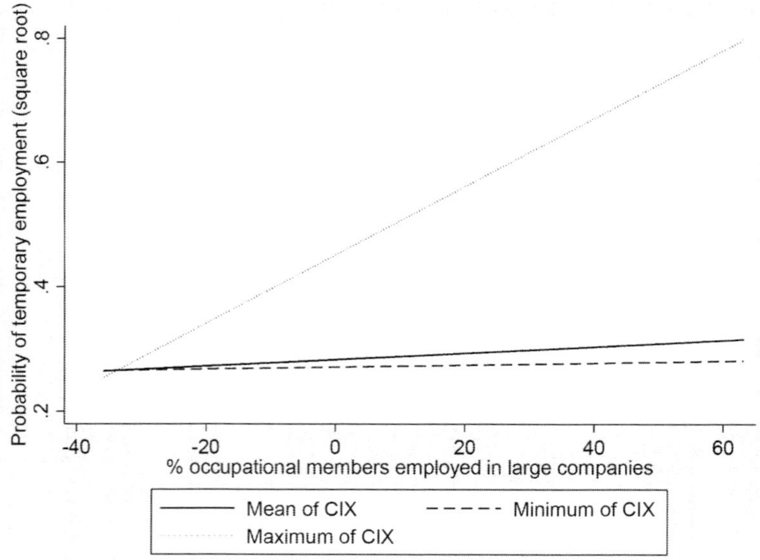

Note: N = 677,080 individuals in 1,118 occupations. All models control for time, skill level, small organizations, large organizations, region, further education, %female, %non-German citizens, and industries. Sources: Statistisches Bundesamt a, b, c, d, e, f, g, h, i, j 1999-2008, own calculations; RDC of the Federal Statistical Office and the Statistical Offices of the Länder, Microcensus, survey years 2000, 2004, 2007, own calculations; Berufenet internet data base of the Federal Labor Office of Germany; Haupt 2012a; survey of the total population of occupational associations conducted by Schroeder, Kalass and Greef, own calculations.

7.3 Occupational Closure and Monitoring Costs

According to the transaction cost approach, governance measures used by employers, like the provision of job security, may also vary according to how difficult it is for the employer to monitor and evaluate the employee's productivity. The relevance of occupational closure might thus differ between occupations that differ in the complexity of their tasks. I use a similar approach as in the last section, and separately interact each of the four levels of task complexity with the closure measures.

Table 10: Pooled linear regression of temporary employment on the different sources of occupational closure—with interactions between managerial tasks (model 9), managerial/skilled tasks (model 10), skilled tasks (model 11), and routine/labor tasks (model 12) with the closure sources, 2000, 2004, and 2007[144]

	Model 9 Managerial		Model 10 Skilled/managerial	
Credential inflation index	0,152	(0,050)**	0,161	(0,048)**
Standardization	-0,015	(0,007)*	-0,007	(0,008)
Width of the sets of tasks	0,059	(0,019)**	0,049	(0,019)**
Commonness of the task sets	0,160	(0,147)	0,176	(0,150)
Associations (omitted category = no association)				
Specific association	0,003	(0,010)	-0,018	(0,011)
General association	-0,012	(0,010)	-0,001	(0,012)
Title licensure	-0,001	(0,000)**	0,000	(0,000)
Unionization (omitted category = no union)				
Trade union	-0,026	(0,016)	-0,036	(0,015)*
Skill-level of tasks x closure strategies:				
Skill level (Skill)	0,040	(0,038)	-0,029	(0,036)
Skill x CIX	0,273	(0,361)	-0,157	(0,251)
Skill x standardization	-0,016	(0,028)	-0,013	(0,036)
Skill x narrow/wide tasks	-0,033	(0,074)	0,099	(0,094)
Skill x unique/common tasks	-1,561	(0,607)**	-1,177	(0,640)
Skill x title licensure	0,005	(0,002)**	-0,007	(0,002)***
Skill x general association	-0,033	(0,048)	0,137	(0,053)*
Skill x specific association	0,021	(0,046)	-0,081	(0,056)
Skill x trade union	0,007	(0,040)	0,126	(0,069)
Constant	0,265	(0,011)***	0,284	(0,010)***
F	12,06***		13,34***	
R squared	0,324		0,338	
Root MSE	0,098		0,970	
Mean vif	3,24		3,21	
F test statistic[a]	3,23**		5,56***	
df	8		8	

---

144   The full table with all control variables is shown in the online appendix (11.5).

	Model 11 Skilled		Model 12 Routine/labor	
Credential inflation index	0,186	(0,048)***	0,186	(0,052)***
Standardization	-0,009	(0,008)	-0,014	(0,008)
Width of the sets of tasks	0,054	(0,019)**	0,050	(0,019)**
Commonness of the task sets	0,422	(0,125)**	0,444	(0,176)*
Associations (omitted category = no association)				
Specific association	-0,017	(0,011)	-0,010	(0,010)
General association	-0,013	(0,012)	-0,008	(0,010)
Title licensure	-0,001	(0,000)**	0,000	(0,000)
Unionization (omitted category = no union)				
Trade union	-0,030	(0,016)	-0,041	(0,017)*
Skill-level of tasks x closure strategies:				
Skill level (Skill)	0,075	(0,043)	0,247	(0,049)***
Skill x CIX	-0,189	(0,154)	-0,037	(0,344)
Skill x standardization	0,018	(0,042)	-0,056	(0,035)
Skill x narrow/wide tasks	0,041	(0,085)	-0,034	(0,076)
Skill x unique/common tasks	1,306	(0,570)*	-0,212	(0,341)
Skill x title licensure	-0,004	(0,002)*	0,005	(0,001)***
Skill x general association	-0,121	(0,060)*	-0,059	(0,047)
Skill x specific association	-0,072	(0,075)	0,011	(0,054)
Skill x trade union	-0,031	(0,065)	-0,151	(0,098)
Constant	0,271	(0,011)	0,292	(0,011)***
F	11,82***		13,75***	
R squared	0,324		0,312	
Root MSE	0,098		0,099	
Mean vif	3,35		3,37	
F test statistic[a]	3,38***		1,99*	
df	8		8	

Note: N = 677,080 individuals in 1,118 occupations; Heteroscedastic consistent Huber-White standard errors in parentheses. All models control for time, skill level, small organizations, large organizations, region, further education, %female, %non-German citizens, and industries. *p<0.05, **p<0.01, and ***p<0.001

[a] The contrast for the model fit statistics is model 6b.

Sources: Statistisches Bundesamt a, b, c, d, e, f, g, h, i, j 1999-2008, own calculations; RDC of the Federal Statistical Office and the Statistical Offices of the Länder, Microcensus, survey years 2000, 2004, 2007, own calculations; Berufenet internet data base of the Federal Labor Office of Germany; Haupt 2012a; survey of the total population of occupational associations conducted by Schroeder, Kalass and Greef, own calculations.

The coefficients of the closure sources remain relatively stable despite the addition of the interaction terms (see table 10). There are, however, some peculiarities: The title licensure measure becomes significant in the model that includes the interaction with managerial tasks and skilled tasks. The occupation-specific trade unions become significant in all but the managerial tasks interaction models. The commonness of the sets of tasks variable drops considerably and becomes insignificant in the managerial tasks interaction model and the managerial/skilled tasks interaction model.

The interactions between title licensure and all four levels of task complexity are significant. The majority of occupational incumbents perform skilled tasks. For these occupations, the association between the two interacting variables and the dependent variable is relatively straightforward. Incumbents of occupations with a low level of protected titles face a steep increase in the risk of temporary employment with each increase in the proportion of skilled incumbents (see figure 27). For incumbents with a low level of protected titles the probability also decreases, but only minutely. A similar picture emerges for the interaction with skilled/managerial tasks. However, the occupational incumbents with high levels of protected titles benefit more strongly from the title protection and have a lower risk of temporary employment along with a higher proportion of skilled/managerial incumbents.

Figure 27: The interaction between the four levels of task complexity and title licensure with regard to the probability of temporary employment

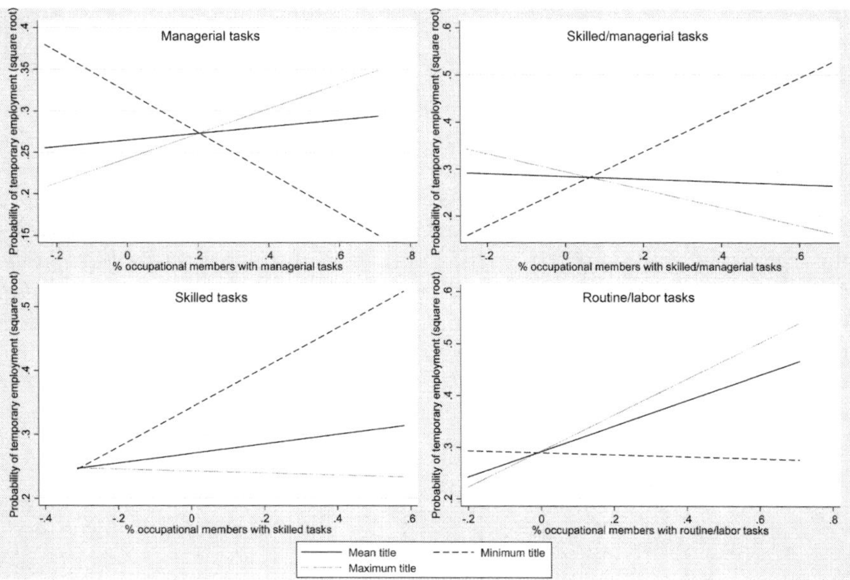

Note: N = 677,080 individuals in 1,118 occupations. All models control for time, skill level, small organizations, large organizations, region, further education, %female, %non-German citizens, and industries.

Sources: Statistisches Bundesamt a, b, c, d, e, f, g, h, i, j 1999-2008, own calculations; RDC of the Federal Statistical Office and the Statistical Offices of the Länder, Microcensus, survey years 2000, 2004, 2007, own calculations; Berufenet internet data base of the Federal Labor Office of Germany; Haupt 2012a; survey of the total population of occupational associations conducted by Schroeder, Kalass and Greef, own calculations.

Occupations with high proportions of incumbents who perform routine/labor tasks do not benefit at all from title protection. Occupations with low levels of title protection have a constant probability of temporary employment, whereas this probability increases for occupations with mean levels of title protection and high levels of title protection. The interaction between managerial tasks and title licensure is very heterogeneous. In occupations where the incumbents mainly perform managerial tasks, low levels of title protection decrease the probability of temporary employment, whereas high levels of title protection increase this probability. However, in occupations where the proportion of incumbents with managerial tasks is average or below average the association between title protection and the probability of temporary employment is reversed. The considerable heterogeneity of the interactions between task complexity and title licensure is worth exploring further, but for my purposes the most important point to note is that title licensure is highly relevant with regard to temporary employment. The measure is, however, confounded, and thus has a low, nonsignificant effect size in the main model (model 6b).

The interaction between the commonness of the sets of tasks and the two levels of task complexity (managerial tasks and skilled tasks) are also significant. The interaction for occupations where there are above-average proportions of incumbents performing managerial tasks is reversed in comparison to the main model (model 6b). For those occupations with relatively unique tasks, their probability of temporary employment increases with each increase in the proportion of incumbents doing managerial tasks, whereas the probability of temporary employment slightly decreases for occupations with common tasks (see figure 28). For occupations whose incumbents mainly perform skilled tasks, the established association between the commonness-of-tasks measure and temporary employment is strengthened and the slopes become steeper.

Figure 28: The interaction between two levels of task complexity and title licensure with regard to the probability of temporary employment

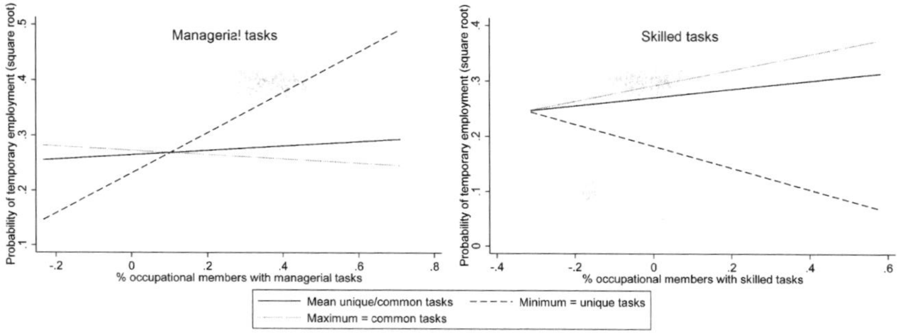

Note: N = 677,080 individuals in 1,118 occupations. All models control for time, skill level, small organizations, large organizations, region, further education, %female, %non-German citizens, and industries. Sources: Statistisches Bundesamt a, b, c, d, e, f, g, h, i, j 1999-2008, own calculations; RDC of the Federal Statistical Office and the Statistical Offices of the Länder, Microcensus, survey years 2000, 2004, 2007, own calculations; Berufenet internet data base of the Federal Labor Office of Germany; Haupt 2012a; survey of the total population of occupational associations conducted by Schroeder, Kalass and Greef, own calculations.

The specific-occupational-association measure also has significant interactions with skilled tasks as well as with skilled/managerial tasks (see figure 29). Incumbents of occupations with above-average levels of skilled/managerial tasks face an increasing risk of temporary employment if they are represented by specific associations, whereas incumbents of occupations without an association benefit from a decreasing probability of temporary employment. This situation is reversed for the interaction between skilled tasks and specific occupational associations. However, the scale of the y-axis reveals that the effect size of the combined measures of task complexity and association representation remains small, even for the maximum values of the respective skill-levels of tasks.

Figure 29:   *The interaction between two levels of task complexity and the representation by specific associations with regard to the probability of temporary employment*

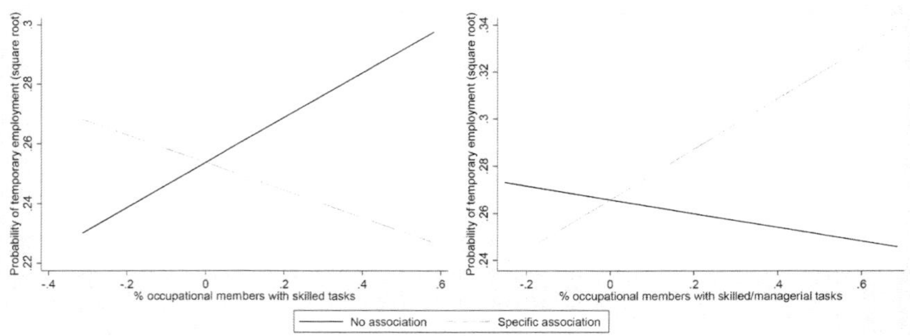

Note: N = 677,080 individuals in 1,118 occupations. All models control for time, skill level, small organizations, large organizations, region, further education, %female, %non-German citizens, and industries.

Sources: Statistisches Bundesamt a, b, c, d, e, f, g, h, i, j 1999-2008, own calculations; RDC of the Federal Statistical Office and the Statistical Offices of the Länder, Microcensus, survey years 2000, 2004, 2007, own calculations; Berufenet internet data base of the Federal Labor Office of Germany; Haupt 2012a; survey of the total population of occupational associations conducted by Schroeder, Kalass and Greef, own calculations.

7.4   Occupational Closure and Additional Distinctive Features of the German Labor Market—Region and Gender Composition

General economic conditions differ considerably between the old and the new German *Länder.* The level of unemployment is very high in the new Länder and the competition for vacant positions is accordingly high. The different economic situation between both parts of Germany might have an impact on the measures of occupational closure.

Table 11: Pooled linear regression of temporary employment on the different sources of occupational closure—with interactions between the new Länder and the closure sources, 2000, 2004, and 2007[145]

	Model 13		
Credential inflation index	0,167	(0,050)	**
Standardization	-0,010	(0,008)	
Width of the sets of tasks	0,051	(0,018)	**
Commonness of the task sets	0,482	(0,111)	***
Associations (omitted category = no association)			
Specific association	-0,001	(0,011)	
General association	-0,010	(0,011)	
Title licensure	-0,001	(0,000)	*
Unionization (omitted category = no union)			
Trade union	-0,020	(0,015)	
New *Länder* x closure strategies:			
New *Länder* (NL)	0,002	(0,001)	**
NL x CIX	0,005	(0,005)	
NL x standardization	-0,002	(0,001)	
NL x narrow/wide tasks	0,001	(0,002)	
NL x unique/common tasks	-0,004	(0,008)	
NL x title licensure	0,000	(0,000)	***
NL x general association	-0,001	(0,001)	
NL x specific association	-0,002	(0,002)	
NL x trade union	0,000	(0,002)	
Constant	0,285	(0,010)	***
F	13,52	***	
R squared	0,330		
Root MSE	0,976		
Mean vif	2,88		
F test statistic[a]	4,94	***	
df	8		

Note: $N = 677,080$ individuals in 1,118 occupations; Heteroscedastic consistent Huber-White standard errors in parentheses. All models control for time, skill level, small organizations, large organizations, region, further education, %female, %non-German citizens, and industries. *p<0.05, **p<0.01, and ***p<0.001

[a] The contrast for the model fit statistics is model 6b.

Sources: Statistisches Bundesamt a, b, c, d, e, f, g, h, i, j 1999-2008, own calculations; RDC of the Federal Statistical Office and the Statistical Offices of the Länder, Microcensus, survey years 2000, 2004, 2007, own calculations; Berufenet internet data base of the Federal Labor Office of Germany;

---

145   The full table with all control variables is shown in the online appendix (11.5).

Haupt 2012a; survey of the total population of occupational associationsconducted by Schroeder, Kalass and Greef, own calculations.

Despite the considerable differences between the old and new *Länder*, the main effects remain surprisingly constant, and only one interaction term indicates different associations between occupational closure and temporary employment in the old and new *Länder* (see table 11). Occupational incumbents with above-average employment in the new Länder and with low levels of title licensure face a steep increase in the probability of temporary employment (see figure 30). This probability decreases for occupations with above-average employment in the new *Länder* and high levels of title licensure. The combined effect of region and title licensure with regard to the probability of temporary employment is very large.

Figure 30:   The interaction between the proportion of incumbents employed in the new Länder and title licensure with regard to the probability of temporary employment

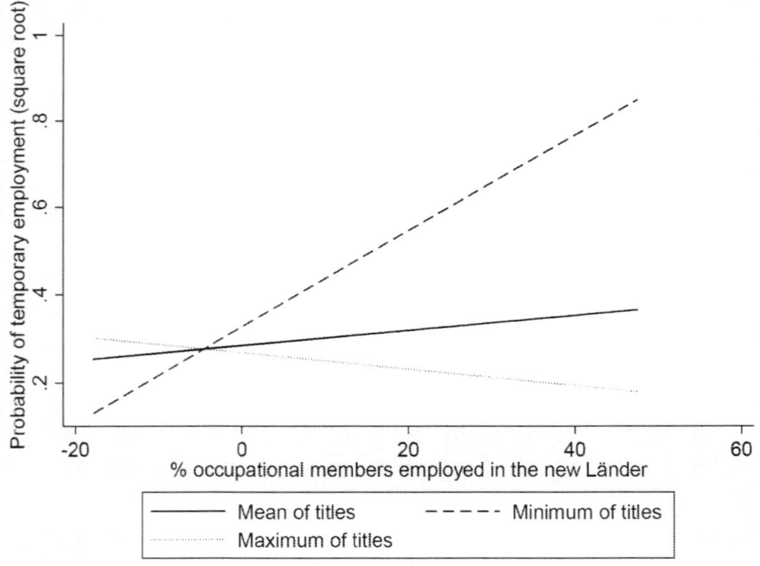

Note: N = 677,080 individuals in 1,118 occupations. All models control for time, skill level, small organizations, large organizations, region, further education, %female, %non-German citizens, and industries.

Sources: Statistisches Bundesamt a, b, c, d, e, f, g, h, i, j 1999-2008, own calculations; RDC of the Federal Statistical Office and the Statistical Offices of the Länder, Microcensus, survey years 2000, 2004, 2007, own calculations; Berufenet internet data base of the Federal Labor Office of Germany; Haupt 2012a; survey of the total population of occupational associations conducted by Schroeder, Kalass and Greef, own calculations.

The gender composition of occupations is another issue frequently discussed with regard to occupations and their characteristics. In particular, the closure measures for occupation-specific credentials might not be gender neutral, because the educational system that awards these credentials is not gender neutral. Table 12 introduces interaction terms for gender composition but does not show substantial changes in the closure variables. However, both credentialism measures are lower after the interaction between the proportion of female incumbents and the closure sources is introduced. Additionally, the coefficient of trade unions increases slightly.

Table 12: *Pooled linear regression of temporary employment on the different sources of occupational closure—with interactions between gender, type of occupations, and the closure sources, 2000, 2004, and 2007[146]*

	Model 14		
Credential inflation index	0,135	(0,048)	**
Standardization	-0,001	(0,008)	
Width of the sets of tasks	0,042	(0,019)	*
Commonness of the task sets	0,438	(0,112)	***
Associations (omitted category = no association)			
Specific association	-0,005	(0,013)	
General association	-0,003	(0,012)	
Title licensure	0,000	(0,000)	
Unionization (omitted category = no union)			
Trade union	-0,037	(0,016)	*
% female x closure strategies:			
% female	0,000	(0,000)	**
% female x CIX	0,004	(0,001)	**
% female x standardization	-0,001	(0,000)	*
% female x narrow/wide tasks	0,000	(0,000)	
% female x unique/common tasks	0,001	(0,003)	

---

146 The full table with all control variables is shown in the online appendix (11.5).

	Model 14		
% female x title licensure	0,000	(0,000)	
% female x general association	0,000	(0,000)	
% female x specific association	-0,001	(0,000)	
% female x trade union	0,001	(0,000)	**
Constant	0,278	(0,010)	***
F	11,49	***	
R squared	0,319		
Root MSE	0,984		
Mean vif	2,98		
F test statistic[a]	3,77	***	
df	8		

Note: N = 677,080 individuals in 1,118 occupations; Heteroscedastic consistent Huber-White standard errors in parentheses. All models control for time, skill level, small organizations, large organizations, region, further education, %female, %non-German citizens, and industries. *p<0.05, **p<0.01, and ***p<0.001

[a] The contrast for the model fit statistics is model 6b.

Sources: Statistisches Bundesamt a, b, c, d, e, f, g, h, i, j 1999-2008, own calculations; RDC of the Federal Statistical Office and the Statistical Offices of the Länder, Microcensus, survey years 2000, 2004, 2007, own calculations; Berufenet internet data base of the Federal Labor Office of Germany; Haupt 2012a; survey of the total population of occupational associations conducted by Schroeder, Kalass and Greef, own calculations.

The interaction terms are significant for both credentialism measures as well as for the trade union measure. Figure 31 shows the interaction between the credential inflation index and the proportion of female incumbents. Credentials that are awarded in an inflationary manner increase the probability of temporary employment considerably. This effect is relatively low or even nonexistent for occupations with below-average proportions of female incumbents, and is large for occupations with above-average proportions of female incumbents. Occupational incumbents whose credentials are not awarded in an inflationary manner, that is, who have mean or minimum values on the CIX, face a relatively constant risk of temporary employment, which is independent of their gender composition.

Figure 31:   The interaction between the gender composition of occupations and the credential inflation index with regard to the probability of temporary employment

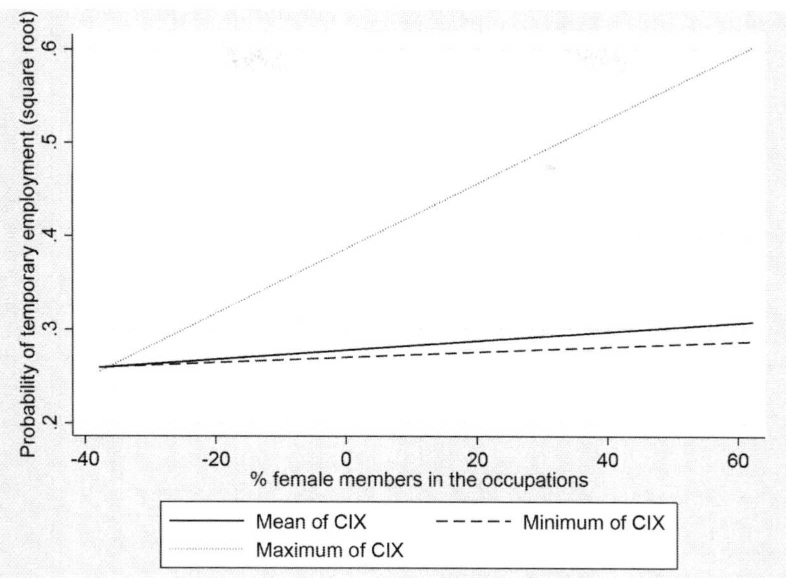

Note: N = 677,080 individuals in 1,118 occupations. All models control for time, skill level, small organizations, large organizations, region, further education, %female, %non-German citizens, and industries.
Sources: Statistisches Bundesamt a, b, c, d, e, f, g, h, i, j 1999-2008, own calculations; RDC of the Federal Statistical Office and the Statistical Offices of the Länder, Microcensus, survey years 2000, 2004, 2007, own calculations; Berufenet internet data base of the Federal Labor Office of Germany; Haupt 2012a; survey of the total population of occupational associations conducted by Schroeder, Kalass and Greef, own calculations.

Figure 32 shows that the standardization of credentials has quite a different impact on the probability of temporary employment for male-dominated occupations and female-dominated occupations. The probability of temporary employment is the lowest for incumbents of male dominated occupations if they have low levels of standardization. On the other side, there are female dominated occupations whose incumbents face the highest risk of temporary employment if their credentials have low levels of standardization. Highly standardized occupations have relatively similar outcomes independent of their sex composition. Their probability of temporary employment is relatively constant.

However, the overall effect size of standardization with regard to the gender composition remains relatively small.

Figure 32:   The interaction between the gender composition of occupations and the degree of standardization with regard to the probability of temporary employment

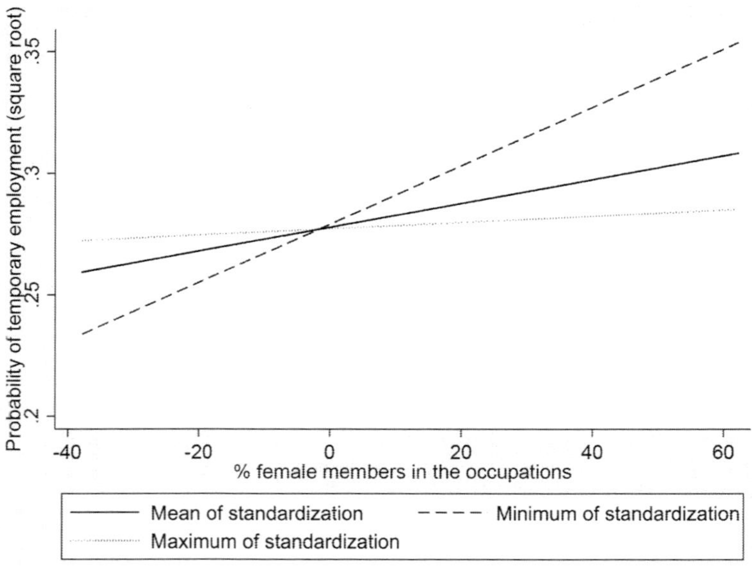

Note: N = 677,080 individuals in 1,118 occupations. All models control for time, skill level, small organizations, large organizations, region, further education, %female, %non-German citizens, and industries. Sources: Statistisches Bundesamt a, b, c, d, e, f, g, h, i, j 1999-2008, own calculations; RDC of the Federal Statistical Office and the Statistical Offices of the Länder, Microcensus, survey years 2000, 2004, 2007, own calculations; Berufenet internet data base of the Federal Labor Office of Germany; Haupt 2012a; survey of the total population of occupational associations conducted by Schroeder, Kalass and Greef, own calculations.

The probability of temporary employment is lower for incumbents of male dominated occupations that are represented by a trade union in comparison to incumbents of female-dominated occupations (see figure 33). The probability of temporary employment is relatively constant and independent from the gender composition for incumbents of occupations without trade union representation. However, the overall effect size of trade union representation is relatively small.

Figure 33:   The interaction between the gender composition of occupations and the representation by trade unions with regard to the probability of temporary employment

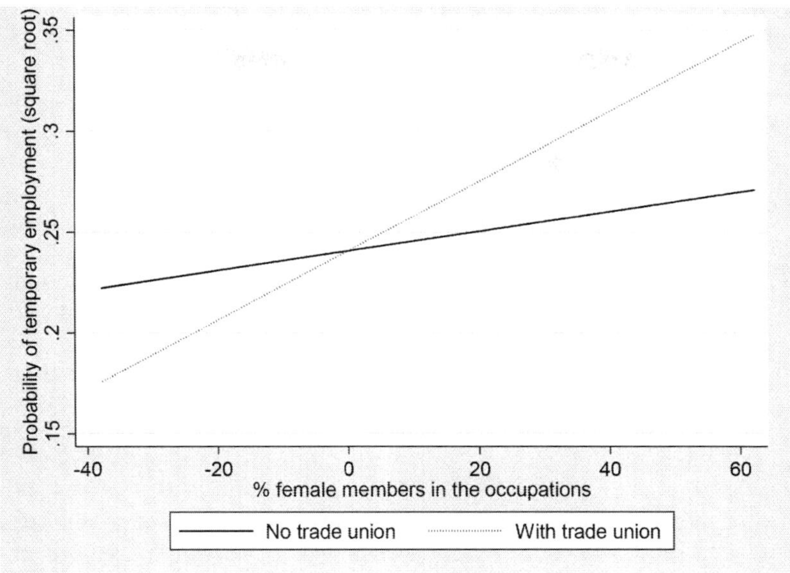

Note: N = 677,080 individuals in 1,118 occupations. All models control for time, skill level, small organizations, large organizations, region, further education, %female, %non-German citizens, and industries. Sources: Statistisches Bundesamt a, b, c, d, e, f, g, h, i, j 1999-2008, own calculations; RDC of the Federal Statistical Office and the Statistical Offices of the Länder, Microcensus, survey years 2000, 2004, 2007, own calculations; Berufenet internet data base of the Federal Labor Office of Germany; Haupt 2012a; survey of the total population of occupational associations conducted by Schroeder, Kalass and Greef, own calculations.

7.5 Occupational Closure and High-Risk Populations

I address two high-risk populations that almost always face a very high risk of temporary employment: poorly qualified individuals and young adults. To explore the potential differences in the impact of the closure sources on these two subpopulations within occupations, I change the dependent variable. The dependent variable now consists of the coefficients of the individual-level first-stage analyses - $\beta\,{}'X_{ot}$ (see equation 1 in section 5.1). I am interested in the coefficient of young occupational incumbents (15-29 years old) in comparison to incumbents of main working age (30-49 years old), and in the coefficient of incumbents with low-level qualifications (completed basic schooling) in comparison to incumbents of the same occupation who have medium-level qualifications (completed upper-secondary education). The coefficients are in the logit metric, which is perfectly suited for linear regression analysis because it is symmetric and without limits[147].

With the change in the dependent variable also comes a change in the number of observations. There are fewer observations now because it is not possible to include occupations without temporary employment in this analytical design. There has to be variance with regards to temporary employment to measure differences between, for example, individuals with low-level and medium-level qualifications. Another reason for the reduction in the sample size is that, for some occupations, no coefficients were provided for the individual-level variables of interest because of the occurrence of perfect predictions.

This change in the analytical design also allows me to check whether occupation-specific trade unions might contribute to the dualization of the workforce. This may happen if the unions concentrate on the core workforce and thereby put labor market entrants or low skilled workers at a disadvantage (hypothesis 10).

Table 13 shows that only one occupational-level closure source explains significant and substantive differences between young and middle-aged occupational incumbents. A change in the unit of the title licensure variable changes the risk of temporary employment for young incumbents by 0.009 logit points. Because logits are not easy and meaningful to interpret, I transform them into odds using the inverse of the logit function. Occupations whose incumbents have a maximum of title licensure (minimum = 0.2 and maximum = 1) thus double the risk of temporary employment for young incumbents in comparison to their middle-aged counterparts $\left(e^{(0.009*80)} = 2.05\right)$. The risk is increased by two thirds for occupations with a mean value on the title licensure variable $\left(e^{(0.009*57)} = 1.67\right)$.

---

147 Both logit variables show approximately normal distribution.

Table 13: *Explaining differences in the probability of temporary employment between young and middle-aged occupational incumbents within occupations using the different sources of occupational closure—a pooled linear regression with the individual-level stage-one logit coefficients of young occupational incumbents as dependent variable[148]*

	Model 15		
Credential inflation index	0,151	(0,466)	
Standardization	0,032	(0,055)	
Width of the sets of tasks	0,046	(0,158)	
Commonness of the task sets	0,413	(1,025)	
Associations (omitted category = no association)			
Specific association	0,046	(0,079)	
General association	0,100	(0,093)	
Title licensure	0,009	(0,003)	**
Unionization (omitted category = no union)			
Trade union	0,070	(0,097)	
Constant	1,503	(0,073)	***
F	9,18	***	
R squared	0,173		
Root MSE	0,813		
Mean vif	3,12		

Note: N = 671,265 individuals in 1,060 occupations; Heteroscedastic consistent Huber-White standard errors in parentheses. All models control for time, skill level, small organizations, large organizations, region, further education, %female, %non-German citizens, and economic sectors. $*p<0.05$, $**p<0.01$, and $***p<0.001$

Sources: Statistisches Bundesamt a, b, c, d, e, f, g, h, i, j 1999-2008, own calculations; RDC of the Federal Statistical Office and the Statistical Offices of the Länder, Microcensus, survey years 2000, 2004, 2007, own calculations; Berufenet internet data base of the Federal Labor Office of Germany; Haupt 2012a; survey of the total population of occupational associations conducted by Schroeder, Kalass and Greef, own calculations.

Table 14 shows that two occupational-level closure variables are significantly associated with the individual-level differences in temporary employment between incumbents of the same occupation with low- and medium-level qualifications: the title licensure measure and general occupational associations. A change in the unit of the title licensure variable changes the risk of temporary employment of the low-qualification group by 0.007 logit points. Occupations with a mean value on the licensed titles variable increase the risk of temporary

---

148   The full table with all control variables is shown in the online appendix (11.5).

employment for incumbents with low-level qualifications in comparison to their counterparts with medium-level qualifications by one half ($e^{(0.007*57)}$ = 1.49)[149]. General occupational associations also increase the temporary employment risk of poorly qualified incumbents in contrast to incumbents with medium-level qualifications by one quarter ($e^{(0.229*1)}$ = 1.26).

Table 14: *Explaining differences in the probability of temporary employment between occupational incumbents with low- and medium-level qualifications within occupations, using the different sources of occupational closure—a pooled linear regression with the individual-level stage-one logit coefficients of occupational incumbents with low-level qualifications as the dependent variable[150]*

	Model 16		
Credential inflation index	0,286	(0,351)	
Standardization	0,130	(0,071)	
Width of the sets of tasks	0,235	(0,179)	
Commonness of the task sets	-1,046	(0,966)	
Associations (omitted category = no association)			
Specific association	0,073	(0,094)	
General association	0,229	(0,109)	*
Title licensure	0,008	(0,003)	*
Unionization (omitted category = no union)			
Trade union	0,119	(0,113)	
Constant	0,754	(0,086)	***
F	12,91	***	
R squared	0,213		
Root MSE	0,914		
Mean vif	3,12		

Note: N = 671,265 individuals in 1,060 occupations; Heteroscedastic consistent Huber-White standard errors in parentheses. All models control for time, skill level, small organizations, large organizations, region, further education, %female, %non-German citizens, and economic sectors. *p<0.05, **p<0.01, and ***p<0.001

Sources: Statistisches Bundesamt a, b, c, d, e, f, g, h, i, j 1999-2008, own calculations; RDC of the Federal Statistical Office and the Statistical Offices of the Länder, Microcensus, survey years 2000, 2004, 2007, own calculations; Berufenet internet data base of the Federal Labor Office of Germany;

---

149 It is not meaningful to display the odds for the maximum value on title licensure because occupations with incumbents with low-level qualifications cannot reach the maximum value.

150 The full table with all control variables is shown in the online appendix (11.5).

Haupt 2012a; survey of the total population of occupational associations conducted by Schroeder, Kalass and Greef, own calculations.

At first glance, it seems odd that general occupational associations increase the risk of temporary employment for poorly qualified incumbents. At second glance it becomes clear, however, that this odds ratio is the result of a decrease in the risk of temporary employment for incumbents with medium-level qualifications, which is induced by general associations.

Both analyses did not show the predicted association between the occupation-specific trade unions and young incumbents or poorly qualified workers (hypothesis 10). Occupation-specific trade unions do not contribute to the dualization of the workforce by concentrating on the traditional core workforce, which would put these two populations at an even greater disadvantage.

7.6 Solving the (Academic) Credentialism Conundrum

I have argued that the conventional credentialism measure—the proportion of occupational incumbents with tertiary degrees—does not theoretically capture the restricting supply closure mechanism. In section 6.2.1, I provided empirical evidence that occupations in which credentials are awarded in an inflationary manner have the highest proportions of members with tertiary degrees. However, Bol and Weeden (2014), Giesecke and Verwiebe (2009), and Groß (2009, 2012) provide empirical evidence for an association between occupational closure and tertiary degrees for Germany. To resolve this inconsistency, I will use the same analytical strategy as in the last section and regress the individual-level logit coefficients of occupational incumbents with tertiary-level qualifications (reference = incumbents with medium-level qualifications) on the various sources of occupational closure.

Table 15: Explaining differences in the probability of temporary employment between highly and moderately qualified occupational incumbents within occupations, using the different sources of occupational closure—a pooled linear regression with the individual-level stage-one logit coefficients of highly qualified occupational incumbents as the dependent variable[151]

	Model 17		
Credential inflation index	-0,860	(0,425)	*
Standardization	0,090	(0,062)	
Width of the sets of tasks	0,264	(0,181)	
Commonness of the task sets	2,039	(1,310)	
Associations (omitted category = no association)			
Specific association	-0,162	(0,092)	
General association	-0,055	(0,111)	
Title licensure	0,005	(0,003)	
Unionization (omitted category = no union)			
Trade union	0,132	(0,110)	
Constant	0,981	(0,100)	***
F	8,77	***	
R squared	0,201		
Root MSE	1,063		
Mean vif	3,13		

Note: N = 671,265 individuals in 1,060 occupations; Heteroscedastic consistent Huber-White standard errors in parentheses. All models control for time, skill level, small organizations, large organizations, region, further education, %female, %non-German citizens, and economic sectors. *p<0.05, **p<0.01, and ***p<0.001

Sources: Statistisches Bundesamt a, b, c, d, e, f, g, h, i, j 1999-2008, own calculations; RDC of the Federal Statistical Office and the Statistical Offices of the Länder, Microcensus, survey years 2000, 2004, 2007, own calculations; Berufenet internet data base of the Federal Labor Office of Germany; Haupt 2012a; survey of the total population of occupational associations conducted by Schroeder, Kalass and Greef, own calculations.

Two closure sources have significant associations with different levels of risk of temporary employment for highly qualified incumbents (completed tertiary education) in comparison to medium-level qualified incumbents of the same occupations: the credential inflation index and specific occupational associations. Specific occupational associations are only significant at a 10 percent level and have a relatively weak impact: They decrease the risk of temporary employment for highly qualified incumbents by one fifth ($e^{-0.162}$) in comparison to incumbents with medium-level qualifications. The credential inflation index

---

151 The full table with all control variables is shown in the online appendix (11.5).

also decreases the risk of temporary employment for highly qualified incumbents in comparison to incumbents with medium-level qualifications. The effect size is large. An increase in CIX of one unit reduces the temporary-employment risk of highly qualified incumbents by -0.86 logit points or more than 100 percent (Odds = 2.3). To put the large effect into perspective: Individuals with tertiary degrees have a higher risk of temporary employment than individuals with nontertiary occupation-specific credentials (see section 6.1). Additionally, for the majority of occupations (eight out of ten), credentials are not issued in an inflationary manner (see section 6.2.1). However, occupations for which credentials are awarded in an inflationary manner do not put incumbents with tertiary credentials at a disadvantage. Quite the contrary: Employers who are faced with an inflation of credentials in a given occupation rely on the signaling value of tertiary degrees when deciding who to hire permanently.

7.7 Sensitivity Checks

I conducted a large array of additional analyses to ensure the stability of the analyses. One series of additional analyses involved the inclusion of additional variables. The check for linear associations between the dependent and independent variables revealed a weak quadratic function for the width-of-task-range variable[152]. Hence, I ran every model with an additional quadratic term. The results remained substantially the same. Because the quadratic function was weak and did not provide additional insights, I decided to only present the more easily accessible models without the additional quadratic term. I also ran all my models with the task licensure variable instead of the title licensure variable. Again, no substantial changes occurred. However, in models where the title licensure variable had significant effects, the task licensure did not[153].

In addition to testing an alternative coding of the licensure closure source, I also tested an alternative coding of the task complexity measures. I tried to implement one comprehensive task complexity variable that replaced the four density measures of task complexity. When I did this, the results of the models changed substantially: Most closure measures had larger effect sizes and almost all closure measures were statistically significant. The reason for this large impact is that the four task complexity levels are not easily transformed into

---

152 A graph of the quadratic association is shown in the online appendix (11.4).

153 There were only two exceptions: Task licensure was significant in the model with interactions between the routine/labor tasks and the closure variables, and was significant on the 10 percent level in the young vs. middle-aged incumbents model.

one joint index. Their impact on temporary employment does not increase in a linear fashion with each level of complexity.

I also tested for time effects. I ran the main model three times and consecutively dropped one of the three years I had pooled in my analyses. All of the results remained substantially unchanged. I also tested for size effects. First, I excluded all occupations with less than 100 incumbents. The results remained stable. Second, I excluded all occupations with more than 1000 incumbents. Again, the main results remained stable. Both sample size reductions roughly equaled a 15 percent reduction in the overall sample size of the occupations. However, excluding small occupations helped the general associations to become significant. Excluding large occupations also made the standardization measure significant. In addition, I directly controlled for the size of occupations by including a relative size measure in the main model, but the results again remained unchanged. No closure measures became (in)significant or changed substantially.

8   Summary

Temporary employment is often associated with low wages, poor working conditions, high labor turnover, and limited career opportunities. Despite the many negative aspects, temporary employment might also act as a bridge into (permanent) employment. Nevertheless, given the choice, 98-99 percent of all temporary employees would prefer to be permanently employed. The fact that, irrespective of their preferences, some employees are temporarily employed while others are not is usually explained using human capital theory, internal labor market theory, and the transaction costs approach. Following the arguments of these theories, the risk of temporary employment is dependent on the amount of general human capital and specific human capital an employee has. It is also dependent on how difficult it is for the employer to evaluate/monitor the productivity of employees directly. Governance structures may separate firm-internal from firm-external labor markets, a process which additionally affects the employees' risk of temporary employment.

In this book, I have expanded on the standard predictions of these theories using arguments drawn from closure theory, which allow for a long-term occupation-specific skill scarcity that is established and maintained by closure barriers. By doing so, I have been able to address two critical gaps in the arguments of these theories and in the research on temporary employment: First, labor markets do not consist of employees who only differ in their level and amount of qualifications and skills. Labor markets consist of employees whose qualifications and skills are related to occupation-specific task fields. Hence, labor markets are segmented by occupations because these qualifications and skills cannot be simply reassigned from one occupational task field to another. Second, the reasons why firms award long-term employment contracts may thus not only relate to problems of investment in specific human capital, employment in firm-internal labor markets, control, and work complexity; they may also be used as part of employers' human resource strategies. Employers use these strategies to manage the outcomes of occupational closure, using permanent employment contracts to secure scarce occupation-specific skills. The outcomes of occupational closure are theoretically based on the restricting supply mechanism, the increasing diffuse demand mechanism, and the channeling demand mechanism, which alter the equilibrium between the supply of and demand for the occupation-specific workforce. In order to adapt Weeden's (2002) original approach to fit this modified research focus—that is, shifting from earning inequalities to temporary employment—I subsumed the signaling quality closure mechanism under the channeling demand mechanism, because occupations that successfully signal quality channel the employers' demand to their incumbents. Based on Weeden's (2002) seminal work, I identified closure sources that might trigger the three closure mechanisms and thereby change the occupational incumbents' risk of holding temporary employment contracts. I constructed a new measure, the credential inflation index, which establishes the link between the credentialism closure source and the restricting supply mechanism. The standardization closure measure addresses the variance of credentials in their signals of quality, which theoretically triggers the channeling demand mechanism. I introduced a closure measure that captures the strength of the boundaries around occupational task niches. Incumbents of occupations with well-defined boundaries cannot easily be substituted by incumbents of other occupations, because their sets of tasks and skills are relatively unique. I constructed a new closure source that measures the degree of occupational task specialization, which triggers the channeling demand mechanism if the sets of tasks and skills are narrow. Task specialization has a signaling value for employers that improves their ability to assess the potential fit between the occupational incumbents' skills and the skill requirements of vacant positions, and thus triggers the channeling demand mechanism. If the sets of tasks and skills are wide, occupations may trigger the increasing diffuse demand mechanism because they theoretically grant access to a wide range of positions. I subsumed both measures—the relative uniqueness of occupations' task niches and the task specialization of occupations—under the new occupational specificity closure source. I included three more closure sources—licensure, association representation, and unionization—that are not novel but are operationalized differently.

Based on a special version of the German Microcensus, I analyzed detailed occupations using a two-step multilevel model. The two-step approach allowed me to circumvent various obstacles related to the binary character of the dependent variable. The results showed great variation in temporary employment across the occupations, with occupations having a minimum of 0 percent temporary employment and a maximum of 64 percent temporary employment. The analyses confirmed the argument that occupational closure influences employees' risk of temporary employment. Specifically, the two measures of occupational specificity and the credential inflation index have substantive and statistically significant effects on temporary employment. The strong impact of unique and common sets of tasks suggests that occupational task niches that are surrounded by well-established boundaries provide their incumbents with relatively unique sets of tasks and thereby restrict employers' choice of alternative workers. Occupational task niches with relatively common sets of tasks do not restrict employers in their choice to replace an occupation's incumbents with members of other occupations and are thus not able to trigger the channeling demand mechanism. The empirical results support the argument that occupations with a high degree of task specialization (narrow ranges of tasks) have a high signaling value that might allow employers to achieve a better fit between the requirements of vacant positions and potential candidates. Because this fit is uncertain for incumbents of occupations with relatively wide ranges of tasks, employers might use temporary employment contracts more often to prolong their probationary periods. The findings also support the argument that an inflationary supply of occupation-specific credentials reduces the competition between employers for these credentials and simultaneously increases the competition between the credential holders, thereby resulting in an increased risk of temporary employment.

The weak effects of associational representation could be interpreted as confirming Weeden's (2002: 91) conclusion that the associations' efforts are largely symbolic. However, the absence of a substantial impact might also be the result of a reversed causal order. In this case, associations would be formed as a response to worsening employment and working conditions. Occupational associations that are well-established and "old" might already have improved the situation for the incumbents of the occupations they represent, whereas "young" associations are just beginning to improve the employment and working conditions. Future research may check the validity of this argument using data on the date of formation of the associations. Occupation-specific trade unions also only have a weak effect. This might be explained by the German tariff uniformity principle (*Tarifeinheit*). This principle allows only one collective bargaining agreement for each organization, which is usually agreed by large industry-level unions. Starting in the 2000s, this principle began to be actively challenged as more and more occupation-specific trade unions started to compete with the large industry-level unions and began to bargain for occupation-specific collective agreements, culminating in the legal suspension of the tariff uniformity principle in 2010. Because my analytical time frame focuses on these formative years, more up-to-date data might show a stronger impact of occupation-specific trade unions on their incumbents' risk of temporary employment because they have successfully confirmed their right to bargain for competing collective agreements[154]. Standardization and licensure each have a weak and nonsignificant impact. However, additional analyses

---

154 The weak effects of associational representation and union representation might also be due to an endogeneity problem: Associations and occupation-specific trade unions both might successfully push for closure through lobbying processes and as a result might change the observable outcomes of the other closure sources. In this case, the main closure effect is already controlled for through the other closure sources.

revealed that this weak impact is due to confounding effects, which can be addressed by adding interaction terms.

Whereas the first set of empirical results lends credit to the closure arguments, I am also interested in expanding the conventional human capital account by analyzing its interrelation with occupational closure. An empirical relationship seems to be inevitable because both theories focus on credentials and skills, albeit from different angles (e.g., Weeden 2002; Werfhorst 2011). Tests of the interrelation between occupational members' participation in further work-related education and training and the degree of standardization of the incumbents' credentials revealed two opposing results. Standardization has its predicted effect on the probability of temporary employment only for occupations whose incumbents rarely participate in further education: Incumbents of occupations with highly standardized credentials face a lower risk of temporary employment than incumbents of occupations whose credentials have a low degree of standardization. Occupations whose incumbents frequently participate in further education are presented with a reverse outcome. Following the main thrust of human capital theory, I have theoretically argued and empirically confirmed that the initial disadvantage of holding unstandardized credentials is offset by further education. The results indicate that the uncertain productive value of occupational incumbents with relatively unstandardized credentials is modified by additional training, and that this additional training results in a sharp drop in the risk of temporary employment faced by these incumbents. Unfortunately, the data do not allow me to distinguish between further education that is financed by the incumbents and by the employing organizations. However, the results indicate that the latter is the case. The main argument of human capital theory—that human capital investments increase the organization's interest in securing these investments—is only true for occupational incumbents whose credentials signal a low or uncertain productive value. Contrary to the theory's arguments, additional increases in human capital barely affect the probability of temporary employment for incumbents of occupations whose credentials already signal a high productive value.

In the theory section I introduced two competing theoretical arguments—Spence's (1973) signaling argument and Iversen and Soskice's (2001) mobility argument—that explain why the composition of occupation-specific tasks and skills might affect their incumbents' risk of temporary employment. By relating the width-of-tasks measure to occupational incumbents' further education, I can rule out parts of the mobility argument. The thrust of this argument is that incumbents of occupations should benefit from having a wide range of skills because it allows their employers to easily reassign them to new positions and tasks if necessity dictates it. However, the initial analysis revealed that occupations with narrow skill and task profiles benefit their incumbents more than occupations with wide profiles. Additionally, only incumbents of occupations with narrow sets of skills and tasks benefit from increases in their human capital. This result suggests the existence of mobility barriers for incumbents of occupations with a narrow range of tasks. These barriers are broken down by additional education and training. The joint effect of the initially high signaling value of occupations with narrow task sets and the enhanced intra-organizational mobility through additional training allows for an easier reassignment of the incumbents if the market or the technology changes. Conversely, incumbents from occupations with wide sets of skills and tasks seem not to benefit from an initially higher intra-organizational mobility and benefit little from additional training, which theoretically would improve the poor initial fit between their skills and their job requirements.

The main sources through which occupations trigger closure mechanisms and thereby bestow benefits on their members could be neutralized by employers, who could instead use additional training and education programs to counter the relative scarcity of occupation-specific skills. Rare skills are either indicated by the credential inflation index or the relatively unique set of tasks in one occupation. Occupations that maintain relatively unique task niches restrict employers' choice of workers from alternative occupations (channeling demand) and thus reduce the incumbents' probability of temporary employment. In contrast to the initial findings, the results are completely reversed for relatively unique occupations whose incumbents strongly participated in further education. Unique tasks niches become a trap when additional education and training courses also provide these relatively unique skills. Their incumbents thus face increased competition. This competition cannot easily be avoided by choosing other kinds of jobs because of the relatively unique nature of the incumbents' tasks. To use an analogy: The relatively impermeable boundaries around the occupations' task niches become semipermeable and let new incumbents in more easily, but they do not let established incumbents out. However, there is no such association between the credential inflation index, further education, and the probability of temporary employment.

Empirical tests of the interrelation between internal labor markets and occupational closure did not provide much in the way of further insights, probably due to the lack of a suitable measure for large organizations. The German Microcensus only allows me to label organizations as large when they have 50 or more employees. However, the findings suggest that the closure theory complements the internal labor market approach: Just because the use of temporary employment contracts is more cost-effective for large organizations does not mean that large organizations use temporary employment contracts more often than small organizations. The empirical findings indicate that large organizations only use temporary employment contracts more often for incumbents of occupations whose credentials are available in excess. For incumbents in the majority of occupations—for which credentials are not awarded in an inflationary manner—employment in large firms barely increases their probability of temporary employment. The result stresses the importance of one of my main closure arguments: Organizations use permanent employment contracts as a means to securing credentialed occupation-specific skills that are not abundantly available.

The most noteworthy point from the exploratory tests for the possible interaction between the skill level of tasks, occupational closure, and temporary employment is that analyzing each skill level of tasks reveals a very different picture than one would find by using a composite measure for the skill levels of tasks. The exploratory analysis shows, for example, that the licensure closure source has an impact on the probability of temporary employment that is different for each skill level of the tasks performed by the occupational incumbents. It also shows that relatively unique sets of tasks are highly disadvantageous in occupations where managerial tasks dominate. These results may point to a new strategy that may be adopted by future research seeking to confirm the suitability of composite skill measures in analyses that include occupational-level phenomena. It might also be a way for future research to further explore the varying associations between temporary employment, licensure, and the skill level of tasks.

Occupational closure is not independent of regional differences in the tightness of the labor markets. The small and insignificant effect size of licensing in the main model becomes large and significant in its effect size when interactions between region and occupational closure are allowed. In tight labor markets with high unemployment rates, every distinguishing signal makes the difference in terms of permanent or temporary employment contracts. Incumbents of occupations who lack these additional signals in the form of licensed titles are at a disadvantage. Further analyses also confirm that the credentialism closure source is not independent of possible gender biases that are induced by the educational institutions providing the occupation-specific credentials. Adding interaction effects between the gender composition of occupations and occupational closure reveals that the standardization of credentials has an impact on temporary employment. It does not show up in the main model because the effect of standardization on temporary employment is reversed for female-dominated and male-dominated occupations. The analysis also shows that credentials awarded in an inflationary manner put the incumbents of female-dominated occupations at a much greater disadvantage than incumbents of male-dominated occupations. The different impact of the credential inflation index on male- or female-dominated occupations might be due to the fact that women are concentrated in relatively few detailed occupations, whereas men are widely distributed. However, it remains an open question why credentials awarded in an inflationary manner are highly disadvantageous for incumbents of female-dominated occupations but not for male-dominated occupations: This could be a promising avenue for future research.

To check whether occupational closure affects all incumbents of the respective occupations equally, or whether the impact varies within the occupations, I extended my analyses as follows: I compared the differences in the probability of temporary employment of poorly qualified individuals with individuals with medium-level qualifications, and also compared the differences in probability of temporary employment of young adults with adults in the prime working age; I then regressed these differences on my closure variables. The analyses of these high-contrast groups indicated that occupational closure does not generally differ within occupations. However, I found two exceptions: Title licensure increased the risk of individuals with low qualifications and young individuals, whereas general occupational associations altered the probability of temporary employment to the detriment of the low-qualified group. The reason for young employees' disadvantage with regard to title licensure might be that employers only benefit from the signaling function of licensed titles when few incumbents have licensed titles. The distinction between occupational incumbents decreases if many or even all incumbents of an occupation have protected titles. If this is the case, and the signaling value of licensed titles is low, employers may rely on alternative signaling sources, like experience. Experience, for example, is clearly age related and would put labor market entrants with a licensed title in highly licensed occupations at a bigger disadvantage than labor market entrants with licensed titles in occupations with a low degree of title licensure. The same argument is broadly true for low-qualified incumbents who do not gain licensed titles because they have no credentials at all. This negative distinction becomes more important and more disadvantageous the more incumbents of an occupation have licensed titles. The results for occupational incumbents with low-level qualifications and for general occupational associations also support the argument that associations increase the diffuse demand for the occupations they represent through advertising and lobbying. However, poorly qualified members of an occupation are usually not represented in the associations' attempts to advertise and lobby for their occupations, as these attempts decidedly emphasize the excellent qualifications and skills of the incumbents they represent. Poorly qualified incumbents will thereby not benefit from the achievements of their occupational associations.

I have theoretically argued and empirically shown that the conventional credentialism measure—the proportion of occupational incumbents with tertiary degrees—does not capture the restricting supply closure mechanism. To determine the relationship between tertiary degrees and occupational closure, I analyzed whether the differences between incumbents with tertiary degrees and incumbents with upper-secondary qualifications in the probability of temporary employment might be explained by the various sources of occupational closure. The analysis revealed that the risk of temporary employment decreases steeply for incumbents with tertiary degrees in occupations where credentials are awarded in an inflationary manner. While credential inflation always increased the probability of temporary employment in the other analyses, it is beneficial for occupational incumbents with tertiary degrees and decreases their risk considerably. In situations where employers face a vast pool of potential candidates who all have credentials that match the requirements of a vacant position, they fall back on other legitimized means of selection[155]. These other forms of selection might be based on the employers' belief in the higher cultural value of academic credentials, or it might just be a practical instrument to limit the potential candidate pool by setting artificially high thresholds and requiring them to have academic degrees (e.g. Collins 1979; Parkin 1979; Bourdieu 1987; Weeden 2002; Werfhorst 2011). Either way, academic credentials signal quality, but only to the benefit of occupational incumbents with academic degrees, and only for occupations with an unrestricted supply of newly credentialed incumbents. Weeden's (2002) argument that academic credentials are linked to occupational closure is therefore true, but limited.

The analyses I presented are unprecedented in four ways. First, it is the first time that the determinants of temporary employment have been analyzed at the occupational level. The results emphasize that occupations constitute labor market segments that affect their incumbents' risk of holding temporary employment contracts by adjusting the equilibrium between the supply of and demand for the occupation-specific workforce. Conventional analyses of the determinants of temporary employment performed previously were not able to account for the fact that skills and qualifications are related to occupation-specific task fields. The occupational specificity of these skills (unique or common skills) determines whether and to what extent these skills are applicable in other occupations. The degree to which occupation-specific credentials are awarded in an inflationary manner is decisive for the competition between the occupational incumbents and the competition between employers over the occupational incumbents. An occupation's relative task specialization signals the potential quality of the fit between the employees' skills and the job skill requirements. Hence, labor market fragmentation follows occupational boundaries.

---

155 Even if the pool of credentialed candidates might be large, candidates nevertheless differ in the training tracks through which they acquired their credentials.

Second, I complement the empirical literature on occupational closure by developing new closure measures. The conventional credentialism measure is only partially able to link the restricting supply mechanism to the credentials. To solve this problem, I utilized the institutionalized link between the education and training system and the labor market in Germany to develop the credential inflation index, which measures the quantity of the newly credentialed labor supply. I also introduce the new occupational specificity closure source. This allowed me to capture the exclusivity of the occupations' task niches. The concept of the task niche is often used in the literature on professions, but it had rarely been applied in quantitative research designs on occupational closure. The new closure source also allowed me the novelty of capturing the occupations' task specialization, a feature that is often the subject of heated discussions with regard to its effect on employees' employment security (e.g., Emmenegger 2009; Streeck 2011). All three measures make substantial contributions to the explanation of the varying probabilities of temporary employment.

Third, I have presented analyses showing that measures of occupational closure are not independent of the varying degrees of economic pressure or the gender composition of occupations. In tight labor markets like the one in the new *Länder,* the relevance of occupational closure theoretically increases. Empirically, I can verify that title licensure has a substantial impact on the probability of temporary employment when the regional differences are allowed to interact with the closure measures. It is also not enough to control for gender composition when the education and training system is not gender neutral and thus provides gendered credentials. Interaction terms are needed to account for the gendered impact of credentialism measures. Additionally, the use of composite skill measures on the occupational level is called into question by the finding that each skill level of tasks varies in its association with the dependent variable as well as with the closure variables. Further research is necessary to examine whether this result is specific to temporary employment or to the skill-level-of-tasks variable, or whether composite skill measures are generally not suitable as control variables in occupational-level analyses.

Fourth, the analyses I have presented complement human capital theory and the internal labor market approach. By extending the analyses from simply controlling for human capital and internal labor market variables to analyses that allowed for interactions between human capital and internal labor market variables, I have increased the reach of these theories by complementing them with closure arguments. I have established the critical link between occupational closure and temporary employment, although much work remains to be done to capture the interplay of closure, human capital, and internal labor markets, both theoretically as well as empirically.

9   Conclusions

Extending closure theory to encompass temporary employment allows us to take a glimpse at the wider picture of labor market inequality and occupational closure. Although we now have insights into some facets of the inner workings of labor markets with regard to earning inequalities, temporary employment, and occupational closure, there is still more to explore. There are more forms of nonstandard work arrangements to be considered, like part-time work, on-call/day-labor work, temporary help agency work, contract work, and self-employment, to which closure theory might contribute new insights. Moreover, occupational closure theory should also provide new insights with regard to the duration and the long-term consequences of nonstandard work. Occupational closure may also be an important determinant in organizations' outsourcing and offshoring decisions. However, before we delve into these specific topics, we still have to extend closure theory to the most basic dimensions of social inequality—individuals' opportunities to actively pursue careers in the labor market. Closure might affect the likelihood of being hired, of participating in employer-provided training, of moving up the career ladder, or it may affect the risk of being laid off.

Established knowledge on the association between the closure sources and individuals' labor market-related risks is still specific to earnings inequalities and individuals' risks of being employed on a temporary basis. Therefore, policy implications should be considered with caution because the various closure sources may differ in their impact on individuals' careers depending on how advanced their career trajectories are. The most prominent illustration of how the various closure sources work differently is the standardization of credentials: It might determine, on the one hand, individuals' chances of being hired. Incumbents of occupations with standardized credentials should experience improved employment chances because the credentials signal instant and high productivity. On the other hand, standardization might directly be linked to individuals' unemployment risks: Standardized credentials reduce employers' search and induction costs and might thereby increase individuals' risk of being laid off by being replaced with competing incumbents from the same or related standardized occupations. Hence there is still a long way to go to provide a concise picture of the impact of occupational closure on individuals' employment security, career prospects, and entire employment biographies.

However, one would be hard pressed to imagine a scenario in which the restricted supply of individuals with occupation-specific credentials results in adverse effects for the incumbents of occupations. I will therefore conclude with two policy implications for this specific closure source. First, the information provided by the credential inflation index could be utilized to identify occupations without a restricted supply of occupation-specific credentials. This information could help individuals to avoid occupational choices that are too popular and that would increase their risk of holding temporary employment contracts. The vocational information and guidance program (*Berufsberatung*) in Germany can use this information to improve the permanent employment and career chances of those seeking advice. Second, the credential inflation index could also be used to introduce modified temporary employment legislation that is targeted towards occupations for which individuals receive their occupation-specific credentials in an inflationary manner. In these occupations, the negative consequences of temporary employment contracts (low wages, poor working conditions, high labor turnover, and limited career opportunities) will prevail, whereas positive effects will be absent (bridge into permanent employment, low unemployment rates). The positive effects will be absent because labor supply and labor demand are not balanced. Targeted legislation could help to alleviate the negative effects of temporary employment in these occupations and at the same time increase the employees' chances of becoming permanently employed by, for example, prolonging the maximum duration of temporary employment contracts without objective reasons to three or four years. By doing so, the potential productivity loss would increase for employers if temporary contracts were not converted into permanent employment contracts, and if experienced workers were replaced by new and inexperienced workers. The prolonged contract time would also increase the chances of temporary employees to use their temporary employment as a stepping stone and finding new employers who regularly use permanent employment contracts. However, Polavieja (2003, 2005) has shown for Spain that targeted temporary employment legislation can be very detrimental for the targeted population because employers not only use temporary employment contracts to increase their external flexibility, but to reduce employment costs, also. To avoid such a substitution scenario where permanent employees are replaced by temporary employees, the legislation on temporary employment should only allow for increased flexibility but not for cost reductions. This can be achieved by increasing the costs of temporary employment contracts for employers, and by increasing employers' contributions to the national unemployment insurance system and the old age pension system.

References

Abbott, A. 1988. The System of Professions. An Essay on the Division of Expert Labor. Chicago: University of Chicago Press.

Abbott, A. 1989. The New Occupational Structure. Work and Occupations, 16(3): 273-291.

Abraham, K. G. 1988. Flexible Staffing Arrangements and Employers' Short-Term Adjustment Strategies. In R. A. Hart (Ed.), Employment, Unemployment and Labor Utilization: 288-311. Boston: Unwin Hyman.

Abraham, M., Damelang, A., & Schulz, F. 2011. Wie strukturieren Berufe Arbeitsmarktprozesse?, LASER Discussion Papers, Vol. 55. Erlangen: LASER.

Achatz, J. 2005. Geschlechtersegregation im Arbeitsmarkt. In M. Abraham & T. Hinz (Eds.), Arbeitsmarktsoziologie. Probleme, Theorien, empirische Befunde: 263-300. Wiesbaden: VS Verlag für Sozialwissenschaften.

Achen, C. H. 2005. Two-Step Hierarchical Estimation: Beyond Regression Analysis. Political Analysis, 13(4): 447-456.

Agresti, A. 2007. An Introduction to Categorical Data Analysis. Hoboken, NJ: Wiley-Interscience.

Alda, H. 2002. Beschäftigungsverhältnisse. In IAB & ISF & INIFES & SOFI (Eds.), Berichterstattung zur sozio-ökonomischen Leistungsfähigkeit der Bundesrepublik Deutschland: 245-269. Wiesbaden: VS Verlag für Sozialwissenschaften.

Allmendinger, J. 1989. Educational Systems and Labor Market Outcomes. European Sociological Review, 5(3): 231-250.

Allmendinger, J., Hipp, L., & Stuth, S. 2013. Atypical Employment in Europe 1996 – 2011, WZB Discussion Paper, Vol. P 2013-003. Berlin: WZB.

Allmendinger, J. & Driesch, E. v. d. 2014. Social Inequalities in Europe: Facing the Challenge, WZB Discussion Paper, Vol. P 2014-005. Berlin: WZB.

Althauser, R. P. & Kalleberg, A. L. 1981. Firms, Occupations, and the Structure of Labor Markets: A Conceptual Analysis. In I. Berg (Ed.), Sociological Perspectives on Labor Markets: 119-149. New York: Academic Press.

Althauser, R. P. 1989. Internal Labor Markets. Annual Review of Sociology, 15(1989): 143-161.

Arrow, K. J. 1972. Models of Job Discrimination. In A. H. Pascal (Ed.), Racial Discrimination in Economic Life: 83-102. Lexington: Lexington Books.

Atkinson, J. 1984. Manpower Strategies for Flexible Organisations. Personnel Management, 16(8): 28-31.

Baethge, M. & Baethge-Kinsky, V. 1998. Jenseits von Beruf und Beruflichkeit? Neue Formen von Arbeitsorganisation und Beschäftigung und ihre Bedeutung für eine zentrale Kategorie gesellschaftlicher Integration. Mitteilungen aus der Arbeitsmarkt- und Berufsforschung, 31(3): 461-472.

Baethge, M. 2001. Beruf - Ende oder Transformation eines erfolgreichen Ausbildungskonzepts? In T. Kurtz (Ed.), Aspekte des Berufs in der Moderne: 39-68. Opladen Leske + Budrich

Baethge, M. 2004. Entwicklungstendenzen der Beruflichkeit - neue Befunde aus der industriesoziologischen Forschung. Zeitschrift für Berufs- und Wirtschaftspädagogik, 100(3): 336-347.

Bals, T. 2006. Vollzeitschulische Ausbildung für Gesundheitsberufe. Ansätze zur Normalisierung. Berufsbildung, 60(100/101): 44-46.

Baranowska, A. & Gebel, M. 2010. The Determinants of Youth Temporary Employment in the Enlarged Europe. European Societies, 12(3): 367-390.

Barbieri, P. 2009. Flexible Employment and Inequality in Europe. European Sociological Review, 25(6): 621-628.

Barley, S. R. & Tolbert, P. S. 1991. At the Intersection of Organizations and Occupations. Research in the Sociology of Organizations, 8: 1-13.

Barry, B. & Crant, J. M. 1994. Labor Force Externalization in Growing Firms. The International Journal of Organizational Analysis, 2(4): 361-383.

Beck, U., Brater, M., & Tramsen, E. 1976. Beruf, Herrschaft und Identität. Ein subjektbezogener Ansatz zum Verhältnis von Bildung und Produktion. Teil I: Die soziale Konstitution der Berufe. Teil II: Kritik des Berufs. Soziale Welt, 27(2): 8-44, 180-205.

Beck, U. & Brater, M. 1978. Berufliche Arbeitsteilung und soziale Ungleichheit. Eine historisch-gesellschaftliche Theorie der Berufe. Frankfurt am Main, New York: Campus Verlag.

Beck, U., Brater, M., & Daheim, H. 1980. Soziologie der Arbeit und der Berufe. Reinbek bei Hamburg: Rowohlt.

Beck, U. 1999. Schöne neue Arbeitswelt. Vision: Weltbürgergesellschaft. Frankfurt am Main, New York: Campus Verlag.

Becker, G. S. 1962. Investment in Human Capital: A Theoretical Analysis. Journal of Political Economy, 70(5): 9-49.

Becker, G. S. 1964. Human Capital : a Theoretical and Empirical Analysis, with Special Reference to Education. New York: National Bureau of Economic Research.

Bellmann, L., Fischer, G., & Hohendanner, C. 2009. Betriebliche Dynamik und Flexibilität auf dem deutschen Arbeitsmarkt. In J. Möller & U. Walwei (Eds.), Handbuch Arbeitsmarkt: 359-401. Nürnberg: IAB.

Bentolila, S. & Bertola, G. 1990. Firing Costs and Labour Demand: How Bad is Eurosclerosis? The Review of Economic Studies, 57(3): 381-402.

Bentolila, S. & Saint-Paul, G. 1992. The Macroeconomic Impact of Flexible Labor Contracts with an Application to Spain. European Economic Review, 36(5): 1013-1047.

Bentolila, S. & Dolado, J. J. 1994. Labour Flexibility and Wages: Lessons from Spain. Economic Policy, 9(18): 55-99.

Bentolila, S. & Saint-Paul, G. 1994. A Model of Labor Demand with Linear Adjustment Costs. Labour Economics, 1(3-4): 303-326.

Berger, P. A., Konietzka, D., & Michailow, M. 2001. Beruf, soziale Ungleichheit und Individualisierung In T. Kurtz (Ed.), Aspekte des Berufs in der Moderne 209-237. Opladen Leske + Budrich.

Berlant, J. L. 1975. Profession and Monopoly. A Study of Medicine in the United States and Great Britain. Berkeley, Cal.: University of California Press.

Bernhardt, J. 2015. Welfare Retrenchment, Social Class, and Policy Feedback: The Impact of the German Hartz IV Reform on Subjective Status Insecurity. Unpublished manuscript.

Bielby, W. T. & Kalleberg, A. L. 1981. The Structure of Occupational Inequality. Quality and Quantity, 15(2): 125-150.

Biersack, W. & Parmentier, K. 2002. Konzepte der quantitativen Berufsforschung im IAB. In G. Kleinhenz (Ed.), IAB-Kompendium Arbeitsmarkt - und Berufsforschung: 475-489. Nürnberg: IAB.

Blanchard, O. & Landier, A. 2002. The Perverse Effects of Partial Labour Market Reform: Fixed-Term Contracts in France. The Economic Journal, 112(480): 214-244.

Blossfeld, H.-P. 1985. Berufseintritt und Berufsverlauf - Eine Kohortenanalyse über die Bedeutung des ersten Berufs in der Erwerbsbiographie. Mitteilungen aus der Arbeitsmarkt- und Berufsforschung, 18(2): 177-197.

Blossfeld, H.-P. 1990. Berufsverläufe und Arbeitsmarktprozesse. Ergebnisse sozialstruktureller Längsschnittuntersuchungen. In K. U. Mayer (Ed.), Lebensverläufe und sozialer Wandel: 118-145. Opladen: Westdeutscher Verlag.

Blossfeld, H.-P., Mills, M., & Bernardi, F. 2006. Globalization, Uncertainty, and Men's Careers : An International Comparison. Cheltenham, UK ; Northampton, MA: Edward Elgar.

Boeri, T. 1999. Enforcement of Employment Security Regulations, On-The-Job Search and Unemployment Duration. European Economic Review, 43(1): 65-89.

Bol, T. 2014. Economic Returns to Occupational Closure in the German Skilled Trades. Social Science Research, 46: 9-22.

Bol, T. & Weeden, K. A. 2014. Occupational Closure and Wage Inequality in Germany and the United Kingdom. European Sociological Review, 0(0).

Bollinger, D., Cometz, W., & Pfau-Effinger, B. 1991. "Atypische" Beschäftigung - Betriebliche Kalküle und Arbeitnehmerinteressen. In K. Semlinger (Ed.), Flexibilisierung des Arbeitsmarktes. Interessen, Wirkungen, Perspektiven: 177-199. Frankfurt am Main, New York: Campus Verlag.

Boockmann, B. & Hagen, T. 2003. Works Councils and Fixed-Term Employment: Evidence from West German Establishments. Schmollers Jahrbuch, 123(3): 359-383.

Boockmann, B. & Hagen, T. 2005. Fixed-Term Contracts as Sorting Mechanisms: Evidence From Job Durations in West Germany. Mannheim: Zentrum für Europäische Wirtschaftsforschung.

Boockmann, B. & Hagen, T. 2005. Die Bedeutung befristeter Arbeitsverhältnisse für die Zugänge und den Verbleib in Beschäftigung. In M. Kronauer & G. Linne (Eds.), Flexicurity - Die Suche nach Sicherheit in der Flexibilität: 149-168. Berlin: Edition Sigma.

Boockmann, B. & Hagen, T. 2006. Befristete Beschäftigungsverhältnisse - Brücken in den Arbeitsmarkt oder Instrumente der Segmentierung? Baden-Baden: Nomos Verlagsgesellschaft.

Boockmann, B. & Hagen, T. 2008. Fixed-Term Contracts as Sorting Mechanisms: Evidence from Job Durations in West Germany. Labour Economics, 15(5): 984-1005.

Booth, A. L. 1997. An Analysis of Firing Costs and their Implications for Unemployment Policy. In D. J. Snower & G. d. l. Dehesa (Eds.), Unemployment Policy: Government Options for the Labour Market: 359-388. Cambridge: Cambridge University Press.

Booth, A. L., Francesconi, M., & Frank, J. 2002. Temporary Jobs: Stepping Stones or Dead Ends? The Economic Journal, 112(480): F189-F213.

Bourdieu, P. & Passeron, J. C. 1971. Die Illusion der Chancengleichheit. Untersuchungen zur Soziologie des Bildungswesens am Beispiel Frankreichs. Stuttgart: Klett.

Bourdieu, P. 1987. Die feinen Unterschiede. Frankfurt am Main: Suhrkamp.

Brater, M. & Beck, U. 1982. Berufe als Organisationformen menschlichen Arbeitsvermögens. In W. R. W. Littek, G. Wachtler (Ed.), Einführung in die Arbeits- und Industriesoziologie: 208-224. Frankfurt am Main, New York: Campus Verlag.

Braude, L. 1975. Work and Workers - A Sociological Analysis. New York: Praeger Publishers.

Braverman, H. 1974. Labor and Monopoly Capital: The Degradation of Work in the Twentieth Century. New York: Monthly Review Press.

Breen, R. 2005. Explaining Cross-National Variation in Youth Unemployment: Market and Institutional Factors. European Sociological Review, 21(2): 125-134.

Brehmer, W. & Seifert, H. 2008. Sind atypische Beschäftigungsverhältnisse prekär? Eine empirische Analyse sozialer Risiken. Zeitschrift für ArbeitsmarktForschung 41(4): 501-531.

Bridges, W. P. & Villemez, W. J. 1991. Employment Relations and the Labor Market: Integrating Institutional and Market Perspectives. American Sociological Review, 56(6): 748-764.

Brint, S. G. 1994. In an Age of Experts: The Changing Role of Professionals in Politics and Public Life. Princeton, N.J.: Princeton University Press.

Brückner, H. & Mayer, K. U. 2005. De-Standardization of the Life Course: What it Might Mean? And if it Means Anything, Whether it Actually Took Place? Advances in Life Course Research, 9: 27-53.

Bryson, A. & Kleiner, M. M. 2010. The Regulation of Occupations. British Journal of Industrial Relations, 48(4): 670-675.

Brzinsky-Fay, C. 2007. Lost in Transition? Labour Market Entry Sequences of School Leavers in Europe. European Sociological Review, 23(4): 409-422.

Brzinsky-Fay, C. 2011. What Difference Does it Make? The Outcome Effects of the European Employment Strategy on the Transition from Education to Work. German Policy Studies, 7(1): 45-72.

Brzinsky-Fay, C. 2013. Der Einfluss von Bildungs- und Arbeitsmarktinstitutionen auf das Ausmaß von Jugendarbeitslosigkeit. In H. Solga, C. Brzinsky-Fay, L. Graf, C. Gresch & P. Protsch (Eds.), Vergleiche innerhalb von Gruppen und institutionelle Gelingensbedingungen – vielversprechende Perspektiven für die Ungleichheitsforschung, Vol. SP I 2013-501: 32-33. Berlin: WZB.

Buchholz, S. & Kurz, K. 2005. Increasing Employment Instability among Young People? Labor Market Entries and Early Careers in Germany since the Mid-1980s, FlexCareer Working Paper, Vol. 3. Bamberg: Otto-Friedrich-Universität Bamberg.

Buchholz, S. & Grunow, D. 2006. Globalization and Women's Employment in West Germany. In H.-P. Blossfeld, M. Mills & F. Bernardi (Eds.), Globalization, Uncertainty, and Men's Careers: an International Comparison: 61-83. Cheltenham, UK, Northampton, MA: Edward Elgar.

Büchtemann, C. F., Schupp, J., & Soloff, D. J. 1994. From School to Work: Patterns in Germany and the United States. In J. Schwarze, F. Buttler & G. G. Wagner (Eds.), Labour Market Dynamics in Present Day Germany: 112-141. Frankfurt am Main, New York: Campus Verlag.

Bukodi, E., Ebralidze, E., Schmelzer, P., & Blossfeld, H.-P. 2008. Struggling to Become an Insider: Does Increasing Flexibility at Labor Market Entry Affect Early Careers? A Theoretical Framework. In H.-P. Blossfeld, S. Buchholz, E. Bukodi & K. Kurz (Eds.), Young Workers, Globalization and the Labor Market: Comparing Early Working Life in Eleven Countries: 3-27. Cheltenham: Edward Elgar.

Busemeyer, M. R. 2009. Wandel trotz Reformstau. Frankfurt am Main, New York: Campus Verlag.

Cabrales, A. & Hopenhayn, H. A. 1997. Labor-Market Flexibility and Aggregate Employment Volatility. Carnegie-Rochester Conference Series on Public Policy, 46: 189-228.

Cahuc, P. & Postel-Vinay, F. 2002. Temporary Jobs, Employment Protection and Labor Market Performance. Labour Economics, 9(1): 63-91.

Campbell, D., Carruth, A., Dickerson, A., & Green, F. 2007. Job Insecurity and Wages. The Economic Journal, 117(518): 544-566.

Caplow, T. 1954. The Sociology of Work. Minneapolis: University of Minnesota Press.

Casey, C. 1995. Work, Self and Society: After Industrialism. London, New York: Routledge.

Clarke, L., Winch, C., & Brockmann, M. 2013. Trade-Based Skills Versus Occupational Capacity: the Example of Bricklaying in Europe. Work, Employment & Society, 27(6): 932-951.

Cohen, P. N. & Huffman, M. L. 2003. Occupational Segregation and the Devaluation of Women's Work across U.S. Labor Markets. Social Forces, 81(3): 881-908.

Collins, R. 1971. Functional and Conflict Theories of Educational Stratification. American Sociological Review, 36(6): 1002-1019.

Collins, R. 1975. Conflict Sociology. Toward an Explanatory Science. New York: Academic Press.

Collins, R. 1979. The Credential Society : A Historical Sociology of Education and Stratification. New York: Academic Press.

Congleton, R. D., Hillman, A. L., & Konrad, K. A. 2008. 40 Years of Research on Rent Seeking. Berlin: Springer.

Corsten, M. 1995. Berufsbiographien als institutionelle Skripte. In E. M. Hoerning & M. Corsten (Eds.), Institution und Biographie: die Ordnung des Lebens: 39-53. Pfaffenweiler: Centaurus Verlagsgesellschaft.

Cox, D. R. 1970. The Analysis of Binary Data. London: Methuen.

Daheim, H. 1967. Der Beruf in der modernen Gesellschaft. Köln: Kiepenheuer & Witsch.

Daheim, H. 2001. Berufliche Arbeit im Übergang von der Industrie- zur Dienstleistungsgesellschaft. In T. Kurtz (Ed.), Aspekte des Berufs in der Moderne: 21-38. Opladen: Leske + Budrich.

Davis-Blake, A. & Uzzi, B. 1993. Determinants of Employment Externalization: A Study of Temporary Workers and Independent Contractors. Administrative Science Quarterly, 38(2): 195-223.

Deaton, A. 1997. The Analysis of Household Surveys : A Micro- econometric Approach to Development Policy. Baltimore, MD: Johns Hopkins University Press.

DiPrete, T. A. 2002. Life Course Risks, Mobility Regimes, and Mobility Consequences: A Comparison of Sweden, Germany, and the United States. American Journal of Sociology, 108(2): 267-309.

DiPrete, T. A. 2005. Labor Markets, Inequality, and Change: A European Perspective. Work and Occupations, 32(2): 119-139.

DiPrete, T. A., Goux, D., Maurin, E., & Quesnel-Vallee, A. 2006. Work and Pay in Flexible and Regulated Labor Markets: A Generalized Perspective on Institutional Evolution and Inequality Trends in Europe and the U.S. Research in Social Stratification and Mobility, 24(3): 311-332.

DiPrete, T. A., Bol, T., Ciocca, C., & Van de Werfhorst, H. G. 2014. School to Work Linkages in the US, Germany, and France. Conference Paper, Population Association of America.

Doeringer, P. B. & Piore, M. J. 1971. Internal Labor Markets and Manpower Analysis. Lexington, Mass.: Lexington Books.

Doherty, M. 2009. When the Working Day is through: The End of Work as Identity? Work, Employment and Society, 23(1): 84-101.

Dostal, W., Stooß, F. S., & Troll, L. 1998. Beruf - Auflösungstendenzen und erneute Konsolidierung. Mitteilungen aus der Arbeitsmarkt- und Berufsforschung, 31(3): 438-460.

Dragendorf, R., Heering, W., & John, G. 1988. Beschäftigungsförderung durch Flexibilisierung. Dynamik befristeter Beschäftigungsverhältnisse in der Bundesrepublik Deutschland. Frankfurt am Main, New York: Campus Verlag.

Dunkmann, K. 1922. Die Lehre vom Beruf. Eine Einführung in die Geschichte und Soziologie des Berufs. Berlin: Trowitzsch.

Dunlop, J. T. 1966. Job Vacancy Measures and Economic Analysis. In NBER (Ed.), The Measurement and Interpretation of Job Vacancies: 27 - 48. New York: NBER.

Durkheim, E. 1988. Über soziale Arbeitsteilung. Studie über die Organisation höherer Gesellschaften. Frankfurt am Main: Suhrkamp.

Durkheim, E. 1991. Physik der Sitten und des Rechts. Vorlesungen zur Soziologie der Moral. Frankfurt am Main: Suhrkamp.

Ebbinghaus, B. & Visser, J. 2000. Trade Unions in Western Europe since 1945. New York: Grove's Dictionaries.

Ebner, C. 2013. Erfolgreich in den Arbeitsmarkt? Die duale Berufsausbildung im internationalen Vergleich. Frankfurt am Main, New York: Campus Verlag.

Edwards, R. C. 1975. The Social Relations of Production in the Firm and Labor Market Structure. In R. C. Edwards, M. Reich & D. M. Gordon (Eds.), Labor Market Segmentation: 3-26. Lexington, Mass.: D.C. Heath.

Edwards, R. C. 1979. Contested Terrain - The Transformation of the Workplace in the Twentieth Century. New York: Basic Books.

Efron, B. 1982. The Jackknife, the Bootstrap, and Other Resampling Plans. Philadelphia, Pa.: Society for Industrial and Applied Mathematics.

Eichhorst, W. & Marx, P. 2012. Whatever Works: Dualization and the Service Economy in Bismarckian Welfare States. In P. Emmenegger, S. Häusermann, B. Palier & M. Seeleib-Kaiser (Eds.), The Age of Dualization. The Changing Face of Inequality in Deindustrialized Societies: 73–99. New York: Oxford University Press.

Eisenmenger, M., Loos, C., & Sedmihradsky, D. 2014. Erwerbstätigkeit in Deutschland - Ergebnisse des Zensus 2011. In S. Bundesamt (Ed.), Wirtschaft und Statistik: 544-560. Wiesbaden: Statistisches Bundesamt.

Elia, L. 2010. Temporary/Permanent Workers' Wage Gap: A Brand-new Form of Wage Inequality? LABOUR, 24(2): 178-200.

Emmenegger, P. 2009. Specificity Versus Replaceability: the Relationship Between Skills and Preferences for Job Security Regulations. Socio-Economic Review, 7(3): 407-430.

Engels, W., Gutowski, A., Hamm, W., Möschel, W., Stützel, W., von Weizsäcker, C. C., & Willgerodt, H. 1986. Mehr Markt im Arbeitsrecht, Schriftenreihe, Vol. 10. Bad Homburg: Frankfurter Institut für Wirtschaftspolitische Forschung.

England, P. 1992. Comparable Worth. Theories and Evidence. New York: Walter de Gruyter.

England, P. 2005. Gender Inequality in Labor Markets: The Role of Motherhood and Segregation. Social Politics: International Studies in Gender, State & Society, 12(2): 264-288.

England, P. & Folbre, N. 2005. Gender and Economic Sociology. In N. J. Smelser & R. Swedberg (Eds.), The Handbook of Economic Sociology: 627-649. New York: Russel Sage Foundation.

Erikson, R. & Goldthorpe, J. H. 1992. The Constant Flux. A Study of Class Mobility in Industrial Societies. Oxford: Clarendon Press.

Erlinghagen, M. 2005. Entlassungen und Beschäftigungssicherheit im Zeitverlauf: Zur Entwicklung unfreiwilliger Arbeitsmarktmobilität in Deutschland. Zeitschrift für Soziologie, 34(2): 147-168.

Firebaugh, G. 1997. Analyzing Repeated Surveys. Thousand Oaks, CA: Sage Publications.

Fischer, A. 1918. Über Beruf, Berufswahl und Berufsberatung als Erziehungsfragen. Leipzig: Quelle & Meyer.

Franzese, R. J. 2005. Empirical Strategies for Various Manifestations of Multilevel Data. Political Analysis, 13(4): 430-446.

Freedman, M. K. 1976. Labor Markets Segments and Shelters. New York, N.Y.: Allanheld, Osmun & Co., Universe Books.

Freidson, E. 1994. Professionalism Reborn. Theory, Prophecy, and Policy. Cambridge: Polity Press.

Fritsch, A. & Schank, T. 2005. Betrieblicher Einsatz befristeter Beschäftigung. Sozialer Fortschritt, 54(9): 211-220.

Fuchs, D. 1999. Soziale Integration und politische Institutionen in modernen Gesellschaften. In J. Friedrichs & W. Jagodzinski (Eds.), Soziale Integration: 147-178. Opladen: Westdeutscher Verlag.

Fürstenberg, F. 2000. Berufsgesellschaft in der Krise. Auslaufmodell oder Zukunftspotential? Berlin: Edition Sigma.

Gallagher, D. G. & Sverke, M. 2005. Contingent Employment Contracts: Are Existing Employment Theories Still Relevant? Economic and Industrial Democracy, 26(2): 181-203.

Gamoran, A. 1996. Curriculum Standardisation and Equality of Opportunity in Scottish Secondary Education: 1984-1990. Sociology of Education, 69(1): 1-21.

Gangl, M., Müller, W., & Raffe, D. 2003. Conclusions: Explaining Cross-National Differences in School-To-Work Transitions. In W. Müller & M. Gangl (Eds.), Transitions From Education to Work in Europe: the Integration of Youth into EU Labour Markets: 277-305 Oxford: Oxford University Press.

Gartner, H. & Hinz, T. 2009. Geschlechtsspezifische Lohnungleichheit in Betrieben, Berufen und Jobzellen (1993–2006). Berliner Journal für Soziologie, 19: 557-575.

Gash, V. & McGinnity, F. 2007. Fixed-Term Contracts - The New European Inequality? Comparing Men and Women in West Germany and France. Socio-Economic Review, 5(3): 467-496.

Gash, V. 2008. Bridge or Trap? Temporary Workers' Transitions to Unemployment and to the Standard Employment Contract. European Sociological Review, 24(5): 651-668.

Gathmann, C. & Schönberg, U. 2007. How General Is Human Capital? A Task-Based Approach, IZA Discussionpaper Series, Vol. 3067. Bonn: IZA.

Gebel, M. 2009. Fixed-Term Contracts at Labour Market Entry in West Germany: Implications for Job Search and First Job Quality. European Sociological Review, 25(6): 661-675.

Gebel, M. & Giesecke, J. 2009. Labour Market Flexibility and Inequality: The Changing Risk Patterns of Temporary Employment in West Germany. Zeitschrift für ArbeitsmarktForschung, 42(3): 234-251.

Gebel, M. 2010. Early Career Consequences of Temporary Employment in Germany and the UK. Work, Employment & Society, 24(4): 641-660.

Gebel, M. & Giesecke, J. 2011. Labor Market Flexibility and Inequality: The Changing Skill-Based Temporary Employment and Unemployment Risks in Europe. Social Forces, 90(1): 17-39.

Gebel, M. 2013. Is a Temporary Job Better than Unemployment? A Cross-Country Comparison Based on British, German, and Swiss Panel Data, SOEPpapers on Multidisciplinary Panel Data Research, Vol. 543. Berlin: SOEP, DIW.

Gelman, A. 2005. Two-Stage Regression and Multilevel Modeling: A Commentary. Political Analysis, 13(4): 459-461.

Gelman, A. & Hill, J. 2007. Data Analysis Using Regression and Multilevel/Hierarchical Models. Cambridge , New York: Cambridge University Press.

Gibbons, R. & Waldman, M. 2006. Enriching a Theory of Wage and Promotion Dynamics inside Firms. Journal of Labor Economics, 24(1): 59-107.

Giesecke, J. & Groß, M. 2002. Befristete Beschäftigung: Chance oder Risiko? Kölner Zeitschrift für Soziologie und Sozialpsychologie, 54(1): 85-108.

Giesecke, J. & Groß, M. 2003. Temporary Employment: Chance or Risk? European Sociological Review, 19(2): 161-177.

Giesecke, J. & Groß, M. 2004. External Labour Market Flexibility and Social Inequality. European Societies, 6(3): 347-382.

Giesecke, J. 2006. Arbeitsmarktflexibilisierung und soziale Ungleichheit: Sozio-ökonomische Konsequenzen befristeter Beschäftigungsverhältnisse in Deutschland und Großbritannien. Wiesbaden: VS Verlag für Sozialwissenschaften.

Giesecke, J. & Groß, M. 2006. Befristete Beschäftigung. WSI Mitteilungen, 59(5): 247-255.

Giesecke, J. & Groß, M. 2007. Flexibilisierung durch Befristung. In B. Keller & H. Seifert (Eds.), Atypische Beschäftigung - Flexibilisierung und soziale Risiken: 83-105. Berlin: Edition Sigma.

Giesecke, J. & Schindler, S. 2008. Field of Study and Flexible Work: A Comparison between Germany and the UK. International Journal of Comparative Sociology, 49(4-5): 283-304.

Giesecke, J. 2009. Socio-Economic Risks of Atypical Employment Relationships: Evidence from the German Labour Market. European Sociological Review, 25(6): 629-646.

Giesecke, J. & Verwiebe, R. 2009. Wachsende Lohnungleichheit in Deutschland. Berliner Journal für Soziologie, 19(4): 531-555.

Goldthorpe, J. H. 2000. Social Class and the Differentiation of Employment Contracts. In J. H. Goldthorpe (Ed.), On Sociology : Numbers, Narratives, and the Integration of Research and Theory: 206-230. Oxford, New York: Oxford University Press.

Gordon, D. M., Edwards, R., & Reich, M. 1982. Segmented Work, Divided Workers. Cambridge: Cambridge University Press.

Goux, D. & Maurin, E. 2000. Labor Market Institutions and Job Stability: A Firm-Level Analysis of Layoff Risk for High and Low-Seniority Workers, CREST-INSEE Working Paper, Vol. 2000-29. Paris: CREST-INSEE.

Goux, D., Maurin, E., & Pauchet, M. 2001. Fixed-Term Contracts and the Dynamics of Labour Demand. European Economic Review, 45(3): 533-552.

Greef, S. & Speth, R. 2013. Berufsgewerkschaft als lobbyistische Akteure. Potenziale, Instrumente und Strategien, Arbeitspapier 275, Vol. 275. Düsseldorf: Hans Böckler Stiftung.

Groß, M. 1999. Die Folgen prekärer Arbeitsverhältnisse für das Ausmaß sozialer Ungleichheit: Einkommensbenachteiligung befristeter Arbeitsverträge. In P. Lüttinger (Ed.), Sozialstrukturanalysen mit dem Mikrozensus: 323-353. Mannheim: ZUMA.

Groß, M. & Wegener, B. 2004. Institutionen, Schließung und soziale Ungleichheit. In T. Schwinn (Ed.), Differenzierung und soziale Ungleichheit. Die zwei Soziologien und ihre Verknüpfung: 173-206. Frankfurt am Main: Humanities Online.

Groß, M. 2009. Markt oder Schließung? Zu den Ursachen der Steigerung der Einkommensungleichheit. Berliner Journal für Soziologie, 19(4): 499-530.

Groß, M. 2012. Individuelle Qualifikation, berufliche Schließung oder betriebliche Lohnpolitik – was steht hinter dem Anstieg der Lohnungleichheit? Kölner Zeitschrift für Soziologie und Sozialpsychologie, 64(3): 455-478.

Grusky, D. B. & Sörensen, J. B. 1998. Can Class Analysis Be Salvaged? The American Journal of Sociology, 103(5): 1187-1234.

Grusky, D. B. & Weeden, K. A. 2001. Decomposition Without Death: A Research Agenda for a New Class Analysis. Acta Sociologica, 44(3): 203-218.

Grusky, D. B. & Weeden, K. A. 2002. Class Analysis and the Heavy Weight of Convention. Acta Sociologica, 45(3): 229-236.

Güell, M. 2000. Fixed-Term Contracts and Unemployment: An Efficiency Wage Analysis, Working Paper, Vol. 433. Princeton: Princeton University.

Güell, M. 2000. The Effects of Fixed-term Contracts on the Duration Distribution of Unemployment: The Spanish Case, Working Paper, Vol. 443. Princeton: Princeton University.

Gundert, S. 2007. Befristete Beschäftigung bei Berufsanfängern und älteren Arbeitnehmern. Berlin: Logos.

Hagen, T. 2002. Do Temporary Workers Receive Risk Premiums? Assessing the Wage Effects of Fixed–term Contracts in West Germany by a Matching Estimator Compared with Parametric Approaches. LABOUR, 16(4): 667-705.

Hagen, T. & Boockmann, B. 2002. Determinanten der Nachfrage nach befristeten Verträgen, Leiharbeit und freier Mitarbeit: Empirische Analysen auf Basis des IAB-Betriebspanels. In L. Bellmann & A. Kölling (Eds.), Betrieblicher Wandel und Fachkräftebedarf, Vol. 257: 199-231. Nürnberg: IAB.

Hagen, T. 2003. Does Fixed-term Contract Employment Raise Firms' Adjustment Speed? Evidence from an Establishment Panel for West Germany. Jahrbücher für Nationalökonomie und Statistik, 223(4): 403-421.

Hall, R. H. 1975. Occupations and the Social Structure. Englewood Cliffs, N.J.: Prentice-Hall.

Hall, P. A. & Soskice, D. 2001. An Introduction to Varieties of Capitalism. In P. A. Hall & D. Soskice (Eds.), Varieties of Capitalism. The Institutional Foundations of Comparative Advantage: 1-68. New York: Oxford University Press.

Haupt, A. 2012. (Un)Gleichheit durch soziale Schließung. Kölner Zeitschrift für Soziologie und Sozialpsychologie, 64(4): 729-753.

Haupt, A. 2016. Zugang zu Berufen und Lohnungleichheit in Deutschland. Wiesbaden: Springer VS.

Hauser, R. M. & Warren, J. R. 1997. Socioeconomic Indexes for Occupations: A Review, Update, and Critique. Sociological Methodology, 27: 177 - 298.

Haynes, W. & Gazley, B. 2011. Professional Associations and Public Service: Do Associations Matter? In D. Menzel & H. White (Eds.), The State of Public Administration: Issues, Problems, Challenges: 54-69. Armonk, NY: M.E. Sharpe.

Heinz, W. 2003. From Work Trajectories to Negotiated Careers. The Contingent Work Life Course. In J. T. Mortimer & M. J. Shanahan (Eds.), Handbook of the Life Course: 185-204. New York: Kluwer Academic/Plenum Publishers.

Heisig, J. P. & Solga, H. 2014. Skills Inequalities in 21 Countries. PIAAC results for prime-age adults, WZB Discussion Paper, Vol. SP I 2014-503. Berlin: WZB.

Henninges, v. H., Stooß, F., & Troll, L. 1976. Berufsforschung im IAB. Versuch einer Standortbestimmung. Mitteilungen aus der Arbeitsmarkt- und Berufsforschung, 9(1): 1-18.

Hevenstone, D. 2010. National Context and Atypical Employment. International Sociology, 25(3): 315–347.

Hipp, L. & Anderson, C. J. 2015. Labor Market Policies and Workers' Attitudes toward Employment Flexibility. International Journal of Social Welfare, 24(4): 335-347.

Hipp, L., Bernhardt, J., & Allmendinger, J. 2015. Institutions and the Prevalence of Nonstandard Employment. Socio-Economic Review, 13(2): 351-377.

Hippach-Schneider, U., Hensen, K. A., & Schober, K. 2011. Germany. VET in Europe – Country Report 2011. In U. Hippach-Schneider & K. A. Hensen (Eds.), ReferNet Reports: BIBB.

Hirji, K. F., Mehta, C. R., & Patel, N. R. 1987. Computing Distributions for Exact Logistic Regression. Journal of the American Statistical Association, 82(400): 1110-1117.

Hirji, K. F., Tsiatis, A. A., & Mehta, C. R. 1989. Median Unbiased Estimation for Binary Data. The American Statistician, 43(1): 7-11.

Hoffmann, J., Damelang, A., & Schulz, F. 2011. Strukturmerkmale von Berufen: Einfluss auf die berufliche Mobilität von Ausbildungsabsolventen, IAB-Forschungsbericht, Vol. 09/2007. Nürnberg: IAB.

Hohendanner, C. & Gerner, H.-D. 2010. Die Übernahme befristet Beschäftigter im Kontext betrieblicher Personalpolitik. Soziale Welt, 61(1): 27-51.

Horn, D. 2009. Age of Selection Counts: a Cross-Country Analysis of Educational Institutions. Educational Research and Evaluation, 15(4): 343-366.

Hosmer, D. W., Lemeshow, S., & Sturdivant, R. X. 2013. Applied Logistic Regression. Hoboken, New Jersey: Wiley.

Houseman, S. N. 2001. Why Employers Use Flexible Staffing Arrangements: Evidence from an Establishment Survey. Industrial and Labor Relations Review, 55(1): 149-170.

Hughes, E. C. & Coser, L. A. 1994. On Work, Race, and the Sociological Imagination. Chicago: University of Chicago Press.

Iversen, T. & Soskice, D. 2001. An Asset Theory of Social Policy Preferences. American Political Science Review, 95(4): 875-894.

Kahn, L. M. 2007. The Impact of Employment Protection Mandates on Demographic Temporary Employment Patterns: International Microeconomic Evidence. The Economic Journal, 117(521): F333-F356.

Kahn, L. M. 2010. Employment Protection Reforms, Employment and the Incidence of Temporary Jobs in Europe: 1996-2001. Labour Economics, 17(1): 1-15.

Kaiser, U. & Pfeiffer, F. 2001. Collective Wage Agreements and Firms' Employment Policies. LABOUR, 15(2): 317-341.

Kalleberg, A. L. & Sørensen, A. B. 1979. The Sociology of Labor Markets. Annual Review of Sociology, 5: 351-379.

Kalleberg, A. L. 2000. Nonstandard Employment Relations: Part-Time, Temporary and Contract Work. Annual Review of Sociology, 26: 341-365.

Kalleberg, A. L., Reynolds, J., & Marsden, P. V. 2003. Externalizing Employment: Flexible Staffing Arrangements in US Organizations. Social Science Research, 32(4): 525-552.

Kalleberg, A. L. 2009. Precarious Work, Insecure Workers: Employment Relations in Transition. American Sociological Review, 74(1): 1-22.

Kalleberg, A. L. 2011. Good Jobs, Bad Jobs: The Rise of Polarized and Precarious Employment Systems in the United States, 1970s to 2000s. New York: Russell Sage Foundation.

Kambourov, G. & Manovskii, I. 2009. Occupational Specificity of Human Capital. International Economic Review, 50: 63-115.

Keller, B. & Seifert, H. (Eds.). 2007. Atypische Beschäftigung - Flexibilisierung und soziale Risiken. Berlin: Edition Sigma.

Kerckhoff, A. C. 2004. From Student to Worker. In J. T. Mortimer & M. J. Shanahan (Eds.), Handbook of the Life Course: 251-267. New York: Springer.

Kerr, C. 1950. Labor Markets: Their Character and Consequences. Economic Review, 40(2): 278-291.

Kerr, C. 1954. The Balkanization of Labor Markets. In E. W. Bakke (Ed.), Labor Mobility and Economic Opportunity: 92-110. Cambridge: MIT Press.

Kilbourne, B., England, P., & Beron, K. 1994. Effects of Individual, Occupational, and Industrial Characteristics on Earnings: Intersections of Race and Gender. Social Forces, 72(4): 1149-1176.

Kim, A. & Kurz, K. 2003. Prekäre Beschäftigung im Vereinigten Königreich und Deutschland. Welche Rolle spielen unterschiedliche institutionelle Kontexte? In W. Müller & S. Scherer (Eds.), Mehr Risiken-mehr Ungleichheit? Abbau des Wohlfahrtsstaates, Flexibilisierung der Arbeit und die Folgen: 167-197. Frankfurt am Main, New York: Campus Verlag.

King, G. & Zeng, L. 2001. Logistic Regression in Rare Events Data. Political Analysis, 9(2): 137-163.

Kitschelt, H. & Rehm, P. 2006. New Social Risks and Political Preferences. In K. Armingeon & G. Bonoli (Eds.), The Politics of Post-Industrial Welfare States. Adapting Post-War Social Policies to New Social Risks: 52-82. London: Routledge.

Kleiner, M. M. 2006. Licensing Occupations: Ensuring Quality or Restricting Competition? Kalamazoo: W.E. Upjohn Institute for Employment Research.

Kleiner, M. M. & Krueger, A. B. 2009. Analyzing the Extent and Influence of Occupational Licensing on the Labor Market, NBER Working Paper, Vol. 14979. Cambridge: NBER.

Kleiner, M. M. & Krueger, A. B. 2010. The Prevalence and Effects of Occupational Licensing. British Journal of Industrial Relations, 48(4): 676-687.

Klemm, E. 2002. Einführung in die Statistik. Wiesbaden: Westdeutscher Verlag.

Knoke, D. & Kalleberg, A. L. 1994. Job Training in U.S. Organizations. American Sociological Review, 59(4): 537-546.

Kohn, M. L. & Schooler, C. 1978. The Reciprocal Effects of the Substantive Complexity of Work and Intellectual Flexibility: A Longitudinal Assessment. American Journal of Sociology, 84(1): 24-52.

Kohn, M. L. 2001. Job Complexity and Adult Personality. In D. B. Grusky (Ed.), Social Stratification: 532-541. Boulder: Westview Press.

Konietzka, D. 1999. Die Verberuflichung von Marktchancen. Die Bedeutung des Ausbildungsberufs für die Platzierung im Arbeitsmarkt. Zeitschrift für Soziologie, 28(5): 379-400.

Korpi, T. & Levin, H. 2001. Precarious Footing: Temporary Employment as a Stepping Stone out of Unemployment in Sweden. Work, Employment and Society, 15(1): 127-148.

Krause, E. A. 1971. The Sociology of Occupations. Boston: Little.

Krüger, H., Born, C., & Kelle, U. 1989. Sequenzmuster in unterbrochenen Erwerbskarrieren von Frauen. Arbeitspapier, Vol. 7. Bremen SFB 186 der Universität Bremen.

Krüger, H. 1996. Die andere Bildungssegmentation: Berufssysteme und soziale Ungleichheit zwischen den Geschlechtern. In A. Bolder (Ed.), Die Wiederentdeckung der Ungleichheit. Aktuelle Tendenzen in Bildung und Arbeit: 252-274. Opladen: Leske+Budrich.

Krüger, H. 2003. Berufliche Bildung. Der Deutsche Sonderweg und die Geschlechterfrage. Berliner Journal für Soziologie 13(4): 497-510.

Kupka, P. 2005. Berufskonzept und Berufsforschung - soziologische Perspektiven. In M. Jacob & P. Kupka (Eds.), Perspektiven des Berufskonzepts: 17-38. Nürnberg: IAB.

Kurtz, T. 2001. Die Form Beruf im Kontext gesellschaftlicher Differenzierung. In T. Kurtz (Ed.), Aspekte des Berufs in der Moderne: 179-208. Opladen: Leske + Budrich.

Kurtz, T. 2005. Die Berufsform der Gesellschaft. Weilerswist: Velbrück Wissenschaft.

Kurz, K., Steinhage, N., & Golsch, K. 2005. Case Study Germany. Global Competition, Uncertainty and the Transition to Adulthood. In H.-P. Blossfeld, E. Klijzing, M. Mills & K. Kurz (Eds.), Globalization, Uncertainty and Youth in Society: 51-82. London: Routledge.

Larson, M. S. 1977. The Rise of Professionalism: A Sociological Analysis. Berkeley: University of California Press.

Lazear, E. P. 2003. Firm-Specific Human Capital: A Skill-Weights Approach, NBER Working Paper Series, Vol. 9679. Cambridge: NBER.

Lewis, J. B. & Linzer, D. A. 2005. Estimating Regression Models in Which the Dependent Variable Is Based on Estimates. Political Analysis, 13(4): 345-364.

Lindbeck, A. & Snower, D. J. 1988. The Insider-Outsider Theory of Employment and Unemployment. Cambridge MA, London: MIT Press.

Lipset, S. M., Trow, M., & Coleman, J. S. 1956. Union Democracy; The Internal Politics of the International Typographical Union. Glencoe, Ill.: Free Press.

Loh, E. S. 1994. Employment Probation as a Sorting Mechanism. Industrial and Labor Relations Review, 47(3): 471-486.

Long, J. S. & Ervin, L. H. 2000. Using Heteroscedasticity Consistent Standard Errors in the Linear Regression Model. The American Statistician, 54(3): 217-224.

Lutz, B., Koehler, C., Gruenert, H., & Struck, O. 2007. The German Model of Labour Market Segmentation: Tendencies of Change. Economies et Sociétés, Série Socio-Economie du Travail, 41(6): 1057–1087.

Marglin, S. A. 1974. What Do Bosses Do? Review of Radical Political Economics, 6(2): 60-112.

Marsden, D. 1992. Institutions and Labour Mobility: Occupational and Internal Labour Markets in Britain, France, Italy and West Germany. In R. Brunetta & C. Dell'Aringa (Eds.), Labour Relations and Economic Performance: 414-438. Houndmills, Basingstoke, Hampshire, London: Macmillan.

Masters, J. K. & Miles, G. 2002. Predicting the Use of External Labor Arrangements: A Test of the Transaction Costs Perspective. The Academy of Management Journal, 45(2): 431-442.

Matthes, B., Burkert, C., & Biersack, W. 2008. Berufssegmente. Eine empirisch fundierte Neuabgrenzung vergleichbarer beruflicher Einheiten, IAB-Discussion Paper, Vol. 35/2008. Nürnberg: IAB.

Matusik, S. F. & Hill, C. W. L. 1998. The Utilization of Contingent Work, Knowledge Creation, and Competitive Advantage. The Academy of Management Review, 23(4): 680-697.

Mayer, K. U. & Blossfeld, H.-P. 1990. Die gesellschaftliche Konstruktion sozialer Ungleichheit im Lebenslauf. In P. A. Berger & S. Hradil (Eds.), Lebenslagen, Lebensläufe, Lebensstile - Soziale Welt Sonderband 7: 297-318. Göttingen: Schwartz.

Mayer, K. U., Grunow, D., & Nitsche, N. 2010. Is Occupational Flexibilization a Myth? How Stable Have Working Lives Been and as How Stable Are they Being Perceived? Kölner Zeitschrift für Soziologie und Sozialpsychologie, 62(3): 369-403.

McGinnity, F., Mertens, A., & Gundert, S. 2005. A Bad Start? Fixed-Term Contracts and the Transition from Education to Work in West Germany. European Sociological Review, 21(4): 359-374.

Mehta, C. R. & Patel, N. R. 1995. Exact Logistic Regression: Theory and Examples. Statistics in Medicine, 14(19): 2143-2160.

Mertens, A. & McGinnity, F. 2004. Wages and Wage Growth of Fixed-Term Workers in East and West Germany. Applied economics quarterly, 50(2): 139-164.

Millerson, G. 1964. The Qualifying Associations; A Study in Professionalization. London, New York: Routledge & Paul, Humanities Press.

Mincer, J. A. 1974. Schooling and Earnings. In J. A. Mincer (Ed.), Schooling, Experience, and Earnings: 41-63. New York: NBER.

Morgan, S. L. & Tang, Z. 2007. Social Class and Workers' Rent, 1983–2001. Research in Social Stratification and Mobility, 25(4): 273-293.

Mortimer, J. T. & Simmons, R. G. 1978. Adult Socialization. Annual Review of Sociology, 4(1): 421-454.

Mortimer, J. T. & Lorence, J. 1979. Work Experience and Occupational Value Socialization: A Longitudinal Study. American Journal of Sociology, 84(6): 1361-1385.

Mouw, T. & Kalleberg, A. L. 2010. Occupations and the Structure of Wage Inequality in the United States, 1980s to 2000s. American Sociological Review, 75(3): 402-431.

Mückenberger, U. 1985. Die Krise des Normalarbeitsverhältnisses. Hat das Arbeitsrecht noch Zukunft? Zeitschrift für Sozialreform, 31(7, 8): 415-434, 457-475.

Mückenberger, U. 1989. Der Wandel des Normalarbeitsverhältnisses unter Bedingungen einer „Krise der Normalität". Gewerkschaftliche Monatshefte, 40(4): 211-222.

Müller, W. & Shavit, Y. 1998. The Institutional Processes of the Stratification Process: A Comparative Study of Qualifications and Occupations in Thirteen Countries. In Y. Shavit & W. Müller (Eds.), From School to Work: 1-48. Oxford: Clarendon Press.

Müller, W., Steinmann, S., & Ell, R. 1998. Education and Labour-Market Entry in Germany. In Y. Shavit & W. Müller (Eds.), From School to Work: 143-189. Oxford: Clarendon Press.

Murphy, R. 1988. Social Closure: The Theory of Monopolization and Exclusion. Oxford, New York: Clarendon Press, Oxford University Press.

Nienhüser, W. 2007. Betriebliche Beschäftigungsstrategie und atypische Arbeitsverhältnisse. Eine Erklärungsskizze aus Sicht einer politischen Personalökonomik. In B. Keller & H. Seifert (Eds.), Atypische Beschäftigung - Flexibilisierung und soziale Risiken: 45-65. Berlin: Edition Sigma.

Oberst, M., Schank, T., & Schnabel, C. 2007. Interne Arbeitsmärkte und Einsatz temporärer Arbeitsverhältnisse: Eine Fallstudie mit Daten eines deutschen Dienstleistungsunternehmens. Zeitschrift für Betriebswirtschaft, 77(11): 1159-1177.

OECD. 1986. Flexibility in the Labour Market. Paris: OECD.

OECD. 1994. The OECD Jobs Study: Facts, Analysis, Strategies. Paris: OECD.

OECD. 1998. Getting Started, Settling in: The Transition from Education to the Labour Market. In OECD (Ed.), Employment Outlook 1998: 81-122. Paris: OECD.

OECD. 2012. Education at a Glance: OECD Indicators 2012 - United States. In OECD (Ed.), Education at a Glance, Vol. 2012. Paris: OECD.

Palier, B. & Thelen, K. 2010. Institutionalizing Dualism: Complementarities and Change in France and Germany. Politics & Society, 38(1): 119–148.

Parkin, F. 1971. Class Inequality and Political Order: Social Stratification in Capitalist and Communist Societies. New York: Praeger.

Pavalko, R. M. 1971. Sociology of Occupations and Professions. Itasca, Illinois: F. E. Peacock Publishers.

Peduzzi, P., Concato, J., Kemper, E., Holford, T. R., & Feinstein, A. R. 1996. A Simulation Study of the Number of Events per Variable in Logistic Regression Analysis. Journal of Clinical Epidemiology, 49(12): 1373-1379.

Pfeffer, J. & Cohen, Y. 1984. Determinants of Internal Labor Markets in Organizations. Administrative Science Quarterly, 29(4): 550-572.

Pfeffer, J. & Baron, J. N. 1988. Taking the Workers Back Out: Recent Trends in the Structuring of Employment. Research in Organizational Behavior, 10: 257-303.

Pfeifer, C. 2005. Flexibility, Dual Labour Markets, and Temporary Employment. Empirical Evidence from German Establishment Data. Management Revue, 16(3): 404-422.

Pfeifer, C. 2006. Warum beschäftigen Firmen befristete Arbeitnehmer und Leiharbeitskräfte? Eine theoretische und empirische Analyse mit Daten aus dem Hannoveraner Firmenpanel. In W. Nienhüser (Ed.), Beschäftigungspolitik von Unternehmen. Theoretische Erklärungsansätze und empirische Erkenntnisse: 197-224. München, Mering: Hampp Verlag.

Plant, J. F. 2000. Codes of Ethics. In T. L. Cooper (Ed.), Handbook of Administrative Ethics: 309-334. New York: Taylor & Francis.

Polavieja, J. G. 2003. Temporary Contracts and Labour Market Segmentation in Spain: An Employment-Rent Approach. European Sociological Review, 19(5): 501-517.

Polavieja, J. G. 2005. Flexibility or Polarization? Temporary Employment and Job Tasks in Spain. Socio-Economic Review, 3(2): 233-258.

Polavieja, J. G. 2006. The Incidence of Temporary Employment in Advanced Economies: Why is Spain Different? European Sociological Review, 22(1): 61-78.

Rabe-Hesketh, S. & Skrondal, A. 2012. Multilevel and Longitudinal Modeling Using Stata, Volume II: Categorical Responses, Counts, and Survival. College Station, TX: Stata Press.

Rifkin, J. 1995. The End of Work: The Decline of the Global Labor Force and the Dawn of the Post-Market Era. New York: G.P. Putnam's Sons.

Rosen, S. 1986. The Theory of Equalizing Differences. In O. Ashenfelter & D. Card (Eds.), Handbook of Labor Economics, Vol. 1: 641-692. Amsterdam, New York, Oxford, Tokyo: North-Holland.

Rothman, R. A. 1998. Working: Sociological Perspectives. Upper Saddle River, NJ: Prentice Hall.

Rotolo, T. & McPherson, J. M. 2001. The System of Occupations: Modeling Occupations in Sociodemographic Space. Social Forces, 79(3): 1095-1130.

Rubery, J. 1989. Precarious Forms of Work in the United Kingdom. In G. Rodgers & J. Rodgers (Eds.), Precarious Jobs in Labour Market Regulation: The Growth of Atypical Employment in Western Europe: 49–74. Genf: International Institute for Labour Studies, Free University of Brussels.

Rubery, J. & Grimshaw, D. 2003. The Organization of Employment. An International Perspective. New York: Palgrave McMillan.

Rudolph, H. 1987. Befristete Beschäftigung - ein Überblick. Mitteilungen aus der Arbeitsmarkt- und Berufsforschung, 20(3): 288-304.

Schäfer, H. 2010. Sprungbrett oder Sackgasse? - Entwicklung und Strukturen von flexiblen Erwerbsformen in Deutschland. IW-Trends, 37(1): 1-18.

Scharmann, T. 1956. Arbeit und Beruf. Eine soziologische und psychologische Untersuchung über die heutige Berufssituation. Tübingen: Mohr.

Schaub, G. 1992. Arbeitsrechts-Handbuch. München: C.H. Beck.

Schaub, G., Koch, U., Linck, R., & Vogelsang, H. 2009. Arbeitsrechts-Handbuch. München: C.H. Beck.

Schelsky, H. 1965. Die Bedeutung des Berufs in der modernen Gesellschaft. In H. Schelsky (Ed.), Auf der Suche nach Wirklichkeit: 238-249. Düsseldorf, Köln: Eugen Diedrichs Verlag.

Scherer, S. 2005. Patterns of Labour Market Entry: Long Wait or Career Instability? An Empirical Comparison of Italy, Great Britain and West Germany. European Sociological Review, 21(5): 427-440.

Schimpl-Neimanns, B. 2009. Schätzung des Stichprobenfehlers im Mikrozensus mit Stata : eine Einführung mit Beispielen zum Campus File Mikrozensus 2002, GESIS-Methodenberichte, Vol. 2009-02. Mannheim: GESIS.

Schömann, K., Rogowski, R., & Kruppe, T. 1998. Labour Market Efficiency in the European Union. Employment Protection and Fixed-Term Contracts. London: Routledge.

Schroeder, W., Kalass, V., & Greef, S. 2008. Kleine Gewerkschaften und Berufsverbände im Wandel. Düsseldorf: Hans Böckler Stiftung.

Schroeder, W., Kalass, V., & Greef, S. 2011. Berufsgewerkschaften in der Offensive. Vom Wandel des deutschen Gewerkschaftsmodells. Wiesbaden: Springer Fachmedien.

Seifert, M. & Pawlowsky, P. 1998. Innerbetriebliches Vertrauen als Verbreitungsgrenze atypischer Beschäftigungsformen. Mitteilungen aus der Arbeitsmarkt- und Berufsforschung, 98(3): 599-611.

Sengenberger, W. 1987. Struktur und Funktionsweise von Arbeitsmärkten. Frankfurt am Main, New York: Campus Verlag.

Sennett, R. 1998. The Corrosion of Character. The Personal Consequences of Work in the New Capitalism. New York, NY: W.W. Norton & Co.

Sesselmeier, W. 2007. (De)Stabilisierung der Arbeitsmarktsegmentation? Überlegungen zur Theorie atypischer Beschäftigung. In B. Keller & H. Seifert (Eds.), Atypische Beschäftigung - Flexibilisierung und soziale Risiken: 67-80. Berlin: Edition Sigma.

Shavit, Y. & Müller, W. 1998. From School to Work. Oxford: Oxford University Press.

Siebert, H. 1997. Labor Market Rigidities: At the Root of Unemployment in Europe. The Journal of Economic Perspectives, 11(3): 37-54.

Simpson, I. H., Simpson, R. L., Evers, M., & Poss, S. S. 1982. Occupational Recruitment, Retention, and Labor Force Cohort Representation. The American Journal of Sociology, 87(6): 1287-1313.

Smith, V. 1997. New Forms of Work Organization. Annual Review of Sociology, 23: 315-339.

Solga, H. & Konietzka, D. 1999. Occupational Matching and Social Stratification. European Sociological Review, 15(1): 25-47.

Solga, H. & Konietzka, D. 2000. Das Berufsprinzip des deutschen Arbeitsmarktes: Ein geschlechtsneutraler Allokationsmechanismus. Schweizerische Zeitschrift für Soziologie, 26(1): 111-147.

Sørensen, A. B. 1983. Processes of Allocation to Open and Closed Positions in Social Structure. Zeitschrift für Soziologie, 12(3): 203-224.

Sørensen, A. B. 1996. The Structural Basis of Social Inequality. American Journal of Sociology, 101(5): 1333-1365.

Sørensen, A. B. 2000. Toward a Sounder Basis for Class Analysis. American Journal of Sociology, 105(6): 1523-1558.

Spence, M. 1973. Job Market Signaling. Quarterly Journal of Economics, 87(3): 355-374.

Standing, G. 2009. Work after Globalization. Building Occupational Citizenship. Cheltenham, Northampton: Edward Elgar.

Standing, G. 2011. The Precariat: The New Dangerous Class. London: Bloomsbury Academic.

Statistisches Bundesamt 1992. Klassifizierung der Berufe. Systematisches und alphabetisches Verzeichnis der Berufsbenennungen. Ausgabe 1992. Wiesbaden: Metzer-Poeschel Stuttgart.

Statistisches Bundesamt & GESIS. 2012. Datenhandbuch zum Mikrozensus Scientific Use File 2007. Bonn, Mannheim: Statistisches Bundesamt, GESIS.

Stolzenberg, R. M. 1975. Occupations, Labor Markets and the Process of Wage Attainment. American Sociological Review, 40(5): 645-665.

Stooß, F. & Saterdag, H. 1979. Systematik der Berufe und der beruflichen Tätigkeiten. In F. U. Pappi (Ed.), Sozialstrukturanalyse mit Umfragedaten: 41-57. Königstein: Athenäum-Verlag.

Stooß, F. 1982. Instrumente zur Analyse und Beschreibung beruflicher Makrostrukturen unter besonderer Berücksichtigung des Tätigkeitsschwerpunkt-Konzeptes des IAB. In D. Mertens (Ed.), Konzepte der Arbeitsmarkt- und Berufsforschung. Eine Forschungsinventur des IAB: 764-794. Nürnberg: IAB.

Streeck, W. 2011. Skills and Politics: General and Specific, MPIfG Discussion Paper, Vol. 11. Köln: MPIfG.

Struck, O. 2006. Flexibilität und Sicherheit. Wiesbaden: VS Verlag für Sozialwissenschaften.

Stuth, S., Hennig, M., & Allmendinger, J. 2009. Die Bedeutung des Berufs für die Dauer von Erwerbsunterbrechungen, WZB Discussion Paper, Vol. P 2009-001. Berlin: WZB.

Stuth, S. & Hennig, M. 2014. Ist der Beruf entscheidend? Zum Einfluss beruflicher Eigenschaften auf die Dauer familienbedingter Nichterwerbsphasen von Frauen, WZB Discussion Paper, Vol. P 2014-006. Berlin: WZB.

Thurow, L. C. 1975. Generating Inequality. Mechanisms of Distribution in the U.S. Economy. New York: Basic Books.

Thurow, L. C. 1979. A Job Competition Model. In M. J. Piore (Ed.), Unemployment and Inflation: Institutionalist and Structuralist Views: 17-32. New York: Sharpe.

Tolbert, P. S. 1996. Occupations, Organizations and Boundaryless Careers. In M. B. Arthur & D. Rousseau (Eds.), The Boundaryless Career. A New Employment Principle for a New Organizational Era: 91-107. New York, NY: Oxford University Press.

Uzzi, B. & Barsness, Z. I. 1998. Contingent Employment in British Establishments: Organizational Determinants of the Use of Fixed-Term Hires and Part-Time Workers. Social Forces, 76(3): 967-1005.

Van de Werfhorst, H. G. 2011. Skills, Positional Good or Social Closure? The Role of Education Across Structural–Institutional Labour Market Settings. Journal of Education and Work, 24(5): 521-548.

Van Maanen, J. & Barley, S. R. 1984. Occupational Communities: Culture and Control in Organizations. Research in Organizational Behavior, 6: 287 - 365.

Vicari, B. 2014. Degree of Standardised Certification of Occupations. An Indicator for Measuring Institutional Characteristics of Ooccupations (KldB 2010, KldB 1988), FDZ-Methodenreport, Vol. 04/2014. Nürnberg: FDZ der BA.

Vittinghoff, E. & McCulloch, C. E. 2007. Relaxing the Rule of Ten Events per Variable in Logistic and Cox Regression. American Journal of Epidemiology, 165(6): 710-718.

Voß, G. G. 1994. Berufssoziologie. In H. Kerber & A. Schmieder (Eds.), "Spezielle Soziologien" Problemfelder, Forschungsbereiche, Anwendungsorientierungen: 128-148. Reinbek: Rowohlt.

Walwei, U. 1990. Ökonomisch-rechtliche Analyse befristeter Arbeitsverhältnisse. Nürnberg: IAB.

Wang, R. & Weiss, A. 1998. Probation, Layoffs, and Wage-Tenure Profiles: A Sorting Explanation. Labour Economics, 5(3): 359-383.

Weber, M. 1978. Economy and Society. An Outline of Interpretative Sociology. Berkeley, CA: University of California Press.

Weber, M. 2001. Wirtschaft und Gesellschaft. Die Wirtschaft und die gesellschaftlichen Ordnungen und Mächte. Nachlaß: Teilband 1, Gemeinschaften. Max Weber Gesamtausgabe. Tübingen: Mohr Siebeck.

Weeden, K. A. 1998. Revisiting Occupational Sex Segregation in the United States, 1910-1990: Results from a Log-Linear Approach. Demography, 35(4): 475-487.

Weeden, K. A. 2002. Why Do Some Occupations Pay More than Others? Social Closure and Earnings Inequality in the United States. The American Journal of Sociology, 108(1): 55-101.

Weeden, K. A. & Grusky, D. B. 2005. Are there Any Big Classes at All? In D. Bills (Ed.), The Shape of Social Inequality: Stratification and Ethnicity in Comparative Perspective: 3-56. Amsterdam: Elsevier.

Weeden, K. A. & Grusky, D. B. 2005. The Case for a New Class Map. American Journal of Sociology, 111(1): 141-212.

Weeden, K. A., Kim, Y.-M., Di Carlo, M., & Grusky, D. B. 2007. Social Class and Earnings Inequality. American Behavioral Scientist, 50(5): 702-736.

Weeden, K. A. & Grusky, D. B. 2012. The Three Worlds of Inequality. American Journal of Sociology, 117(6): 1723-1785.

Weeden, K. A. & Grusky, D. B. 2014. Inequality and Market Failure. American Behavioral Scientist, 58(3): 473-491.

Williamson, O. E. 1981. The Economics of Organization: The Transaction Cost Approach. American Journal of Sociology, 87(3): 548-577.

Williamson, O. E. 1985. The Economic Institutions of Capitalism. Firms, Markets, Relational Contracting. New York, NY: The Free Press.

Willms-Herget, A. 1985. Frauenarbeit: zur Integration der Frauen in den Arbeitsmarkt. Frankfurt am Main, New York: Campus Verlag.

Witte, J. C. & Kalleberg, A. L. 1995. Matching Training and Jobs: The Fit between Vocational Education and Employment in the German Labour Market. European Sociological Review, 11(3): 293-317.

Wolf, E. 1999. Dynamik der Arbeitszeitstruktur: Welche Rolle spielt der Strukturwandel? In P. Lüttinger (Ed.), Sozialstrukturanalysen mit dem Mikrozensus: 119-148. Mannheim: ZUMA.

Wooldridge, J. M. 2002. Econometric Analysis of Cross Section and Panel Data. Cambridge, MA: MIT Press.

Zijl, M., van den Berg, G. J., & Heyma, A. 2004. Stepping-Stones for the Unemployed: The Effect of Temporary Jobs on the Duration until Regular Work, IZA Dicscussion Paper Series, Vol. 1241. Bonn: IZA.

Zimmermann, H. 1997. Befristete versus unbefristete Arbeitsverträge: eine theoretische und empirische Untersuchung zur Anwendung unterschiedlicher Beschäftigungsformen in privatwirtschaftlichen Unternehmen. Frankfurt am Main: Lang.

Index

access 36, 37, 41, 44, 49, 51, 62, 72, 78, 81, 83, 122, 131, 160
additional education and training 50–52, 129, 131, 132, 134, 163
advertising 47, 165
apprenticeship 24, 49, 55, 56, 62, 63, 65, 68, 69, 80–82, 86, 88, 93, 103
asymptotic methods 73, 74
attitude 24

bargaining 21, 33, 49, 55, 68, 69, 93, 125, 134, 161
bias 73, 78, 82, 92
bridge 28, 159, 170

career 21, 29, 159, 169
certificate 41
closure mechanism 23, 38, 40, 44, 46–48, 53, 63–65, 113, 155, 159, 163, 165
– channeling demand 39, 40, 43, 45, 46, 48, 53, 61, 63–66, 125, 159–161, 163
– increasing diffuse demand 39, 44, 45, 47, 53, 125, 131, 159, 160
– restricting supply 38, 49, 53, 61, 125, 155, 159, 160, 165, 167
– signaling of quality 38–40, 125
– signals of quality 39, 63, 160
closure source 23, 24, 40, 43, 61–63, 67–69, 77, 79, 95, 102, 121, 125, 130, 152, 157, 160, 164, 167, 170
– common sets of tasks 46, 89, 105, 106, 116, 122, 133, 160
– credentialism 23, 24, 40, 41, 43, 49, 53, 61–64, 69, 76, 77, 79, 100, 102, 113, 121, 147, 148, 155, 160, 164, 165, 167
– licensing 40, 43, 44, 50, 53, 64, 79, 88, 108, 109, 164
– narrow range of tasks 45, 163
– occupational associations 23, 40, 46–48, 53, 67, 79, 90, 91, 111, 112, 125, 153–156, 165
– occupational specificity 23, 24, 40, 53, 65, 66, 72, 79, 105–108, 115, 121, 122, 129, 132, 160, 166, 167
– standard 24, 27, 42, 43, 49, 55, 57, 75–77, 87, 95, 97, 113, 119, 121, 126, 128, 159, 169
– standardization of credentials 104, 116, 149, 164, 169
– task licensure 114, 116, 117, 123, 124, 127, 157
– task specialization 23, 53, 160, 161, 166, 167
– title licensure 111, 113, 115, 121, 125, 126, 128, 136, 139–143, 145, 146, 148, 152–154, 157, 165, 167
– union 49, 52, 56, 68, 91, 113, 114, 116, 117, 123–125, 127, 128, 136, 139, 140, 145, 147, 148, 150, 153, 156, 161
– unionization 49, 53, 68, 123–125, 127, 128, 136, 139, 140, 145, 147, 153, 156
– unique tasks 45, 46, 105, 106, 142
– wide range of tasks 44, 45, 108, 114, 122
collective action 28, 40
competence 43, 56
competition 27, 29, 30, 35, 37, 39, 42, 46, 48, 51, 52, 69, 132, 134, 144, 161, 163, 166
constitution 64, 86
control 25, 31, 33, 35, 40–43, 48, 76, 91–93, 115, 126, 159, 167
core workforce 49, 152, 155
correlation 79, 95, 115, 116
craft 34, 36, 47, 56, 66, 116
curricula 41, 43, 63, 64, 82, 86, 87, 103

dismissal 58
division of labor 32, 35, 40
dual system 80, 84

economic cycles 27
employee 22, 27, 38, 45, 71, 85, 95, 97, 137, 138, 159
employer 22, 27, 29, 31, 33, 39, 42, 59, 138, 159, 169
employment protection legislation 24, 55, 58, 92
employment relations 27, 29, 33, 36, 55, 57, 93
equilibrium 22, 23, 28, 31, 33, 47, 159, 166
exact logistic regression 74
examination 41, 42
examinations 41, 43, 64
exchangeable 33, 62
exclusive 41, 44, 46

experience 22, 33, 51, 81, 131, 165, 169

field of study 76, 83
flexibility 21, 24, 27, 51, 55, 92, 131, 170
fluctuations 27, 81
fragmentation 22–24, 29, 31–33, 37, 46, 166

gender 69, 91, 93, 120, 147–151, 164, 167
German Dictionary of Occupational Titles 72, 79, 82
governance 29, 30, 138

hire 22, 32, 43, 47, 49, 64, 157
human capital 22–24, 28–33, 49, 50, 66, 91, 92, 120, 128, 129, 131, 134, 159, 162, 163, 167
– general human capital 22, 29, 31, 159
– specific human capital 22, 29–31, 128, 159
human resources 22, 28, 33

induction costs 45, 169
industry 68, 93, 115, 126
internal labor market 29, 30, 49, 50, 53, 159, 163, 167
involuntary 57

job 21, 22, 29–32, 35, 39, 45, 56, 65, 88, 96, 122, 131, 138, 163, 166
job security 21, 23, 31, 138, 169

labor intensity 21
labor shortage 28
labor turnover 21, 159, 170
layoffs 58
legislation 58–60, 65, 72, 86, 87, 108, 109, 170
lobbying 46, 47, 67, 125, 161, 165
logistic regression 73, 74
logit coefficients 119

management 28, 52, 62, 104, 111
manpower 27, 35
marginal costs 52, 92, 137
master craftsman 65, 88
Microcensus 24, 57, 71, 72, 74, 76, 79, 81, 83–85, 88, 90–92, 95, 96, 160, 163
military ranks 65, 77
mobility 27, 33, 42, 45, 46, 51, 56, 62, 66, 96, 122, 131, 162
monitor 29, 30, 40, 138, 159
monopolizing 44
monopoly 125
multilevel 24, 25, 72, 74–77, 95, 119, 160

niche 51, 66, 132, 167
norm 27, 57
normative 24, 27, 37, 55, 57
number of events 73, 77

objective reasons 58, 59, 170
on the job 29
organization 28, 29, 31, 33, 44, 45, 51, 59, 64, 67, 80, 83, 135, 161, 162

power 33, 38, 44, 52, 65, 67, 134
prestige 41, 55
probationary periods 28, 131, 161
productivity 21, 22, 27–30, 39, 43, 45, 49, 50, 91, 129, 138, 159, 169, 170
professional ethics 46, 48, 67, 125
professions 34, 36, 56, 167
promotion 59
public service 65, 88, 93

qualification 27, 41, 62, 74, 76, 93, 97, 98, 120, 153

regulation 58, 60, 64, 96
rents 33, 38, 49

sample size 72, 73, 76, 77, 152, 158
scarcity 22, 31, 33, 34, 41, 42, 52, 62, 79, 134, 137, 159, 163
schooling 29, 42, 61, 69, 80, 84, 86, 93, 97, 152
schools of the healthcare sector 80, 81, 84, 86
screening 28
search costs 33
shelter 24, 32, 40
signal 32, 34, 39, 40, 43, 44, 63, 122, 160, 162, 164, 166, 169
skill 33, 114, 139, 140
small-sample bias 73, 74
social closure 37, 38, 40, 42
social credit 43, 46–48
social security 27
specificity 30, 49, 66, 89, 105, 106
standard work arrangements 57
standards 41, 47, 48, 63, 125
strikes 49, 125

tertiary degree 62
tertiary education 62, 80–84, 86, 93, 156
titles 29, 44, 64, 65, 72, 88, 109, 110, 113, 115, 125, 141, 153, 164, 165
track 42, 69, 80, 82–84, 86, 87, 103

trade, technical, and master's schools 80, 81, 84, 86
transaction costs 28, 29, 31, 159

unemployment 69, 95, 144, 164, 169, 170
universities 48, 60, 65, 81, 83, 86, 88
university degree 32

vacancies 31, 37, 39, 40, 43, 45, 46, 55, 62, 69, 84, 144, 160, 161, 166
vocation 52, 65, 80, 81, 86

vocational full-time schooling 80, 86
vocational school 80

wage 21, 23, 29, 33, 34, 36, 38, 46, 55, 69, 91, 93, 96, 159, 169, 170
work complexity 33, 159
workforce 42, 46, 49, 60, 62, 152, 155, 159, 166
working conditions 21, 39, 49, 69, 91, 125, 159, 161, 170